WRITING IN CRISIS

In memory of Alf and Kerstin Helgesson

WRITING
IN CRISIS

Ethics and History in Gordimer, Ndebele and Coetzee

Stefan Helgesson

UNIVERSITY OF KwaZulu-Natal PRESS

Writing in Crisis: Ethics and History in Gordimer, Ndebele and Coetzee

ISBN 1 86914 044 3

© Stefan Helgesson 2004

Published by University of KwaZulu-Natal Press
Private Bag X01
Scottsville 3209
South Africa
Email: books@ukzn.ac.za

Editor: Andrea Nattrass
Cover designer: Sumayya Essack
Typesetter: Manoj Sookai

Printed and bound by Interpak Books, Pietermaritzburg

Contents

Acknowledgements

This book has been long in the making. In its first life, it emerged as a doctoral thesis and was defended in May 1999 at the Department of Literature at Uppsala University. For that, and for sharing their formidable literary-critical experience so generously, I express my heartfelt gratitude to Bengt Landgren, my supervisor, as well as my assistant supervisor Torsten Pettersson. At work-in-progress seminars a number of colleagues shared their insights with me, notably Patrik Mehrens, Anna Cullhed, Magnus Ullén, Gachugu Makini, Sigrid Klaman, Ann Öhrberg, Annika Olsson and Sara Danius. The weaknesses of this work are my own doing; what strengths there may be are largely thanks to their various interventions.

As cherished friends and colleagues – both outside and within the teaching machine – Stefan Jonsson, Ola Larsmo, Louis Faye and Moa Matthis were at different stages instrumental in convincing me that this project was worth its while, even in Sweden. Their passion, intelligence and erudition has been my benefit.

The current moment of publication in South Africa is none the less a homecoming of sorts. In its embryonic phase my thesis enjoyed the support and keen criticism of Leon de Kock at the University of South Africa, as well as of the staff at what was still the English Department in Pietermaritzburg, notably Anton van der Hoven, Jill Arnott, Colin Gardner and Kathrin Wagner. David Attwell has been a particularly important reader, given that he fulfilled the crucial function of 'opponent' at the defence of the thesis in Uppsala, a privilege of rare magnitude.

In Johannesburg, both Mike Marais at the Rand Afrikaans University and Ivan Vladislavić, my long-time interlocutor on matters literary and stylistic, have consistently been more accommodating than I could ever ask them to be.

In the later phase of publishing this book, I have become greatly indebted to the University of KwaZulu-Natal Press, particularly to my editor Andrea Nattrass, whose thorough professionalism has made my burden in making the thesis publishable light to bear.

Thanks are due to the university libraries at Pietermaritzburg, Durban and Uppsala (both Carolin Rediviva and the Nordic Africa Institute), as well as to Kerstin Landgren for her deft administration of my finances. The sources of these funds must likewise be acknowledged, principally SIDA, but also Knut & Alice Wallenbergs Stiftelse, Karl & Warburgs Fond för Litteraturhistorisk Forskning and Jan Stenkvists Minnesfond.

Finally, as always, where would I have been without Bibi's perseverance and care? Half the work has been hers as we have juggled the responsibility and joy of bringing up Sonya, Clara and Samuel, whose invigorating disruptions have always reminded me that a person is a person thanks to other people.

Stefan Helgesson
Pietermaritzburg, January 2004

Foreword

J.M. Coetzee's description, in his Jerusalem Prize Acceptance Speech in 1987, of apartheid South African literature as the kind of writing that one would expect from a prison-house evinces an acute awareness of the 'worldliness' of the literary text, its inevitable contamination by the discursive determinants of the cultural and historical context from which it emanates. Although Coetzee does not dwell on literary criticism in this address, what he has to say about creative writing has obvious implications for critical writing. One is forced to consider, for instance, the ways in which the South African 'interpretive community' of the apartheid era was affected by historical forces.

In *Writing in Crisis*, Stefan Helgesson touches on this question in his prefatory summation of the heated critical debate on literary representation, artistic integrity and political responsibility in the South Africa of the 1980s – a debate which eventually divided the literary culture of the country into 'aesthetic' and 'activist' factions, that is, into proponents of a Eurocentric model of formal sophistication in literary production, on the one hand, and proponents of an engaged mode of literary writing, which would respond unambiguously to the exigencies of the political realities of the time, on the other. As Helgesson puts it, 'we would be hard pressed to find *any* writer or critic at the time who is unaffected by the conflict' (12).

He is, of course, quite right. Indeed, the heavily polarised positions occupied by these factions did not allow for much in the way of clear thinking – for a recognition, for instance, of the point that Helgesson goes on to make in his study, that is, that form *has* content, is *always* political, and that content is, in fact, *constituted* by form. To this part of Helgesson's discussion may be added an observation which, I think, helps to clarify the importance of his contribution to the study of South African literature: namely, that the 1980s was also a time in which continental literary theory slowly began to influence local debates in the English academy. Significantly, both the literary positions to which Helgesson refers responded, albeit for different reasons, antipathetically to this 'new' direction in thinking about literature. Perhaps the 'aesthetic' faction's antipathy may be ascribed to a New Critical aversion to what was perceived to be 'extrinsic' approaches to literature that were bound to compromise the internal integrity of the literary work. In the case of the 'activist' faction, such antipathy was quite simply the product of a suspicion of post-structuralist reading strategies which reflect on the instability of language, complicate representation – particularly the stability of history as an a priori structure – and, in the process, problematise the notion of subjective agency. While the country was burning, quite literally in places, literature had to strike a blow for freedom and it was the critic's moral and political duty to assist in, rather than confound, this endeavour.

However, it is not only the 'activist' and 'aesthetic' factions that responded with a measure of antipathy to the infiltration of post-structuralist theories into literary studies in South Africa. Much local criticism on South African literature, as Helgesson rightly points out, 'has tended to begin with a broad historical argument which is then applied to the text – the meaning of which is already assumed by the argument' (4). In fact, the kind of criticism that is here at issue assumed that language transparently reflects a history that is directly accessible to the writing subject. Tellingly, in this regard, some practitioners of this form of criticism routinely conflated author and character in their commentaries, and treated the narrative events in the texts which they appraised as historical incidents. In such a critical context, to consider the sheer ambivalence of language, particularly literary language, and the discursive mediation of history, was to open oneself to the accusation of frivolous abstraction from some quarters. One of the inevitable corollaries of this fairly widespread suspicion of theory was a certain parochialism in the study of South African literature. Although there are quite definite signs of change in this regard, it is interesting to note that, to date, a self-evidently useful approach to the study of South African literature such as post-colonialism has enjoyed rather limited currency in this country.

It is here that Helgesson's work, which originated as a doctoral thesis at Uppsala University, constitutes an invaluable contribution to the study of South African English literature. His post-colonial approach to the texts which he considers erodes precisely the oppositions between form and content, 'theoretical' criticism and 'historical' criticism, to which I have referred above and, in so doing, reveals the false premises on which they have been constructed. What you will find in *Writing in Crisis* is a critical practice that is at once theoretically sophisticated, without ever being abstruse, *and* uncompromisingly historicist, without ever reducing the text to a mere supplement of history. Moreover, his sublation of the specious opposition between theoretically-grounded and historically-grounded criticism culminates in a mode of close reading that is not premised on a separation between form and content (and therefore on the questionable and dangerously conservative assumptions of aesthetic transcendence and universalism that this distinction enables), but which ceaselessly historicises the entire text.

It is, of course, not only *in* but also *through* achieving this dialectical critical practice that Helgesson's work constitutes a real and fresh contribution to South African literary criticism. Only through collapsing the above-mentioned oppositions, is he able to arrive at some of the pivotal insights attendant on the thesis of this study, namely the ways in which Ndebele's *Fools and Other Stories*, Gordimer's *A Sport of Nature*, and Coetzee's *Life & Times of Michael K*, in the 1980s, negotiated the 'beyond', that is, 'a subjective and/or social space that was not defined, circumscribed or constricted by the currently dominant historical force of apartheid' (4), and attempted 'to achieve a symbolic solution to the prevailing pressures on subjectivity and writing in the 1980s' (4). Such attention to the texts' representation of subject-positions and the aesthetic conditions of possibility for these representations was simply precluded by the closely-guarded, narrow parameters within which many previous commentators read the works of these writers. Indeed, as much of the early Coetzee criticism attests, commentators who subscribed to the 'activist' and 'aesthetic' factions of the critical community of the 1980s simply could not adequately respond to texts which included both these positions.

To a large extent, then, Helgesson's study of Ndebele, Gordimer and Coetzee provides revisionist readings of these writers: a retrospective re-assessment of the ways in which their works responded to the political and aesthetic pressures of the period in which they were produced. While this, in itself, makes his book a timely and major critical intervention in South African literary studies, it is the sophisticated form of close reading through which his revisionist consideration proceeds that sets it apart from anything else that I have read on South African literature in recent years. In its attention to matters of form, Helgesson's text-centred approach articulates that which has languished in near silence for some time now in criticism of South African literature, namely the aesthetic dimension of the text. This step towards a rediscovery of the aesthetic can only be welcomed.

Finally, it should be noted that Helgesson's critical practice is informed by a highly sophisticated understanding not only of the theories of Bhabha and Spivak, but also of the ethical philosophy of Lévinas. As such, his close readings of Ndebele, Gordimer and Coetzee establish a crucial nexus between post-colonialism and ethics, and in the process examine the interface between politics, ethics and aesthetics. In this regard, the contribution to criticism and theory made by this study far exceeds a narrow interest in the literature of a region.

Michael Marais
Johannesburg, January 2004

Introduction

IN HER CAPACITY as dissident writer, and for the benefit of a foreign readership eager to hear subversive truth from the land of apartheid, Nadine Gordimer described her own context in 1982 in the following way:

> I live at 6,000 feet in a society whirling, stamping, swaying with the force of revolutionary change. The vision is heady; the image of the demonic dance – and accurate, not romantic: an image of actions springing from emotion, knocking deliberation aside. The city is Johannesburg, the country South Africa, and the time the last years of the colonial era in Africa (1988: 262).

These were drastic words, yet not unparalleled. That same year, her colleague André Brink assessed that 'despite the deceptively calm surface – the South African situation in 1982 is decidedly worse than during the Soweto riots of 1976' (1983: 238). Brink sensed that 'attitudes have polarized alarmingly' and that a 'siege mentality has emerged quite chillingly from the relative openness of the 1970s' (1983: 238).

Although their emotional responses to the situation varied, Gordimer and Brink shared the perception that a sea-change was underway in South Africa. Their observations were prescient. Four years later, the critic Lewis Nkosi would conclude: 'There is hardly any doubt that from the '70s, and more acceleratingly in the '80s, the battle against apartheid has finally moved into the streets and that the rock and the fire-bomb have become its most potent sign' (1986: 43). Politically, Nkosi welcomed the turbulence, but there was more to this than politics – it also 'plunged South African literature into its worst crisis in years' (1986: 43). In Nkosi's view, this irony was inevitable. Literature could not provide a space for 'that personal contact with a revolutionary impulse which can only be achieved at a more intimate level of collective action' (1986: 43). If we follow his suggestion, then the word 'crisis' would apply differently in the respective contexts of politics and literature, reviving the former and paralysing the latter. But is it viable to split the notion of crisis in this way? Aren't we dealing in *both* cases with a major *historical* crisis that redefines, at great cost, the terms and conditions of any social or aesthetic activity, the upshot being that crisis simultaneously, albeit in a qualified fashion, makes difference imaginable?

In other words, is it possible to find South African literary texts of the period that both respond to the crisis of the 1980s and deconstruct their own grounding in the conflicts that dictate the crisis, thus enabling the reader to imagine subject-positions, aesthetic options and conceptual horizons that lie 'beyond'? Texts that become 'sports' that engage a received cultural form and deviate from it at the same time? If so, how is it done? And how, if at all, do such texts relate to one another? In tackling these questions, this book focuses on three specific works: *Fools and Other Stories* by Njabulo Ndebele (1983); *A Sport of Nature* by Nadine Gordimer (1987); and *Life & Times of Michael K* by J.M. Coetzee (1983).

The 1980s belong to a dire chapter in South African history. Throughout the decade the political turmoil that had initially erupted with the Soweto uprising in 1976 was intensified by the government's increasingly draconian strategies and measures to quash any resistance to its policies. These were the years – additionally aggravated from the first State of Emergency in 1985 onwards – when the police and military resorted not only to mass detentions and torture, but also to systematic assassinations, border raids, and undercover support for vigilante gangs. The catch-word for official policy at the time was 'total strategy', a term coined late in the 1970s by the Minister of Defence Magnus Malan in response to what was symmetrically dubbed the 'total onslaught' on South Africa by supposedly communist forces (Davenport, 1991: 397). As far as the fundamental issue of the 'black' majority's right to full citizenship and political power was concerned, the government would not budge an inch. When President Botha called for elections in 1983 and 1987, minimal concessions were made to the 'Indian' and 'Coloured' groups (who were allowed separate chambers of parliament), while in fact 'white' supremacy was maintained throughout – politically and economically. A precarious state of ignorance among large sections of the 'white' population was upheld by means of anti-communist propaganda, media censorship and, not least, the general desire to remain ignorant. Conversely, on the international scene, the image of South Africa was almost exclusively of a spectacular, televised genre in which 'the rock and the fire-bomb' were perceived as South African reality itself, and not just its signs.[1]

In the midst of this interregnum, to use the Gramscian phrase appropriated by Nadine Gordimer (1988: 261–284), and subsequently widely accepted,[2] South African literature and literary criticism was, inevitably, affected. More specifically, the 1980s brought a number of critical debates on representation, artistic integrity and political responsibility to a head, debates in which the three writers I will discuss played a crucial role. Likewise, in the fiction published around this time – without necessarily causing or being caused by the critical debates – a sense of crisis was more than traceable. At the representational level, a number of novels published around the turn of the decade envisioned the breakdown of the current social order and, in some cases, ventured prophetically to the beginnings of what lay 'beyond'. Paying special attention to Gordimer's *July's People* (1981), Coetzee's *Life & Times of Michael K* (1983) and Mongane Serote's *To Every Birth its Blood* (1981), Stephen Clingman suggested that 'in South African fiction, as in South African culture and politics more generally, the future is *the* presiding question of the 1980s' (1990: 43). Interestingly, he offered a materialist explanation to this state of affairs by comparing it with earlier moments in resistance history: 'in the 1950s, the movements opposed to apartheid were nonetheless active *within* the framework of what already existed. Fully believing in the potential of South African democracy, what the opposition movements of the time wanted primarily was its *extension*, to include blacks and everyone else within it' (1990: 44). Although it is far too reductive to view South African literature as a mere supplement to political history, Clingman's remark exemplifies the paradigmatic shift from thinking 'within' to thinking 'beyond' that clearly affects (and is effected by) the literature of the 1980s – whatever the overdetermined motivations behind such a shift. The spatial metaphor also shows that this not only concerned 'the future' in the strictly temporal sense of word. Without moving ahead in time, a number of novels and stories also persistently constructed scenarios of the 'beyond', that is, of a subjective and/or social space that was not defined, circumscribed or constricted by the currently dominant historical force of apartheid. However, such an ambition could not be carried through – unproblematically – in terms of straightforward representation, since the forms of representation available in English language literature themselves bore (and bear) the mark of the history that was to be challenged. Thus, identifying representational convention itself as part of the problem, several writers implicitly (like Njabulo Ndebele) or explicitly (like J. M. Coetzee) addressed the crisis by disrupting representational and generic expectations in their fiction.

Given this critical moment in the history of South African literature, I intend in this work to investigate how Ndebele, Gordimer and Coetzee each in his or her own way negotiates the 'beyond' and attempt to achieve a symbolic solution to the prevailing pressures on subjectivity and writing in the 1980s. The readings are two-tiered: they are concerned with the representation of subject-positions but equally with the formal/literary conditions of possibility for such representations.

While virtually all criticism on South African literature to have emerged from the 1970s onwards insists on some notion of resistance through writing, this book differs from other scholarship on four counts. Firstly, in adherence to an heuristic model of knowledge, it involves an at times microscopically close reading practice. While much work in this field has tended to begin with a broad historical argument which is then applied to the text – the meaning of which is already assumed by the argument – it is my ambition to proceed *through* and *against* the literary text and see how such a reading may produce, deconstruct or evade a particular understanding of the subject in history.[3]

This approach is perhaps particularly appropriate to the principal context in which this work emerged – a university in Sweden – given that the notion of 'South African history' tends to be ossified or simplified when removed from the unfolding historical process in South Africa. Of course, such an approach cannot do without some primary assumption of a historical context, but by privileging the reading process it is my ambition to disrupt the primary assumption, as in the case of *A Sport of Nature* where a close reading leads to a discussion of postmodern and post-colonial globality far removed from the conventional reading of the 'struggle' normally applied to Gordimer's fiction. The chapter on Ndebele is something of an exception, given that I start off with a theorisation of the 'black' writer's historical position in South Africa, but this ties in specifically with my discussion of *Fools* in Part 2.

My text-centered approach means, furthermore, that I regard form as a constitutive element of the literary artefact. On such an understanding, form cannot be divorced from meaning – in the sense that generic assumptions, style, choice of language, etc. all contribute, earnestly or ironically, to the way in which a specific text is read, indeed, to its very readability. This is not to be mistaken for a strict formalism which reduces the text to this aspect only, but rather as an insistence on how each moment of writing engages form.

Secondly, whilst I underpin this book on the notion of 'South Africa' and 'South African literature', I make a point of destabilising these concepts by intervening with transnational points of intellectual anchorage. While this may be *comme il faut* in Coetzee's case, studies of Ndebele and Gordimer – and of South African literature in general – often restrict themselves to a South African horizon.[4] This can be harmful insofar as it risks reducing these works of fiction to parochial 'special cases' of scant interest to the mainstream metropolitan literary establishment, thus preventing the mode of critique or knowledge offered by these works of fiction from leaking out from the South African enclosure. Such a re-stricted horizon would, moreover, reproduce the isolation which is inseparable from the troubled historical construction of 'South Africa' and which has obscured its embeddedness in the global history of Western imperialism. Therefore, even as it is being con-structed in progressive political terms – as a utopian project in the 1980s and a distinctly pragmatic project in the 1990s – 'South Africa' as a concept needs to be deconstructed in all its hetero-geneity. The unity of the concept is patently questionable, but so is the sense of its uniqueness. The specific conjunction of interests, histories and conflicts that converge on 'South Africa' is of course just as unique as any other national configuration, but to reify 'South Africa' would ultimately prohibit any attempt to discuss in a demystifying fashion literary attempts to imagine it. (Just as the cliché 'but this is Africa,' always short-circuited European criticism of apartheid. Meaning: unique conditions call for unique measures.)

It is for these reasons that I mobilise post-colonial theory: so that I may connect specific texts to an ongoing global debate while steering clear of any easy, Western universalism. More than that, I use each reading as an occasion to engage in a theoretical discussion – not as a 'method' that I apply to a supposedly inert text, but as a condition of possibility of the reading itself and as a form of understanding that unfolds along with the reading. I particularly focus on Homi Bhabha's and Gayatri Spivak's under-standing of post-colonial irony: the necessity to articulate resistance through language and forms that have historically been employed to disable such resistance.

Thirdly, and by the same token, I consistently regard the categories 'black' and 'white' as provisional. My choice of writers forms part of an ambition to cut through the compartmentalisation of 'white' and 'black' writing. This is not to say that the terms 'white' and 'black', and their various synonyms, are devoid of social significance (they are, of course, entirely disqualified as *racial* categories[5]) in the sense that they have determined at base level the status and options of each individual in South Africa – a deter-mination that was formalised and exacerbated during the apartheid era. Indeed, Zoë Wicomb even suggests that

> [o]ne of the more refreshing qualities of apartheid was the abandon with which we all talked about and identified ourselves in terms of race, a situation which compares rather favourably with European cultures where official 'anti-racism' [. . .] stifles its own discourse with a fastidious reluctance to speak of white or black (1998: 363).

Wicomb states this not out of an essentialist longing, but because terminological frankness would arguably make it easier to expose the constructedness of the labels. Indeed, if we examine the categories sanctioned by the apartheid state, we will find that they had constantly to manage a semantic crisis of their own making. How else to account for the 'reclassification' of several hundred individuals each year which magically transformed 'Coloured' into 'white', 'white' into 'Chinese', 'Indian' into 'Coloured', 'Coloured' into 'African', etc.? (Lelyveld, 1986: 85). If anything, these regular 'adjustments' to satisfy the classificatory zeal of the apartheid state demonstrated with bizarre precision the fictive nature of the categories. To constantly foreground the constructedness of the terms 'black' and 'white' while just as insistently acknowledging their conflictual social significance is therefore even more important when dealing with writers and texts that try to move 'beyond' the conceptual horizon of apartheid South Africa. Such semantic vigilance can be traced genealogically to Fanon's statement that 'The Negro is not. Any more than the white man', offered at the tail end of his brilliant exposition of the burden of 'blackness' in *Peau noire, masques blancs* (1986: 231). Therefore, if we follow Fanon, resistance to categorisation is not a question of ignoring the colonial construction of 'blackness', but of working one's way through and ultimately out of this construction.[6] A comparable instance is Simone de Beauvoir's analysis of gender in *Le deuxième sexe*. Published a mere three years before Fanon's book, Beauvoir's treatise places 'woman' under erasure in the same way as Fanon does 'blackness', that is, by squarely confronting the social and semantic force of the notion of 'woman' (1949: 11–32).[7]

Fourthly, I attempt to intervene in the post-colonial debate through a successive process of abstraction which arrives, in Chapter 14, at the ethical philosophy of Emmanuel Lévinas. As I shall argue, much of what is gathered under the heading of 'post-colonial theory' resonates in crucial ways with the work of Lévinas. The relation between the two, which hinges on the ethical response to alterity, was long overlooked, despite the fact that it clarifies and enriches the critique of the Western subject that has gained global currency through post-colonial studies.[8] This process of abstraction – some would call it a retreat from historicism – was not premeditated as I began this project, but has emerged as one compelling way to elaborate the philosophical underpinnings of post-colonial theory.

Outline

The general outline of this book is simple. In Part 1, I expand on the theoretical premises of my readings. In Part 2, I discuss *Fools and Other Stories* at length, investigating not only its epistemological critique, but also the deployment of form and the prefiguration of a 'body' located outside of colonial discourse. In Part 3, I explore the construction and representation of *A Sport of Nature*'s protagonist Hillela at three different levels: semiotically, as a sign fulfilling specific functions in a narrative; realistically, as a character bearing the symbolic burden of fulfilling a desire to transcend 'white' determinations in South Africa; and allegorically, as a fantastical figure standing in for the conjunction of incommensurable elements in the web of global relations. Part 4 investigates the 'life' and the 'times' as these are represented and deconstructed in *Life and Times of Michael K.* The narrative is viewed metacritically – more so than in the previous cases – and read from the perspective of Levinasian ethics.

I wish to make it clear that I do *not* assume that there is a qualitative progression from Ndebele through Gordimer to Coetzee. What sense of progression there may be has only to do with any measure of increased maturity on my part in matters theoretical. I happened to begin with Ndebele and finish with Coetzee, and found my bearings in the process. Apart from that, each work of fiction places different demands on me as reader and cannot be reduced to a position in a progressivist narrative. Having said this, however, I do make comparisons along the way which I reflect on in the Conclusion. These comparisons are to be understood as addressing each narrative in its own right, rather than placing them in a hierarchy of literary value. Above all, the comparisons pertain to the broader discussion of South African literature in the 1980s, its predicaments, its limits, and its capacities.

PART 1

Negotiating the 'Beyond'

Theoretical Considerations

History is what hurts, it is what refuses desire.

Fredric Jameson (The Political Unconscious, *1981: 102*)

CHAPTER 1

Exploring 'History' and 'Writing'

IN MICHAEL CHAPMAN'S ANALYSIS, the critical debate in South Africa in the 1980s centred on the very status of 'literature' (1996: 424–425). What in retrospect can be regarded as the aesthetic complacency of certain 'white' literary circles was challenged by a more inclusive notion of literature that denounced Western standards and took, above all, the oppositional voice of 'black' performance poetry on board. This wasn't 'merely' a polemical or academic concern. Rather, there were a number of events and conditions at the collective level, connected to the political developments outlined in the Introduction but with cultural consequences, that eventually forced the hand of South African critics and intellectuals.

There was the pervasive yet unpredictable fact of censorship, which tended automatically to endow the act of writing with a certain *gravitas*;[1] there was the international boycott on cultural exchange with South Africa which gained momentum towards the middle of the decade; and there was the (ANC-aligned) United Democratic Front's campaign in 1985 for a 'people's culture' which, as far as literature was concerned, prescribed an 'accessible' and oppositional social realism that depicted the lives of the oppressed (Attwell, 1990: 102).

All of these factors – and I deliberately restrict myself to some of the most immediate, synchronic points – contributed to the polarised context of the critical debate. It evolved into a stalemate between supposedly 'aesthetic' and 'activist' conceits, so that '[in] reply to the cultural activists' charge that the poets of contemplation were Eurocentric, elitist and conservative in their professed liberalism, the poets of contemplation defended the exploratory value of language removed from cliché and slogan' (Chapman,

1996: 425). Typical antagonists in this struggle were, on the activist side, the marxist poet Jeremy Cronin and, on the aesthetic side, the staunch literary idealists Lionel Abrahams and Stephen Watson – but we would be hard pressed to find *any* writer or critic at the time who is unaffected by the conflict (Abrahams, 1988: 307–333, 1989: 27–30; Chapman, 1996: 424–426; Watson, 1990: 82–99).

I find that the three works of fiction that I deal with in this book each in its own way accommodates both the activist and the aesthetic positions. In the chapters that follow I try to demonstrate just how precarious and hard-won such an inclusive position can be. Ndebele, Gordimer and Coetzee's texts all bear the mark of untenable pressures, of an immense historical burden bearing down on their narrative desire. This claim dismisses any facile version of liberal pluralism, and assumes instead that the capacity of these texts to say something different, to transcend the polarisation of the political and literary culture at the time, begins with the recognition that 'aesthetics' and 'politics' are, at this moment in South African history, irretrievably involved with one another. What becomes of this recognition is a different matter, but once the recognition is made, the idealist conception of, for example, Lionel Abrahams's 'standards' becomes hard to sustain (Chapman, 1996: 424).[2]

Ndebele, Gordimer and Coetzee all contributed to these po-lemics. Their interventions as intellectuals do not pre-empt their fictional writings, but they do help us to determine in greater detail the contested field against which the potential significance of the narratives as socially symbolic acts can be read. In one of the most pointed moments of the protracted debate, J.M. Coetzee offered a condensed interpretation of the field:

> in times of intense ideological pressure like the present, when the space in which the novel and history normally coexist like two cows on the same pasture, each minding its own business, is squeezed almost to nothing, the novel, it seems to me, has only two options: supplementarity or rivalry. It cannot be both autonomous and supplementary. If the novel aims to provide the reader with vicarious first-hand experience of living in a certain historical time, embodying contending forces in contending characters and

filling our experience with a certain density of observation, if it regards this as its goal [. . .] then its relation to history is self-evidently a secondary relation.

What, by contrast, would be meant by a novel that occupies an autonomous place, that is what I call a rival to history?

I mean – to put it in its strongest form – a novel that operates in terms of its own procedures and issues in its own conclusions, not one that operates in terms of the procedures of history and eventuates in conclusions that are checkable by history (as a child's schoolwork is checked by a schoolmistress). In particular I mean a novel that evolves its own paradigms and myths, in the process [. . .] perhaps going so far as to show up the mythic status of history – in other words, demythologising history. Can I be more specific? Yes: for example, a novel that is prepared to work itself out outside the terms of class conflict, race conflict, gender conflict or any other of the oppositions out of which history and the historical disciplines erect them-selves (1988a: 3).

In Coetzee's view, history and the novel belong to different orders of understanding. The difference between them is so significant that it should be foregrounded rather than suppressed. The way in which he foregrounds this difference is revealing: he grants both terms an agency of their own. Coetzee writes after 'the death of author'[3] and seems to imply that the writer may choose between two discursive contexts that function differently but can scarcely hope to command either context. Of course, Coetzee himself is not indifferent to the moment of choice. No reader of his article can doubt that he is advocating 'rivalry' as against 'supplementarity'. But although this means that he grants the writer the capacity to choose between two alternatives, this is an implied, heavily qualified form of agency.

When contrasted with the major strain of oppositional literature in South Africa, which emphasised the construction and recon-struction of (political) agency, and did not regard discourse as a constitutive and thus ineluctable element of agency, we can understand that Coetzee's argument was provocative at the time. It stands out against the realist bias of resistance literature and the 'people's culture' campaign, but it also has a highly specific address, namely Nadine Gordimer and her more prominent exegeses. A year before, Stephen Clingman had published his influential study on Gordimer's novels and established the view that Gordimer's writing, in the spirit of Lukácsian 'critical realism', deliberately seeks to engage with history and illuminate it 'from within'. Her novels should primarily be read in referential terms, as vessels for their characters rather than as self-reflexive texts. The characters should, in turn, be understood as 'figures who [. . .] both condense broader social and historical patterns and, in their individuality, engage with them in intense and extreme form. They are characters who fully become 'subjects' of history, and in turn explore it as far as their capacities and situation will allow' (Clingman, 1986: 9).

This resembles Coetzee's description of the supplementary novel as much as it echoes Nadine Gordimer's own critique of Coetzee's *Life & Times of Michael K*. This novel failed in Gordimer's opinion because of its refusal to engage with the historical thrust of the time. She concluded that 'Coetzee's heroes are those who ignore history, not make it' (1984: 3). By Gordimer's standards, such a novelist is guilty not of a political transgression but of disloyalty to the demands of being a writer: 'the organicism that Georg Lukács defines as the integral relation between private and social destiny is distorted here more than is allowed for by the subjectivity that is in every writer' Gordimer, 1984: 6). This position, which centres on the notion of responsibility, is developed at length by Gordimer in her essay 'The Essential Gesture', in which she underscores society's demand that the writer be 'more than a writer':

> The creative act is not pure. History evidences it. Ideology demands it. Society exacts it. The writer loses Eden, writes to be read, and comes to realise that he [*sic*] is answerable. The writer is *held responsible:* and the verbal phrase is ominously accurate, for the writer not only has laid upon him responsibility for various interpretations of consequences of his work, he is 'held' before he begins by the claims of different concepts of morality – artistic,

linguistic, ideological, national, political, religious – asserted upon him. He learns that his creative act was not pure even while being formed in his brain: already it carried congenital responsibility for what preceded cognition and volition: for what he represented in genetic, environmental, social and economic terms when he was born of his parents (1988a: 285–286).

This amounts to a version of original sin. As a consequence thereof, the writer of any integrity must recognise 'society's right to make demands on the writer as equal to that of the writer's commitment to his artistic vision' (Gordimer, 1988a: 289). Gordimer insists that this conflictual position – the required excess of being both a writer and more than a writer – can, ideally, be harmonised precisely through writing. But such reconciliation is hard to achieve. It forces the writer to confront both aspects of this responsibility rather than to evade them: 'To gain his [*sic*] freedom the writer must give up his freedom' (Gordimer, 1988: 293).

Thus we find Gordimer *answering* precisely to those demands of history that Coetzee, at roughly the same moment, tries his utmost to *refute*. The conflict between the two positions seems clear enough and would enable me to construct, as has been done many times before, a cut-and-dried opposition between Coetzee and Gordimer as the two exemplary figures of 'contemporary South African literature in English'. In this opposition, the 'rival' Coetzee is generally seen as the more aesthetically minded of the two, whereas the 'supplementary' Gordimer is regarded as the more politically responsible. Their positions form a neat antithetical pair that may subsequently be applied to readings of their respective works.[4] However, this view – which I simplify somewhat – risks eliding a crucial point of resonance: the fact that both of them *address* the relation between history and writing, and that both find this relation problematic as well as potentially rewarding. Their positions could be read as negative imprints of each other in which 'agency' functions as the submerged counterpart of 'history': whereas Gordimer's readiness to accept the primacy of history stems from her conviction that the writer, indeed, the *author*, can enter history without effacing his or her independent agency, Coetzee grants history even greater power over the writer, and tries for that very reason to salvage a sliver of differential agency on behalf of the writer. Nevertheless, even in Coetzee's harsh formulations there is a sense in which rivalry with history elevates the novel, since history is the precondition for that rivalry. His argument on the autonomy of the novel is literally not conceivable outside the difference between history and novel. The novel cannot have any intrinsic autonomy because, in Coetzee's words, 'the difference is everything'; the autonomy of the novel is an effect of difference (1988a: 4).

As for Gordimer, although her engagement with history is deliberate and desired, it always tends to be countered by a romantic faith in the elevated stature of writers and writing.[5] Just as individual agency is an absolute in her reasoning, so she grants literature, the concept of literature, an absolute status which is then matched more or less successfully by the individual author – but this depends on how the author answers to the demands of history.

A third point of entry in this debate (and one that takes us beyond the pedestrian juxtaposition of Coetzee and Gordimer) is offered by Njabulo Ndebele. A 'prophet of the post-apartheid condition', in Graham Pechey's description (1995: 1), Ndebele emerged in the 1980s as one of the country's foremost thinkers on cultural matters. He combined from the start a 'dispassionate' intellectual approach with an intense engagement with local history and literature. His subject-position as 'black' – albeit in exile – was in this regard an advantage, compared with Gordimer and Coetzee whose 'white' subject-positions prohibited any easy identification with or severe critique of 'black' dissent.

Coetzee's paper certainly reads as a critique of much 'black' writing, but this is understated: his argument is held in abstract terms and makes few explicit claims on its own behalf. By contrast, Ndebele could afford to be both specific and severe in his interventions. In a number of essays, of which the first was published in 1984, he argued that 'black' South African literature was stuck in a counter-productive mode of representation. His founding assumption was that the horizon of knowledge in 'black' literature tended to be delimited by the dominant 'white' society even when such literature explicitly resisted apartheid. Protest literature had reproduced, rather than challenged, the obvious facts of oppression. For example, the representation of victims and oppressors in Alex la Guma's stories confirmed the system rather than resisted it. This resulted from a focus on 'anticipated surfaces' (Ndebele, 1991: 27), and produced an art that became 'grounded in the very negation that it [sought] to transcend' (1991: 23).

The claim that 'black' writers primarily wanted to make their living conditions *known* did not hold, in Ndebele's view, since their journalistic, sensationalist approach restricted their epistemological horizon to what was already set in place by the 'white' establishment. This included liberal institutions whose morally motivated focus on the devastating surface effects of apartheid perpetuated the image of powerless victims and an omnipotent state (Ndebele, 1991: 24). As against this, Ndebele stressed the need for what we might call *epistemological transformation*. He argued for an alternative mode of representation where 'blacks' are situated as subjects rather than objects; a literature that deals with processes and personal histories rather than reified symbols of good and evil; imaginative storytelling rooted in social contexts simultaneous with yet not defined by apartheid.

As can be seen, Ndebele's analysis is delicately poised between an almost Foucauldian conviction that discourse conditions the resistance against it, and an insistence on the capacity of critical reflection and communal identification to foster a truly resistant agency. This doubleness, which covers elements of both Coetzee's and Gordimer's positions, is characteristic of Ndebele's entire project. He writes in 'flawless' English about the virtues of vernacular orality; he resists apartheid by criticising resistance literature; he is an urban intellectual who speaks on behalf of rural experience. But instead of undercutting his authority, these tensions, as Tony Morphet argues, enhance it. This is because 'black' historical experience in South Africa spans, also at the individual level, precisely such contradictions. When Ndebele 'speaks from the breach' and his language 'moves between two fields of thought' he is more attuned to the historical imperatives of his position than had he used a supposedly purer approach (Morphet, 1992: 139).

This double articulation also operates in his most explicit statement on artistic autonomy:

The central problem here appears to lie in the often confusing paradox that art is an autonomous entity which, at the same time, derives its objective validity from and within society. This latter condition would then, by definition, appear to deny artistic autonomy. Something there is, therefore, in art that determines its autonomy; and something there is that appears necessarily to undercut that autonomy. Writers might therefore fall into two camps: according to whether they emphasise what makes for artistic autonomy, on the one hand; or, on the other hand, according to whether they emphasise the undercutting elements (Ndebele 1991: 22).

Ndebele's analysis – which underlies his plea for a socially responsive literature that takes its autonomy seriously – inscribes yet again the bipolar field in which both Gordimer and Coetzee position themselves. In other words, differences in emphasis and choice of words notwithstanding, all three writers explicitly concede a tension between *history* and *writing*.

It is in this troubled yet productive relation that I locate the founding assumption of this book. History, each of these writers will claim or imply, determines writing, but it is the task of writing to exceed that determination, to differ, to imagine something other than what the historical present already has articulated for them. 'Writing' is an act with the potential to clear a space for desire, even as that desire is being resisted by history. Writing is a utopian act, even if the Utopia in question is a purely negative one and manifests itself as a desire to escape the pressures of history. In other words, I suggest that the three works of fiction under discussion enact a persistent doubleness, which is, with necessary changes, precisely what I trace and discuss in this book. In my opinion, it is crucial to maintain the tension between 'history' and 'writing', rather than to consummate Gordimer's synthetic project – as did Stephen Clingman – or valorise the autonomy of writing – as Teresa Dovey (1988) tended to do in the first monograph on Coetzee.

Defining 'history' and 'writing'
'History' and 'writing' are both extremely porous terms that call for

elaboration. As Michael Green has shown, 'history' has been taken to mean a number of things by South African writers, in much the same way as the academic understanding of the term has shifted (1997: 14–27). In the 1980s, the main faultline within both literary and academic debates – the distinction isn't always clear – went between the 'realist' notion of social history which emerged from the revisionist (materialist) attack on liberal historiography, and the discursive notion of history, as represented above by Coetzee.⁶ These two positions remain clinched in conflict, not least because their respective terms of debate are incommensurable. Whereas the sociohistorical position regards 'history' in ontological terms, which makes the writing of history a straightforward but secondary and always imperfect pursuit of the primary truth about collective human endeavours – 'Queen History', as Charles van Onselen (1996: 11) calls it – the discursive position offers a formal, epistemological critique without really addressing the ontological issue at all. The flaw in the sociohistorical position, for the discursively minded intellectual, is the idealist notion that a signified ('history') could precede a system of signification. But this is a way of disqualifying rather than resolving the ontological issue. To use Coetzee's own imagery, he is only concerned with the two cows called 'novel' and 'history', whereas the social historians are interested in the pasture, no matter which cow leads them there.

What remains of the discursive position after its gesture of rejection are two crucial points: firstly, the irreducibly formal nature of historiography and the generic conventions that go with such a practice and, secondly, the power that is accorded the idea of history. The two options that Coetzee grants the novel could be described as, on the one hand, accepting the generic assumptions of historiography in order to claim some small part of its power and, on the other hand, as disrupting these same assumptions so as to safeguard another, more elusive discourse called 'the novel' or 'storytelling'.

This is not identical with the notion of history that informs this book. Rather, in order to gather Njabulo Ndebele, Nadine Gordimer and J.M. Coetzee under one roof, it is imperative that we surpass the narrowly formal view of history. Neither should 'history' as I use it be taken simply to mean 'that which is past', not in its ontological sense, nor in the strict temporal sense that it only refers to the *past*. Instead, I wish to understand history in terms of *historicity*. From this perspective, history becomes a dynamic concept which necessarily involves the present. This is what enabled Stephen Clingman to give his monograph on Gordimer the subtitle *History from the Inside*. Despite the fact that her novels are set exclusively in the present, the historical sensibility that Clingman reads from them concerns the historicity of any particular moment in society: its changeability, its strangeness, its conflictual nature, its relative difference from any other moment.

The term 'historicity' involves a shift of focus from history *per se* to the *effects* of history. The text offers an interface of historicity. Although it is the 'end product' of a vast web of determinations, I choose to place it first and proceed from there. Moreover, in order to grasp historicity we must historicise; to reach the noun we must go by way of the verb, which gracefully cuts the present discussion down to scale. If 'history' is a nebulous term referring to some process (or every process) 'out there', 'historicisation' is a hermeneutic activity that cannot be referred to independently of its agent. Historicisation only occurs in the doing. It cannot be given a fixed definition, since there is no conclusive way to seal off the historicity of a text. As Ferdinand Braudel has stated,

> History exists at different levels. [. . .] There are ten, a hundred levels to be examined, ten, a hundred different time spans. On the surface, the history of events works itself out in the short term: it is a sort of microhistory. Halfway down, a history of conjunctures follows a broader, slower rhythm. [. . .] And over and above the 'récitatif' of the conjuncture, structural history, or the history of the *longue durée*, inquires into whole centuries at a time (1980: 74).[7]

My reading is consequently marked by choice, by what I decide are the significant aspects or levels of historicity in these narratives. But since this choice is, in its inconclusiveness, threatened by a *mise en abyme*, it is also conditioned by a prior understanding – akin to Gadamer's *Vorverständnis* or 'pre-understanding' (1960: 252–253) – of what consitutes recent South African history. Such an understanding is already evident in the fact that I label the writers Ndebele, Gordimer and Coetzee 'South African'. It is likewise evinced by my privileging of the term 'post-colonial' as shorthand for an overdetermined complex of cultural and historical contradictions. There is also a foregone understanding embedded in the reception of these writers, and in the arguments they themselves present in their essayistic work. Choice and determination are, in other words, collusive and could lead me to posit an a priori historical grid upon which I simply project the narratives. I accept that such contextualisation is indispensable to a degree, but it is my ambition to *disrupt* the process by paying microscopic attention to the shifts and turns of the narratives themselves, in the conviction that something always remains that eludes the prior understanding. It is this something, this excess, that my readings attempt to bring into play.

The excess can be described as the resistant potential of writing, its resistance to its own historicity (and this includes but also exceeds Coetzee's rivalry with the *discourse* of history). I am hereby engaging four concepts: historicity, writing, writer, and reader, with writing as the most indeterminate concept cutting through the other three. At the most basic level, I claim that history determines the writer's writing, but that the writer attempts, through writing, to be free (Barthes, 1953: 17–44 adopts a similar schema). Or, better, that the writer negotiates historical determination through writing. This is not unlike Coetzee's suggestion that 'to write' is a verb in the 'middle voice', that is, neither active nor passive but in-between (1992: 94–95).

Consequently, the writing subject should be seen as separate from the act of writing, yet implicated in it. Similarly, history is separate from the act of writing, yet implicated in it. In so far as history is that which refuses desire, writing constitutes a site where desire can, at best, come into play. It is in this struggle with and against the inertia of historicity that the written narrative emerges.[8] Paradoxically, however, and this is the paradox of writing, the emergence of the narrative can only be manifested afterwards by readers, at a remove from the proper moment of emergence. This is more than just a sly observation, since it involves my 'rights' as a reader. If writing is semi-autonomous, and if writing is the only trace available to me of a specific moment of a writer's struggle with history, I must invest writing itself (and my reading of it) with a measure of agency. My first loyalty is therefore to the text, irrespective of how it may contradict what a writer says about his or her work. This does not unequivocally sever the ties between writer and writing, and thus disable the writer's agency, but the relationship between writer and written text is not one of unmediated authority. Thus, whereas the writer may mobilise writing as a mode of agency that symbolically challenges, negates or deconstructs history, a chosen text may, conversely, indicate how the act of writing is pressured, conditioned and enabled by an ongoing historical process. Writing is therefore not a fixed objective, but rather a performative mode which enables history and desire to clash, allowing the formal qualities of written narrative (such as irony, self-reflexivity, the representation of multiple subjectivities, the suspension and contraction of time) to momentarily displace the daunting imperatives of the historical process. This sense of a disjunction between literary narrative and historical narrative is strong in all three of the texts under discussion.

It operates in *Fools*, in its rewriting of the social and cultural space of 'South Africa'; it emerges as a particularly powerful theme in *A Sport of Nature*, which stitches together disparate temporalities into a 'new' entity; and it is explicitly thematised in *Life & Times of Michael K*, where both the terms and ostensible contents of history are displaced through, and for the benefit of, writing.

My focus on writing as an indeterminate yet historically pressured phenomenon, rather than a straightforward mode of expression for the individual author, enables me as critic to speak of texts as worldly – to use Said's term (1983: 35) – and discuss them in relation to the writer's historical position without taking recourse to rather embattled notions of intention and causality (Said, 1983: 47–48). The subjective/social position of the writer at the time of writing and publication is therefore by no means immaterial to the reading of a specific text, but the critic must distinguish between precisely such a *position* – the writer's legal status in society, his or her public interventions in current debates, his or her inscription in the colonial encounter, etc. – and the distinctly private, psychological realm of intentions, grudges, loves.

I remain agnostic with respect to the private realm: it is not easily retrieved nor self-evidently relevant to the signification of the text. It might even be argued that the very definition of 'private' is defunct in the light of feminist and subject-theoretical insistence on the social constructedness of subject-positions. The 'private realm' is consequently a less than appropriate object for me to pursue.

Positionality, by contrast, refers to the writing subject's intersection with society and the public domain and may legitimately be included in a discussion on the worldliness of a particular text, without reducing it to these factors or causes.

CHAPTER 2

Blankness, Irony, Ambivalence

A CRUCIAL SYMBOLIC SPACE in the three narratives where intratextual concerns and worldliness tend to merge is the body. The body is foregrounded in divergent ways, but there is a common historical factor at work here: the political charging of the body in the context of colonialism/apartheid. This was first theorised by Fanon in *Peau noire, masques blancs* and has later become a mainstay of post-colonial studies. The racial construction and degradation of the 'black' body – its absolute negativity in the daily drama of racist society – is the first and obvious theme, but as already Fanon implied, the 'black' body is also the 'white' body's condition of possibility (1952: 207). Thus, we find that in *A Sport of Nature* 'whiteness' is thematised through the explicitly corporeal Hillela, whereas in *Fools*, the 'black' body is redefined. In *Life & Times of Michael K* categorisations as such are challenged and the protagonist's body emerges as a vessel of qualified freedom.

In brief, I argue that the body constitutes an absolute limit of subjectivity in the narratives under discussion, and that it is to the extent that the body is seen to resist and/or re-channel representation that it ultimately prefigures an-other, post-colonial subject-position. At specific moments – such as the whipping of Zamani in 'Fools', Hillela's allegorical re-mapping of Africa through her purportedly corporeal, sensual sense of style, and Michael K's purely 'bodily' resistance to the instructions at the rehabilitation camp – it will appear that the body represented blocks out expectations inherent in the representational mode, expectations which are coded in binary terms and have already assigned positions for diverse bodies along the lines of oppression/protest, evil/good, white/black. In blocking out these expectations, the resistant body becomes marked by blankness. It cannot affirm, unironically and within its representational context, its alterity *vis-à-vis* this very context, but it can gesture towards it through its blankness, whether convincingly or not.

Such an argument focuses less on the 'battle-cry for freedom' (Carusi, 1989: 81) common in much South African writing of the period – and indispensable as part of a political struggle – and more on the challenge to the discursive underpinnings of apartheid, a challenge issued simultaneously from within and against this discursive context in such a way that it, in Annamaria Carusi's words,

> allows for an understanding of the materiality of a 'body', traversed by plural and sometimes contradictory lines of determination, which constitute it as a subject capable of action[. This notion of a] subject-effect thus provides for the positioning of a subject as a discursive instance which is the effect of a variety of structures or discursive practices (1989: 91).

Proceeding from such an understanding,

> the colonized body becomes the subject of its own history and turns the table on [imperialistic] humanism by *appropriating* its positivism from the position of its own negativity and heterogeneity. This is what we see at work in the appropriation of, for example, the categories of Western literature (realism, responsibility etc.) by a 'subject-effect' which is at once both within and without that tradition and that culture (Carusi, 1989: 92).

Resistance is seen as articulated by way of subject-positions already circumscribed by a history dominated by colonialism/apartheid. The blankness of the body that I trace in these specific examples is therefore ironic even prior to conception.

This argument bears affinity with feminist theories which claim that the female body may achieve a mode of agency by refurbishing and deconstructing the codes and structures of patriarchal language, but is barred from affirming and representing the position beyond patriarchy within language. For the most part, I tacitly assume this affinity between feminism and post-colonial theory, but there are also junctures where the gender issue tends to be elided on behalf of the post-colonial project. Such points of conflict, which make it imperative to ask how the racially defined body relates to the gendered body of 'woman', are discussed in the corresponding chapters. In *Fools*, for example, women stand as the champions of communal sharing and cultural cohesion, but are also the hidden term behind the utopian moment of the story 'Uncle'; in *A Sport of Nature*, the utopian transgressions of the protagonist are apparently achieved at the cost of succumbing to patriarchal eroticism. The feminist perspective qualifies in this way the post-colonial discussion. The opposite may be equally true, as evidenced by Gayatri Spivak's (1988: 134–153) sharp critique of the ethnocentrism of French feminism, but since I locate the Archimedean point of this book in post-colonial theory, it is this, rather than feminism, that I choose to confront and elaborate.

Catachresis and mimicry

The complex position of the body in the narratives serves as a paradigm for the condition of (im)possibility of the texts' resistance to their historicity. Its ambivalence and blankness is consequently marked by the ironies of post-coloniality.

Two of the most distinct terms that are used to describe this ironical predicament of post-colonial writing are Gayatri Spivak's 'catachresis' and Homi Bhabha's 'mimicry'. Both these terms convey a distinctly anti-foundational understanding of resistance and decolonisation. With reference to the deployment of 'Western' concepts such as nationhood, constitutionality and democracy in decolonised space, Spivak says the following:

> Within the historical frame of exploration, colonization, decolonization – what is being effectively reclaimed is a series of regulative political concepts, the *supposedly* authoritative narrative of the production of which was written elsewhere, in the social formations of Western Europe. They are being reclaimed, indeed claimed, as concept-metaphors for which no historically adequate

referent may be advanced from postcolonial space, yet that does not make the claims less important. A concept-metaphor without an adequate referent is a catachresis (1993: 60).

In Spivak's analysis, historical circumstances have forced post-colonial nations to found themselves on catachreses, that is, Western concepts that have become both necessary and inadequate. This split position determines not only the nation, but equally its subjects, its cultural institutions, and so on:

> The so-called private individual and the public citizen in a decolonized nation can inhabit widely different epistemes, violently at odds with each other yet yoked together by way of the many everyday ruses of *pouvoir-savoir*. 'Literature', straddling this epistemic divide, cannot simply remain in the 'private' sphere (Spivak, 1993: 47–48).

Spivak refers explicitly to the decolonised context, but the notion of a split position applies equally well to the still-colonised subject who enters the public sphere. Catachresis refers then to the displacement of concepts proper to colonial history, concepts that we must inhabit and persistently critique at the same time (Spivak, 1993: 61). The ambivalence of simultaneous repetition and difference fosters what I shall call *catachrestic agency*, allowing the subject the qualified option of disrupting what Spivak calls 'the Enlightenment episteme', that is, the set of knowledges, truth criteria and sociocultural values pertaining to modernity and transferred through Western imperialism (1993: 48).

With reference to my argument on history and writing, catachresis is that element – part strategy, part historical necessity – which makes writing's (post-colonial) resistance to its historicity possible. By virtue of being an inevitably double mode of signification, catachresis emerges in the texts that I investigate partly as a refurbishment and reassemblage of generic conventions and historically charged concepts (such as 'land'), but also as the inability of these (or similar) conventions and concepts to signify adequately. The blankness which I refer to most particularly in *Life*

& Times of Michael K should therefore also be regarded as a mark of catachresis.

Although I prefer 'catachresis' to Homi Bhabha's 'mimicry', which has a specific Indian/British imperial connotation,[1] Bhabha covers similar ground to Spivak with a psychoanalytic emphasis. Indeed, Bhabha could be accused of reducing a historically changeable phenomenon to a transhistorical psychodrama, which is what Anne McClintock objects to in her call for a more historicising, diversified approach to mimicry (1995: 62–65). Her reading is useful in its own right, but fails to acknowledge that Bhabha's notion of mimicry is *by definition* relational and historically situated, and already distinguished (as in the quotation below) from some other form of 'dependent colonial relations'. Just as with catachresis, mimicry *seems* to adhere to colonial precedence but actually constitutes a moment of independence:

> What I have called mimicry is not the familiar exercise
> of *dependent* colonial relations through narcissistic identi-
> fication so that, as Fanon has observed, the black man stops
> being an actional person, for only the white man can
> represent his self-esteem. Mimicry conceals no presence or
> identity behind its mask: it is not what Césaire describes as
> 'colonization-thingification' behind which there stands the
> essence of the *présence Africaine*. The *menace* of mimicry is
> its *double* vision which in disclosing the ambivalence of
> colonial discourse also disrupts its authority (Bhabha, 1994:
> 88).

Bhabha rejects the foundational notion of a pristine 'native' waiting to emerge from under the sordid layers of colonial discourse. Rather, the 'native' position is *produced* by colonial discourse. Mimicry, rather than nativism, would therefore be a more promising/menacing threat to colonial authority, since it exposes the ambivalence of the latter's intention to (re)create subjected persons, 'mimic men', in its own image. Thus, mimicry unsettles the master discourse from within its own logic and offers a possible avenue of resistance in the face of impossible alternatives:

it is difficult to agree entirely with Fanon that the psychic choice is to 'turn white or disappear'. There is the more ambivalent, third choice: camouflage, mimicry, black skins/ white masks. [. . .] To the extent to which discourse is a form of defensive warfare, mimicry marks those moments of civil disobedience within the discipline of civility: signs of spectacular resistance. [When] the words of the master become the site of hybridity – the warlike, subaltern sign of the native – then we may not only read between the lines but even seek to change the often coercive reality that they so lucidly contain (Bhabha, 1994: 88).

Both catachresis and mimicry indicate slippage in what is ostensibly repetition, difference in what appears to be identity. I must reiterate, however, that this is an intensely historical form of resistance. It only bears relevance at points of conflict between different epistemic orders, that is, at those sites where colonial/ imperial history has had such a decisive influence that it determines the conditions of discourse. Colonialism (and its derivatives) must, in other words, not be regarded as a monolithic structure that renders all foregoing epistemic orders null and void. This is the view *ascribed* to post-colonial theory by its most fervent critics: that colonialism, at the very moment of its putative deconstruction, returns as the beginning of all history; that what was previously the Third World is now a 'post-colonial' world, defined in its naming as a mere appendix to the master-narrative of the erstwhile coloniser (Dirlik, 1994: 328–356; McClintock, 1995: 11). These are important reminders of the pitfalls inherent in an analysis of post-colonial ironies, but they hardly do justice to either Spivak or Bhabha. In my reading, the lesson of these theorists is that the differentiated historical impact of colonialism cannot be dismissed, however much we wish it were otherwise. Moreover, the paradoxical notions of catachresis and mimicry indicate that colonialism's influence has tended to be strategic: it has endowed certain modes of public exchange with an absolute value (and thus power), rendering other, indigenous modes less valuable or valueless, but by way of displacement, not necessarily eradication. One such privileged mode is written literature in (originally) European languages, and it comes as no surprise that the bulk of post-colonial studies has been devoted to writing in English and French. But this is not just a matter of choosing an academic and theoretical approach at will. Rather, the dominance of English and French in, particularly, African literatures is a historical predicament that consistently affects or disrupts each premeditated return to a 'native' voice. The fact that Ngugi wa Thiongo's and Mazisi Kunene's respective insistence on writing in their mother tongues is an issue *at all* – and a highly charged issue, at that – confirms this: the 'vernacular' is available as an alternative for African writers, but its status as a literary medium is not unaffected by recent history.[2] In South Africa, according to Kunene, access to the vernacular has been particularly distorted due to educational policies under apartheid: 'The weeding out of African students at the early level guaranteed cheap unqualified labour, people only semiliterate in the mother tongue. The result was that the African literature produced often was and is of low quality and centred on insignificant and innocuous themes' (1996: 16).

The 'Second World'

In the light of the foregoing argument, Ndebele's *Fools and Other Stories* falls squarely within the scope of a catachrestic reading. It straddles Spivak's 'epistemic divide', repeats a form inherited from the epistemic disruption of colonialism, but puts this form to such use as to counter that discourse and open up its ambiguity – a point which comes across vividly, as we shall see, in the displacement of 'science' in *Fools*. This formal aspect is matched by Ndebele's own subject-position as one of the erstwhile colonised at the receiving end of racist discourse. So far, so good. But if we stick to the catachrestic perspective, does that not discount Gordimer's and Coetzee's narratives? Historically, both Gordimer and Coetzee are marked by complicity with the colonisers/settlers, and both have been, by epidermal fluke, beneficiaries of apartheid. It would thus appear that Gordimer's and Coetzee's work is generated by a continuation rather than a disruption of an epistemic order. In Tim Brennan's words,

Nadine Gordimer or John Coetzee [. . .] are probably better placed in some category of the European novel of Empire because of their compromised positions of segregated privilege within colonial settler states. They are too much like the fictional 'us' of the so-called mainstream, on the inside looking out (1989: 35–36).

Gordimer's and Coetzee's position on the 'inside' of Western tradition would therefore demand a different readerly approach than the one suggested by catachresis, even if we pay due respect to the oppositional element of their writing. But is this the only way to theorise the predicament of 'white' writers? In response to Brennan's claim, Stephen Slemon has argued that we should conceptually divorce the experience of 'settler' communities from metropolitan history as much as from the experience of the colonised (1990: 30–41). Slemon's chosen term for this liminal context – 'Second World' – is awkward, since it once referred to the 'communist bloc', but I endorse the substance of his argument.

Instead of either being conflated with First-World writing or simply being ignored, 'settler' literature should be assigned a place of its own in post-colonial studies. In fact, Slemon argues, nowhere does the ambivalence of anti-colonial literary resistance emerge as forcefully as in this context: 'the *illusion* of a stable self/other, here/there binary division has *never* been available to Second-World writers, and that as a result the sites of figural contestation between oppressor and oppressed, colonizer and colonized, have been taken *inward* and *internalized* in Second-World post-colonial textual practice' (1990: 38). Therefore, although their writing does not bear the mark of a radical epistemic rupture, it is already unsettled by the ambivalence inherent in metropolitan-colonial relations, and unsettled once again by its resistant desire. When Coetzee appears to be rehearsing values embedded in the Western canon, for example, it is more likely that he is engaged in a catachrestic deconstruction of the same.

Theory is a late-comer in this regard. In 1959, speaking as much from a 'breach' as Ndebele, Nadine Gordimer articulated a tortured liminality that forms the thematic basis of virtually all her fiction: 'I myself fluctuate between the desire to be gone – to find a society for myself where my white skin will have no bearing on my place in the community – and a terrible, obstinate and fearful desire to stay' (1988: 34). Three decades later, Coetzee characterised early South African writing by 'whites' as being 'generated by the concerns of people no longer European, not yet African' (1988b: 11). Ambivalence was there from the start and has remained ever since. Even in the 1980s, apparently, the only responsible gesture by 'white' South African writers was to renounce the assumption that an African identity was theirs for the taking. As Stephen Slemon confirms, the 'ambivalence of emplacement is the *condition* of their possibility; it has been since the beginning' (1990: 39).

Thus, in so far as ambivalence and irony are defining marks of the post-colonial resistance that I trace, *A Sport of Nature* and *Life & Times of Michael K* are just as appropriate to a catachrestic reading as *Fools*. I do not want to imply, however, that their moments of ambivalence are identical. Each text addresses a different set of problems. Specifically, there is a shift from an ambivalent appropriation of modernity in Ndebele's case, to an ambivalent disavowal of the same in Coetzee's. In Gordimer's novel we find a likewise ambivalent – and particularly problematic – appropriation of 'africanness'. As these remarks already indicate, there is a necessary split between 'white' and 'black' positions here that hinges on the issue of authority (both literary and subjective): in *Fools*, the challenge is to acquire the authority that is refused by apartheid/colonial history; in *Life & Times of Michael K* and *A Sport of Nature* it is a question of renouncing the authority *offered* by the same set of historical circumstances and, in the latter novel, to construct an alternative grounding for authority. Amidst these differences, however, they still fall under the larger heading of resistant writing.

Rather than seeking the one and only correct way to 'resist', my interest lies in the multiplicity of textual/literary responses to a specific historical (and likewise heterogeneous) challenge.

CHAPTER 3

The Post-Colonial Metanarrative

IT IS COMMONLY held that the task of post-colonial theory is to undermine Western metanarratives. The emphasis in such a 'mission statement' tends, moreover, to weigh more heavily on the notion of 'metanarratives' as such – of 'progress', 'civilisation', 'class struggle', etc. – that is defined as detrimental and imperialistic, the main charge being that any metanarrative functions in such a way as to structure hierarchy and elide difference.[1] However, this position itself relies on a minimal metanarrative that validates the project of radical heterogeneity, just as any postmodern scepticism towards metanarratives must, in Kim Worthington's account, engage values such as 'individual liberty, intersubjective tolerance, and the respect for difference' (1996: 47). For this reason, while nurturing suspicion towards the clandestine workings of colonial metanarratives, I shall pragmatically posit my discussions within what I regard as the implied metanarrative of post-colonial theory: the demise of the Western subject. This is also where I locate the extended significance of the literary narratives themselves.

The anti-humanist critique that snowballed in France in the 1960s and encompassed widely divergent figures such as Roland Barthes, Louis Althusser and Alain Robbe-Grillet had a potentially, and sometimes explicitly, post-colonial bias. Indeed, the announcement that the human sciences should dissolve 'man' rather than constitute him was first made by the structural anthropologist Claude Lévi-Strauss, ultimately as a result of his work in non-Western societies (1962: 326). The death of 'man' would later be hailed by Foucault and more or less taken for granted by Jacques Derrida, who dismissed the notion of a governing, controlling subject in favour of the endless and uncontrollable displacements of 'writing'. In his pivotal philosophical intervention *De la grammatologie*, Derrida explicitly associated what he called logocentrism, the authority that the humanist tradition has granted the spoken word, with ethnocentrism (1967: 11). Derrida's deconstruction of the authority of logocentrism is consequently directed towards/against 'Western metaphysics and thought' (Said, 1983: 185) and corresponds with Spivak's contention that '[t]here is an affinity between the imperialist subject and the subject of humanism' (1988: 202).

But although anti-humanism in the strict sense has had a formative influence on post-colonial theory, the post-colonial metanarrative exceeds it. In the wake of the Second World War, a number of mainly francophone thinkers attacked Western thought without dismissing the humanist belief in the autonomous individual. Jean-Paul Sartre in particular – the very target of Lévi-Strauss's anti-humanist declaration – levelled a sharp anti-colonial critique against France whilst maintaining his position as the 'last' great humanist.[2] Frantz Fanon likewise articulated a strongly critical argument against the purported universalism of 'Western man' without sparing Sartre himself in the process, yet desired ultimately the transcendent subjectivity prefigured by Sartre's existential-ism (Fanon, 1952: 108–133, 190–208). On another track, Lévinas, whom I shall soon discuss, dealt uncompromisingly with the philosophical foundation of the occidental sovereign subject, yet retained humanism by inverting it, by conferring it on the other instead of on the self.

Restricting ourselves at first to anti-humanism, its arguably grandest moment – of great consequence to subsequent anti-foundational post-colonial theory – is Foucault's closing chapter in *Les mots et les choses* (1966: 355–398). This is where Foucault claims that 'man' is a recent invention. He arrives at his startling conclusion at the end of a highly complex analysis of the history of knowledge in Europe from the Renaissance onwards. Distinguishing between three 'epistemes' (conditions for the definition and production of knowledge proper to a specific historical juncture), covering the Renaissance, the Classical period, and the modern era beginning in the late eighteenth century, Foucault argues that 'man' was constructed as both the object and subject of knowledge by the European sciences in the nineteenth century. The constitutive sciences in this respect are biology, economics and philology, each of which determine a representational limit for 'man', and at the same time push towards a field that lies beyond representation. Man thus emerges continually out of the dark (as opposed to the structured clarity of knowledge in the classical period, which knew no dark fields) and returns constantly to himself, to 'the Same'.

Although Foucault chooses for the most part to speak of 'man' pure and simple – it is more provocative that way – he is clearly referring to *occidental* man within the *occidental* episteme, and the life-span of this particular species happens to coincide with the heyday of Western imperialism. Once this recognition is made, however, it also becomes possible to see how imperialism offers a context where the construction of 'man' overreaches itself. In fact, Foucault privileges ethnology, along with psychoanalysis and linguistics, as one of the sciences that ultimately dissolve 'man'. Ethnology emerges with imperialism, at the moment of Europe's historical sovereignty, and constitutes the epistemological relationship of the occidental *ratio* with 'other' cultures:

> ethnology itself is possible only on the basis of a certain situation, of an absolutely singular event which involves not only our historicity but also that of all men who can constitute the object of an ethnology [. . .]: ethnology has its roots, in fact, in a possibility that properly belongs to the history of our culture, even more to its fundamental relation with the whole of history, and enables to link itself to other cultures in a mode of pure theory. There is a certain position of the Western *ratio* that was constituted in its history and provides a foundation for the relation it can have with all other societies, even with the society in which it historically appeared (Foucault, 1970: 376–377).[3]

Yet, once the possibility of this structural relation with 'others' arises, ethnology will ultimately fail to affirm the philosophical foundation of 'man', namely 'human nature'. By moving beyond the representational limit of occidental man, it sets out to penetrate the enigma of human nature, but returns with an enumeration of so many versions of humanity and tends therefore, at the theoretical level, to incapacitate the idea of human nature. This, I daresay, is the enduring point of Foucault's words on the disappearance of 'man': not that humanity will be wiped out, but that the authority of occidental man will dissolve.

As I read it, Foucault's critique of 'man', despite its marginal focus on the colonial encounter, occupies a central position in the post-colonial metanarrative and works towards the dissolution of those epistemological relations between 'the West and the rest' that imperialism erected. It comes as no surprise that seminal post-colonial investigations such as Edward Said's *Orientalism* (1978) and V.Y. Mudimbe's *The Invention of Africa* (1988) have been directly influenced by Foucault, particularly the Foucault of *Les mots et les choses*. Likewise, much of the epistemological critique in my discussions of Ndebele and Gordimer operates within this field, in the sense that knowledge is seen not as a neutral space, but as being constituted through specific, historically differentiated epistemes.

In Part 4 I extend the critique of knowledge and the Western subject by engaging the work of Emmanuel Lévinas. He is seldom placed in this context – with crucial exceptions such as Robert Young (1990: 12–18), Tzvetan Todorov (1982: 254), and Walter Mignolo (2002) – but his thinking is perfectly apposite to the post-colonial metanarrative. Like Foucault, Lévinas refers to Western epistemology and subjectivity in terms of 'the Same'. The structures of knowledge ensure that the subject always returns to itself: this is Lévinas's basic assumption and the philosophical dilemma that he attempts to resolve.[4] As opposed to Foucault, Lévinas does not make historical differentiations, but argues purely at a philosophical level. He is loyal to the tradition of Plato, Descartes, Hegel and Husserl yet tries to exceed it, given that he identifies this tradition as the adventure of the ego. Western philosophy's unheeded enlargement of the realm of the subject – 'the Same' – has led to the elision of difference, or 'alterity'. Western philosophy has functioned according to an imperialistic logic. The only way to resist eliding the other is by focusing on the ethical encounter rather than philosophical (and technological, scientific, etc.) appropriation. In so doing, we will find that the other in fact precedes the subject.

Rather than being a supplement to, or an effect of the subject, the other always escapes the subject while simultaneously holding it *hostage*. In Jacques Derrida's reading of Lévinas:

> the hostage is the one who is delivered to the other in the sacred openness of ethics, to the origin of sacredness itself. The subject is responsible for the other before being responsible for himself as 'me.' This responsibility to the other, for the other, comes to him, for example (but this is not just one example among others) in the 'Thou shalt not kill' (1991: 112).

This inescapability of the other underlies Lévinas's insistence that 'ethics', understood as the responsible encounter with the other, precedes the enlargement of the self in 'philosophy'. On such an understanding, it is ethics and not philosophy that is capable of taking the other (in his or her otherness) into account. However, as long as we employ philosophical terms or, indeed, affirm any knowledge linguistically, we will need precisely a philosophical strategy that renders the certainties of knowledge provisional. Lévinas's solution to this dilemma, in his major work *Autrement que l'être ou au-delà de l'essence* (1974), is to clear a space continuously for 'Saying' (*le Dire*) in the realm of 'the Said' (*le Dit*). 'The Said' refers to the stasis of knowledge and conceptualisation, to that which is said and will not admit change or disruption, whereas 'Saying' should be seen as the processual ethical encounter, as the moment which cannot be reduced to fixed concepts or themes, but which vanishes as soon as the encounter is conceptualised (Lévinas, 1974: 6–9). In Simon Critchley's discussion (via Derrida) of how this actually is 'done', it emerges primarily as a *rhetorical* strategy which, in a deconstructive manoeuvre, doubles back on itself and disturbs the hypostasis of philosophical discourse (1992: 107–144). Although Lévinas's thinking should hardly be reduced to a question of rhetoricity, Critchley's observation validates the employment of Lévinas in a literary analysis which focuses on style and form.[5]

I enter Lévinas's mode of reasoning by way of *Life & Times of Michael K* in which the Levinasian frame of reference helps to resolve a number of issues bearing on the novel's relation to alterity, in which representation and interpretation assume the same position as 'philosophy' in Lévinas's critique. Specifically, the elusiveness of Michael K and the representations of a civil war in South Africa are invested with new reading options when examined from this perspective. It might appear that such an analysis moves away from the dynamics of post-colonial reading but, as I have argued, Lévinas should be regarded in the light of a larger process. His own awareness of this larger process is indicated, for instance, by the essay 'La signification et le sens' where he discusses the impossibility of grounding meaning outside of the specific, culturally situated body that apprehends meaning:

> Whereas the Platonic soul, liberated from the concrete conditions of its corporeal and historical existence, can reach the heights of the empyrean to contemplate the Ideas, whereas a slave, provided that he 'understands Greek' which enables him to enter into a relationship with the master, reaches the same truths as the master, our contemporaries require that God himself, if he wishes to be a physicist, have spent his time in the laboratory, go through the weighings and measurings, the sensible perception, even the infinite series of aspects in which a perceived object is revealed.
>
> The most recent, boldest, and most influential ethnography maintains the multiple cultures on the same plane. *The political work of decolonization is thus attached to an ontology* – to a thought of being, interpreted in its multiple and multivocal cultural meaning. And this multivocity of the meaning of being – this essential disorientation – is perhaps the modern expression of atheism (1996: 44, emphasis added).[6]

'Atheism' thus construed, with its tacit reference to Lévi-Strauss, should not be read theologically, but rather culturally, as the loss of faith in the Western subject as God, as Greek master, the objective arbiter of universal truth. This resonates once again with Foucault, who (five years later) not only pointed out the radical implications of ethnography, but also equated Nietzsche's 'death of God' with the 'death of man'. Despite the differences in their respective philosophical approaches, both thinkers locate themselves in the larger process of the critique of the Western subject. In Lévinas's case, the cited passage demonstrates how he explicitly links decolonisation to seemingly arcane philosophical critique.

Even if we disregard Lévinas's own reference to decolonisation, sustained reflection on his thinking will confirm its affinity with post-colonial theory. In so far as his arguments hinge on the issue of responsibility for the other – and this theme runs through all his work – they address the key problematic of colonial discourse theory and post-colonialism: the assignation of otherness, the exclusion of the other. In Lévinas's inversion of the imperialistic relationship between self and other, the singular encounter with the other confers an absolute responsibility on the self. This responsibility, in so far as it is held in honour, prohibits violence, prohibits the self from dominating, appropriating or even knowing the other. Racism, conquest, colonialism – all instances of the imperialism of the Same, of the incessant inflation of the ego – are obvious antitheses to such a conception of ethics. As could be noted above, however, Lévinas and a number of post-colonial thinkers do not converge specifically on the negation of the ethical imperative through *physical* violence, but rather on the conviction that certain structures of institutionalised Western thought itself are culprits in the history of imperialism. Thus, when Spivak refers to the appropriation of the subaltern by the imperial humanist subject (1988: 201–207), her argument resonates with Lévinas's inscription of the imperialism of Western philosophy. Likewise, when Homi Bhabha refers to Lévinas, it is with a clear sense that the latter moves on the outside of classical Western aesthetics (1994: 15–17). Most importantly, in so far as post-colonial theory constitutes an ethical project, Lévinas enables an articulation of ethics as sublimity – as inappropriable, as resistant to conceptualisation – within this current-day context, which is what I discuss in Part 4 on Coetzee.

Limits to the post-colonial

During the course of my work on this book (and the thesis from which this project emanates), the field of 'post-colonial studies' has not only grown exponentially, it has also undergone transformation and diversification to the point that 'post-colonial' risks being an unusable term, marred as it is by suspicions of political duplicity and the perception that it harbours mutually incommensurable positions.[7]

In an astute meditation on the subject, Ella Shohat has argued that the semantic structure of the term differs from other 'post' terms in the academe. Whereas 'poststructuralism' or 'postfeminism' have a strictly academic reference and indicate a movement beyond particular philosophies or schools of thought, 'the "post-colonial" implies both going beyond anti-colonial nationalist theory as well as a movement beyond a specific point in history, that of colonialism and Third World nationalist struggles' (1992: 101). There is, in other words, an inherent ambiguity in the term. For Shohat, this is a problem, since the historical sense of 'post-colonial' blurs the lines of conflict, ignores the difference between colonisers and colonised, and gives the impression that colonial relations have been transcended. Used in the sense of 'after' formal colonial relations, the term can indeed be scandalous: it would make Ian Smith, in what used to be Rhodesia, as much of a post-colonial leader as, for example, Agostinho Neto in Angola. For that reason, Shohat suggests that only the academic sense of the term should be granted currency.

In response not only to the political critique of Shohat and others, but also to those critics on the other side of the fence who deride post-colonial theory for being too rigidly binaristic and confrontational, Stuart Hall has turned the tables on this critique and has argued for the usefulness of 'post-colonial' precisely as a *vague* periodisation. Drawing on Peter Hulme, he sees it as a reference to a process rather than an accomplished fact. Its lack of specificity is in this case an advantage, in that it directs our attention to 'the many ways in which colonisation was never simply external to the societies of the imperial metropolis. It was always inscribed deeply within them – as it became indelibly inscribed in the cultures of the colonised' (Hall, 1996: 246). Colonisation/ imperialism is thus seen as a primary category of modernity itself, and 'post-colonial' may justifiably refer to Britain as well as Iraq, Australia as well as Mozambique – *but in different ways*. The concept allows for a mapping of fragmented temporalities that still relate to each other in hybridised, translational and agonistic ways that cannot be conceptualised entirely outside of the historical narratives of colonisation. This consolidates both the temporal and academic aspects of the term, because if 'post-colonial' were to refer strictly to a theoretical trajectory beyond the binarism of anti-colonial critique, the trans-disciplinary, transnational, ethical, and socio-political purchase of the theories themselves would be contradicted. Rather, it is to the extent that post-colonial theory contributes to making post-colonial 'times' readable, that its relevance exceeds the limitations of an internal academic debate. Stuart Hall argues, furthermore, that the limited theoretical view of the 'post-colonial' distinguishes between power and knowledge in a way that the theory disallows: 'It is precisely the false and disabling distinction between colonisation as a system of rule, of power and exploitation [that is, as a historical process], and colonisation as a system of knowledge and representation, which is being refused' (1996: 254). Even when Hall finds that theorists have been inexplicably reluctant to discuss the relations between the post-colonial moment and global capitalism – which I nonetheless think is an unfair assessment of work done by, for example, Spivak and Anne McClintock – this does not divest 'the post-colonial' of its explanatory force. The term remains a necessary element in the conceptual framework needed to come to grips with 'the transverse linkages between and across nation-state frontiers and the *global/local* inter-relationships which cannot be read off against a nation-state template' (Hall, 1996: 250).

How do I locate South Africa in this vague post-colonial context? My previous distinction between Ndebele's mode of catachresis and the 'Second World' context of Coetzee and Gordimer has already supplied part of the answer: South Africa is not situated in any *single* way in 'the post-colonial'. Instead, it is precisely in the play and conflict of differences, in the impossibility of reading South Africa as a unified narrative, that it is most profoundly post-colonial. Thus, purported moments of South African independence – the Union in 1910, the Republic in 1961 (Davenport, 1991: 220–225, 360–361) – cannot be valorised as moments that easily transcend colonial history, but neither can the powerful and paradoxical anti-colonial sentiments of the Afrikaner establishment simply be ignored. By the same token, neither can the postponement of a democratic breakthrough until 1994 be taken to mean that the colonised status of the 'black' majority was homogeneous and unchanged throughout the years of 'white' rule. Rather, the multiplicity and transformation of 'black' resistance strategies throughout the nineteenth and twentieth centuries is perhaps best understood in terms of post-colonial hybridity, as responses to colonisation within colonial time that bend the limits of the colonial.

Thus, South Africa, with its wealth of intellectual and cultural histories, is 'post-colonial' in the sense that it is embroiled in relations affected or defined by the colonial encounter, and yet these relations already displace the binary logic offered by colonialism. This argument for 'post-colonial' as a general but inevitably fractured heading, which indicates links between history, epistemology, and political and cultural resistance, may then be followed by further distinctions. In terms of periodisation, it seems reasonable to follow Graham Pechey's suggestion that South Africa's specific form of post-coloniality this century has been *neo*-colonialism; that South Africa in 1910 became the first (bar Liberia) neo-colonial state in Africa (Pechey, 1994: 152). Indeed, the advent of even stricter segregation in 1948 could well be read as a 'strategy of containment'[8] designed to manage the emergent post-war crisis of decolonisation for the 'white' population and allow it to ossify the structures set in place by European imperialism. In its 'grand design' for rendering the majority invisible – while simultaneously exploiting it – and effectively retaining Europe as the reference point for all historical and cultural discourse (a move disguised by ostentatious Afrikaner nationalism) apartheid refined the tools of imperialism in a Second World context. In the 1960s, the term proposed to describe this condition was 'internal colonialism', in which the metropolis and colony were not spatially separated but situated 'one on top of the other in the same territory' (Pechey, 1994: 154). The term 'colonialism' is duly censured by Pechey for theoretical incoherence, particularly since it fails to negotiate the contradiction between colour-blind 'class' and colour-coded 'nationalist' narratives, but with that qualification in mind, it remains the single most adequate term to characterise South Africa's predicament in the twentieth century.[9]

However, with regard to the writing with which I am concerned, it would be untenable to label it 'neo-colonial' or, worse, 'colonial'. All three writers attempt to negotiate the colonial predicament in ways that mark their writing as a vector pointing outside of the already unstable colonial enclosure. This is what makes it justifiable to call their writing 'post-colonial'. But does it also mean that the movement indicated by the vector is or even can be carried through? The following chapters will, hopefully, multiply the number of answers to that question.

PART 2

Significant Others

Modes of Knowledge and
Resistance in Njabulo Ndebele's
Fools and Other Stories

I am my own foundation.

Frantz Fanon (Black Skin, White Masks, *1986: 231*)

CHAPTER 4

'Black' Writing in South Africa

IT WAS ONCE called 'the most radical piece of fiction to come out of South Africa in recent years', due to its alternative approach to resistance in writing (Neill, 1990: 172). Instead of the static portrayal of oppressor vs. oppressed, Njabulo Ndebele's *Fools and Other Stories* resituates the oppressed, or the subaltern,[1] as subjects at the centre of their own world. No 'whites' enter this book, save for one crucial exception at the end. Charterston location, the scene of each story, is by and large a self-contained community with its own network of relations, dependencies, and conflicts. It is a clearing in the hostile political bundu of apartheid-era South Africa – the mid-1960s, if we follow the indication of 'Fools' – a symbolic space which allows for the insertion of subject-positions other than those delimited by colonial discourse.

This textual strategy was radical in the early 1980s, but also risky. While refraining from sheer reproduction of the bleak reality of colonial power relations, the stories had to intensify the struggle against colonial/apartheid hegemony at a discursive level in order not to revert to the idyllic mode and mystify the determining forces in South African society. How was this strategy constructed and with what success, or lack of success?

Ndebele's stories focus on various aspects of subaltern subject-ivity. Rather than *re*-present the surface effects of apartheid, they engage with the troubled relationship between 'Western' and 'African' epistemologies, the place of the intellectual and the artist in the subaltern community, as well as the interdependency between bodily and intellectual freedom.

Fools and Other Stories has so far drawn a rather limited amount of academic attention, at least in terms of published material;[2] the stories tend to be overshadowed by Ndebele's essays. The first of few

47

major attempts to grasp the implications and contradictions of Ndebele's literary project was made by Michael Vaughan. In probing fashion, Vaughan asked whether the populist bent of Ndebele's writing was credible. He chose Ndebele's own statements on the significance of 'storytelling' as a point of departure:

> Political commitment has overlooked culture; it has confined itself to a comparatively narrow range of attitudes and slogans, shared or debated amongst the intelligentsia. This is where Ndebele's conception of 'storytelling' comes in as an antidote. Storytelling requires precisely the cultural insight or capacity for imaginative analysis – analysis which engages seriously with the resonances of popular experience – that has been wanting in the literature of African writers (1990: 188).

Ndebele's prime example of a 'storyteller' is the Turkish writer Yasar Kemal whose familiarity with the local, orally based culture enables him to engage 'imaginatively' yet critically with the social processes of his country. On such an account, however, Vaughan found Ndebele's own work lacking. Due to an English-language education, Ndebele is no more nor less than a skilful writer in the tradition of Western realism. There is, according to Vaughan, no significant formal element in the stories that is extraneous to this tradition. Yet at the same time Ndebele the critic gives no quarter to writers who depend on Western or 'white' models. His practice contradicts his theory. This is an overt contradiction, however, that obscures the deeper problem that it is impossible for the person who *writes* to fuse 'organically' with oral culture to begin with. Instead, Vaughan's argument implies, writing is necessarily a hybrid act. In direct speech, for example, Ndebele accommodates township idioms, but he must do so through translation. The affirmation of 'the vernacular' goes by way of its negation: a conclusion which brushes close to my opening assumptions on 'catachresis' and postcolonial irony. In fact, we might say that my analysis begins where Vaughan's ends.

As I shall argue further, the specific problems identified by Vaughan arise from his attempt to erect a homologous relationship between Ndebele's essay 'Turkish Tales and Some Thoughts on South African Fiction' in *Rediscovery of the Ordinary* (1991) and his stories. This restricts the scope of Vaughan's reading. When the stories are released from this restriction and inserted in a theoretical framework concerned more with the productivity of narratives (and less with their correspondence with programmatic statements), I am convinced that they have an even more intriguing tale to tell.

Apart from Vaughan, a number of critics have briefly passed judgement on *Fools and Other Stories*. In a review article, Lewis Nkosi approved of Ndebele's attempt to move beyond the 'protest' paradigm, but lamented what he saw as 'the ultimate collapse of ["Fools"] into dreadful sentimentality', due to the weak character Zamani who is 'incapable of supporting the ethical structure of the story' (1986: 45). Elmar Lehmann has argued against Lewis Nkosi's negative assessment of the ending of 'Fools' – in which Zamani is whipped by a Boer, but refuses to resist – and saw instead an accurate description of 'the state of affairs in racist South Africa' (1990: 140). More elaborately, Michael Neill has likewise re-appraised the ending of 'Fools' and indeed *Fools* as a whole. Neill reads the inconclusiveness of the stories sympathetically, as 'part of Ndebele's strategy against the teleological determinations of white history' (1990: 177).

One of the most concerted attempts so far to read the full collection of stories has been made by Lokangaka Losambe. In a speculative yet intriguing moment, Losambe suggests that the overall project of the stories should be described as an attempt to fuse the 'arborescent' and 'rhizomatic' dimensions of being (1996: 78). Drawing on Deleuze and Guattari's distinction, 'arborescent' refers to the rootedness and firmness of cultural identity, whereas 'rhizomatic' indicates those ongoing connections, social, political, material, etc., that have no beginning or end, and are always in-between terms or stages. Opposed to Deleuze and Guattari, who claim that the terms are irreconcilable, Ndebele (in Losambe's reading) creates an image of their harmonious co-existence. From this highly evocative theoretical beginning, however, Losambe proceeds to perform what is mostly paraphrase. By summarising the stories he restates the positions on culture, africanism and resistance represented by the various protagonists.

This amounts to a conscientious reading, but there appears to be a diffidence on Losambe's part which prevents him from bringing the argument one step beyond what is already plainly stated in the stories. Losambe is not suspicious of the harmonising tendency of form, nor does he discuss the problematical implications of the culturalist vision offered by the stories.

CHAPTER 5

Ambivalence and Alienation

WHAT MARKS OUT the South African writer striving to attain a post-colonial subject-position from within subaltern culture is the profound ambivalence of his or her position, which echoes in a curious way the logic of the colonial stereotype that he or she sets out to transcend. In Homi Bhabha's words, it is

> the force of ambivalence that gives the colonial stereotype its currency: ensures its repeatability in changing historical and discursive conjunctures; informs its strategies of individuation and marginalization; produces that effect of probabilistic truth and predictability which, for the stereotype, must always be in *excess* of what can be empirically proved or logically construed (1994: 66).

Drawing on Freudian and Lacanian terminology, Bhabha speaks of a fetishistic ambivalence. The stereotype, he claims, is a fetish which masks the anxiety of recognising difference (fear of castration for Freud). In handling fear of this difference, skin becomes a visual signifier in the service of racial fantasy. Difference becomes absolute, but also ambivalent; 'the native' is at once the ultimate lack, the negation of all values (Fanon, 1968 [1961]: 10),[1] and the site of the coloniser's wish-fulfilment, of fantasies of power, knowledge, and sexuality. It is this peculiar duality which allows for 'the native' to be an absolute other and entirely knowable at the same time.

Both coloniser and colonised are caught in the web of this discursive order. The subaltern is invariably assigned the role of 'the bantu', 'the coolie', etc. in the quotidian drama of colonial society, whereas the owner of a whitish skin and a European pedigree is automatically privileged. But colonial discourse not only defines the field of domination and subjugation – it also determines the site, if not the substance, of resistance and opposition.

Following my initial argument on 'catachresis', post-colonial discourse may be understood as the process through which new questions are formulated within or against dominant forms, but always in some relation to them. These forms are not so much a matter of choice, because even when critiqued, changed, or rejected, they are present in their absence as facts of history. If this dynamic is ignored or underestimated, post-colonial writing runs the risk of reduplicating the unintentional ironies of *négritude*, to mention the most famous example.[2]

Recent historical and literary research on the epistemological impact of colonial encounters in South Africa has begun to assess, in a less binaristic mode than was previously the case, the forms of violence, appropriation, exchange, resistance and reversal that they gave rise to. Some key historical figures in this regard are Tiyo Soga (the first 'black' clergyman), William Ngidi (Bishop Colenso's advisor), and, in the early twentieth century, Sol Plaatje, H.I.E. Dhlomo and John Dube (Attwell, 1994; Couzens, 1985; Guy, 1997: 219–242; Willan, 1984). Differences and specificities notwithstanding – which fall beside the scope of the present study – it is possible to locate some consistent tensions in the histories of these encounters. The subaltern subject is shown to occupy a split position between the attempt to redeem an 'African' identity condemned by the Manichean logic of colonial orthodoxy, and the desire and necessity to partake in the 'civilising project' with its seemingly universal promise of betterment.

Leon de Kock has demonstrated how the colonial enterprise, in its various and even contradictory aspects, generated this split subject-position in what is today the Eastern Cape. In the nineteenth century, missionaries and colonial administrators systematically placed distinctive cultural traits of the Xhosa under erasure. The use of money, trousers, square houses and writing were to varying degrees substituted for barter, red cosmetic clay, round houses and oral narrative (1996: 50–55). This devaluation, eradication or appropriation of discursive markers proper to Xhosa culture was carried out with physical as well as epistemic violence, with each mode of domination dependent on the other. The history of the apparently gentle and civilised realm of 'English' in South Africa is imbricated with the sheer brutality of frontier wars – the most emblematic example being when lead type at Lovedale was recast into bullets during the War of the Axe (De Kock, 1996: 31). It is easy to imagine how the ideology of a civilising mission, with its virtuous self-image and strong othering of indigenous cultures, helped to justify acts of military violence. This, in turn, created the facts of destitution and subordinacy among the Xhosas, serving to verify the 'truth' of European cultural superiority. Colonial discourse fuelled itself in a tautological circle.

Thus, the indigenous Xhosa experienced their own specific 'middle-passage' – a term otherwise used to describe the passage of Africans into slavery in America – into subaltern status as their forms of response to the British were gradually rendered ineffectual. At the time of the disastrous Cattle-Killing Movement in 1856 to 1857 – which in itself was syncretic rather than 'purely' African[3] – all avenues to a non-colonial version of autonomy closed. Now only colonial modernity, under the double sign of English and Christianity, seemed to offer a path to self-definition. The emphases in such a description differ when applied to various parts of South Africa (as, for example, the history of KwaZulu-Natal differs from that of the Eastern Cape), but it seems safe to generalise the ironic observation that mission education's programme of re-culturation, with its heavy emphasis on English letters, articulated a promise of emancipation at the same moment as it exercised epistemic violence (Attwell, 1994; Couzens, 1985: 40–81; De Kock, 1996: 50–55).[4] A growing, franchised elite was, by way of mission education, to be carved out of the subaltern collective. This 'civilisatory promise' has, even as it has been transferred to the secular space of liberalism, continued to haunt South Africa, and 'black' South African writing in particular, to this day. In Njabulo Ndebele's analysis:

> [t]he much vaunted traditions of English and American democracy have promised an attractive world of 'freedom and opportunity' to all those who would enter that world. Yet, many of those who entered, mainly as colonial subjects, soon discovered that the newly promised freedom was pre-

mised ultimately on the subject's unfreedom. The colonial
subject had to give up much of what constituted his own
sphere of freedom (1991: 101).

Some of the major disruptions to the Enlightenment project may be
ascribed to South Africa's peculiar Second World status as both
settler colony and sovereign state with a majority population of
colonised subjects. As the 'motherland' of a significant minority
of European descendants (including of course the antagonists of
the British – the Afrikaners), the 'standard' procedure of British
imperialism, that is, the creation of native elites to administer the
colonies (and eventually rule them as independent states without
upsetting the class-system set in place by the British), was never
carried through. Instead, through the advent of large-scale mining
capitalism at the end of the nineteenth century, the civilisatory
ideals were overrun by the need for cheap labour, which entailed
massive, racially defined proletarianisation. The Native Land Act of
1913, the labour laws of the 1930s, the advent of apartheid in 1948
and, as an ultimate negation of the civilising mission, the
introduction of Bantu Education in 1953 and subsequent closing of
the mission schools in 1955, excluded to an increasing degree
participation by the 'black' population at any but the lowest
echelons of society (Davenport, 1991: 231–297).

The hampering of the subaltern's social aspirations bears directly
on the status of 'black' South African writing in English throughout
this century.[5] Sol Plaatje's novel *Mhudi* found no publisher until
1930, ten years after its completion (Couzens, 1978: 6–7). The
playwright H.I.E. Dhlomo, who died in 1956, was virtually
forgotten until Tim Couzens published his biography in 1985. A
score of writers – including Dennis Brutus, Nat Nakasa, Arthur
Nortje, Bessie Head, Ezekiel Mphahlele – went into exile when
conditions were further aggravated by censorship, bannings and
imprisonment in the 1950s and 1960s (Alvarez-Péreyre, 1984:
134–135, 154; Gordimer, 1988: 58–67). These personal circumstances tended then to be matched by a corresponding change,
rupture or displacement in their published work.[6] Although such
examples all fit neatly inside the embryonic South African canon,
the same picture of a severely frayed and maltreated tradition is

suggested by the archives of 'lesser' writing, such as periodicals (Alvarez-Péreyre, 1984: 1–39).

In this foreshortened perspective, a triply removed image of 'black' South African writing emerges. Firstly, indigenous African culture is negated by the dual, if somewhat divergent, forces of imperialist violence and the civilising mission. Secondly, when individuals from the subaltern majority begin to occupy the same symbolic spaces as colonial culture – in particular various forms of written English – they are ignored or ousted from these spaces by the racist state. Thirdly, the individual writers and readers of a specific period are cut off from the writing of preceding periods; and the already frail tradition of writing breaks down into discontinuities.

However, as I argued in Part 1, writing thus burdened by history is not merely submerged in its historicity, but may also be read as a negotiation of the same, as a multi-faceted attempt at symbolically overcoming the ruptures and displacements just described. It talks back to history agonistically, in a fashion which far exceeds the notion of 'protest literature' and deals with issues relating to subjectivity, epistemology and modernity.[7] Consequently, it is in *writing* that the shortcomings of a Manichean definition of colonial history become evident. Rather than passively acquiescing to their objectified status, 'black' writers have for a century and a half assumed authority through the act of writing and attempted to 'negotiate the difficult passage of their compatriots from traditional oral cultures to literacy and modernity' (Pechey, 1995: 2). This task has been marked by much of that openness and indeterminacy that Derrida ascribes to writing (1967: 15–41), and has involved the invention and (symbolic) performance of new and ambiguous forms of agency. In Graham Pechey's words,

> colonisation had [. . .] transformed the prize of battle beyond recognition, and irreversibly. The best that could be done was to seek a full role in deciding the direction that the process was to take; to forestall the loss, in the rush to modernisation, of old indigenous stories and meanings; and to suggest by their own example the hybridised forms of collective and individual self-fashioning that might yet be its most desirable outcome (1995: 2).

'Collective' and 'individual' are central terms here: a vast problematic in *Fools and Other Stories* concerns the tension between the monolithic subalternity forced upon the 'black' community (which, ironically, forms the basis of united political resistance against 'white' oppression) and the internal differences made evident by Ndebele's restricted focus on the community itself. Racist logic projects 'blackness' as a unified, subordinate category, whereas the actual historical experience of those defined as 'black', the most extreme experience condensed into single life-spans, has produced subject-positions marked by a number of fissures and disjunctures. This is, as we shall see, what Ndebele simultaneously represents and tries to overcome.

CHAPTER 6

Know the Write Thing

NDEBELE'S NOVELLA 'Fools', which makes up nearly half of his collection of stories, concerns the alienation described in Chapter 5 or, in more positive terms, the struggle for self-determination under circumstances which easily, almost inevitably, strip a person of his or her dignity. The latter description is one that the reader may arrive at only eventually, since the narrator's fall from grace appears to be of his own doing. Zamani, an ageing teacher in Charterston township, is a pitiful character, constantly thrown between self-justification and self-hatred.

One morning at Springs Station
The story of Zamani's life is contained in the first section of the novella, when he and the budding revolutionary Zani first meet on a railway platform. Not only is it actually uttered during the course of their conversation, but the trajectory of this part of the story is itself patterned on the teacher's degeneration.

By making Zamani the narrator, Ndebele places him squarely at the centre of the story. It begins: 'When I first saw him in the waiting room on platform one at Springs Station, I wanted to know him' (1983: 152).[1] Here is the I/eye, the sovereign subject of first person narrative, poised to create, through writing, the narrative as such. He is at his leisure to observe and construct knowledge about others. After noting Zani's fine clothes, the teacher concludes: 'There was a detachment about him that I found impressive: such detachment as I had never seen in any of our young men in all the countless years I had been teaching' (1983: 152). Zamani here plays the part of the patronising elder who allows himself to be impressed by a younger person while all the time being the latter's judge. But not for long.

Very soon an uneasiness enters the narrative; Zamani is anxious to make a flattering appearance, but cannot control the visual impression he makes on Zani. (Ndebele evokes the image of a newly-awakened Zamani with traces of spittle at the corner of his mouth.) His stubborn attempts to hold his ground by producing 'knowing' analyses of Zani is undercut by a growing sense of resignation. From aloof, analytical observation – 'He looked relaxed and confident again; but something of the intimidating look I had seen earlier still remained. He looked at me as if he was trying to make up his mind about something' (1983: 160) – the gaze of the narrative is quickly averted and thrown back on Zamani: 'He chuckled, while I seethed inside. But a deep sense of powerlessness made me sit back and listen. There was something in him that drained me of any will to challenge him' (1983: 161). After one last attempt at self-assertion – 'I decided to feel amused. He seemed so sure of himself. He had asked a perfectly good question, of course. A perfectly good question: "Do you still peel off skins?" I didn't do it anymore. I stopped three years ago. But the urge was there to begin again with that boy [Zani] sitting in front me. He was just the kind of boy I liked to break' (1983: 162) – the tables are definitely turned.

In an ironic inversion of Zamani's position as sovereign narrator, it is Zani who tells us about the teacher's embezzlement of church funds, his political impotency, and, above all, his abduction of a young schoolgirl (Zani's sister). At this point, Zamani is no longer a teacher, someone who absorbs and dispenses knowledge, but rather the object of knowledge himself. From having been the observer, he has become someone whom others not only look down upon but actually see through. 'So rarely in my life had I felt so small before a young person' (1983: 165), he claims when Zani starts to unleash his accusations. Two pages further on his subjection to Zani's gaze is complete: 'The accuracy of his observations made me numb. [. . .] I felt so naked before him, like a frog that was being dissected alive, and there was nothing in the world it could do about its misfortune' (1983: 167).

In a corresponding manner, the other protagonist of the story also undergoes change in these opening pages. The confidence observed at first by Zamani is gradually magnified. After being worthy of a certain admiration, but no more, Zani's assertiveness becomes overwhelming. Having been to boarding-school in Swaziland, having received an education far superior to what was available in Charterston township, he returns with the makings of a leader. 'I was struck by the actual heavy possibility of achievement', (1983: 170) Zamani notes. In this way, Zani gets the upper hand. He and Zamani may stand as equals at the very beginning – sovereign narrator observes aloof youngster – but they soon fulfil their first narrative duty as 'potential' and 'spent potential', respectively. In such a reading of the first section of the story, their individual trajectories never cross, instead, they diverge from approximately the same level. If, however, we extend our epistemic reading – that is, the enquiry into how knowledge is defined and evaluated, and who is the site of this knowledge – to the character Zani, a chiastic movement is registered. As described above, Zamani's status switches from teacher/subject into pupil/ object. Zani, by contrast, is at first a pupil returning from school. Not only that – he even depicts himself as a seven year-old boy terrified of the prospect of having Zamani as teacher:

'The children used to say: "Panyapanya [Zamani's nick-name] will let you lie face down on a bench, and then have the bigger boys of the class hold your arms and legs fast. And then he will get hold of his notorious cane, Happy Days, with his right hand; and with the left, he will flick his fingers just over your buttocks as if he was seasoning them with salt and pepper. And then the cane will rain down on you." That's what the children used to say' (1983: 161).

The object-status of the pupil is obvious from such a paragraph, and could even be mistaken for caricature in places where corporal punishment is no longer the order of the day. But from this position of terror, Zani's lowest point, the narrative quickly turns Zani into a teacher – and has already done so, in fact, some pages before, where he reprimands Zamani for his shallow analysis of the blacks' predicament – and announces that soon he will spell out the disgrace of Zamani: '"I know so many things about you."' (1983: 165)

African education

My preoccupation with the terms 'teacher', 'pupil' and 'knowledge' is well motivated by the text. It is startling to notice the intimate connection between knowledge and power, education and physical violence in the narrative. The title, 'Fools', also indicates a dominant concern with the question of knowing and not knowing. As my brief discussion of the epistemic capture of the indigenous subject implied, the question of knowledge ranks as a major post-colonial dilemma, and it is necessary for me to expand on this point – beyond the South African horizon – in order to appreciate Ndebele's response to it properly.

In post-independence Africa emphasis has generally been placed on the spreading rather than the production of knowledge. In Kwame Nkrumah's Pan-African treatise *Africa Must Unite* we read: 'The burning desire for education among both children and adults received little encouragement from the colonial powers, and one of the worst legacies of colonialism has been the absence of a trained body of African technicians and administrators' (1963: 43). In similar fashion, Julius Nyerere observes: 'Since long before independence the people of this country [. . .] have been demanding more education for their children' (1968 [1967]: 44). A decade later in Mozambique, Frelimo, regarding education as fundamental for 'the triumph of the revolution', nationalised the education system after its takeover of power, with the ambition to extend primary education to all children in the country (Johnston, 1989: 128–129).

Conversely, in South Africa, the educational policies of the Nationalist government were cause for outrage and resistance throughout the apartheid era. In other words, the emancipatory, nation-building movements in Africa have all seen the lack of education as the most severe drawback for the progress of the continent. Schools were to be the paving on the highway to modernity – the benign version of modernity, to be sure, with its promise of affluence, health, national sovereignty and social welfare. The trick has been to spread education to all layers of society, and to raise 'standards' in accordance with modern (European) rationality.[2] Hence, when Zani in Ndebele's story proclaims that he *believes in science* and wants to 'spread knowledge and science to the people' (1983: 164), we witness a representative moment in the struggle for African self-determination.

Does the importance attached to education justify a privileging of 'the means of communication' as *the* main post-colonial conflict, as Ashcroft, Griffiths and Tiffin idiosyncratically claim? Arguably, yes – provided that we gloss 'communication' as 'the dispersal of knowledge' (Ashcroft et al., 1989: 83–84). What such a contention presupposes, however, is that there already exists a more or less unproblematic 'something' to communicate. It requires that we see knowledge as an ideal entity, a given, rather than something which is produced and reproduced at the moment of its enunciation. This has of course caused a great deal of debate. Julius Nyerere's policy paper 'Education for Self-Reliance' is an attempt at defining the forms of education and knowledge that are valuable in post-colonial Tanzania. His analysis of the colonial system echoes the intro-ductory discussion of Chapter 4:

[Colonial education] was a deliberate attempt to change those values and to replace traditional knowledge by the knowledge from a different society. It was thus part of a deliberate attempt to effect a revolution in the society; to make it into a colonial society which accepted its status and which was an efficient adjunct to the governing power (1968 [1967]: 47).

Add to this, yet again, the fact that education as an *institution* (schools and universities, as opposed to the initiation ceremonies and various forms of tutelage in indigenous communities) was set in place in Africa primarily by the imperial powers, and it should be clear that the problems attached to 'education' and 'knowledge' in independent Africa by far exceed the material challenges in-volved – which in themselves are daunting.

Nyerere's and other political leaders' policy statements notwith-standing, the ambivalent value of colonial education, and the need for a post-colonial version of education has been most forcefully addressed by African *writers*. The intimate connection between education and writing in twentieth-century Africa is striking. As Abdulrazak Gurnah writes:

The [. . .] theme – colonial education – has echoes in a remarkable number of African works of the immediate post-colonial period [. . .] For instance, Nwoye in *Things Fall Apart* [Achebe, 1958] actively subverts sacred Umuofia customs both to express his rejection of the toleration of such cruelties as the murder of Ikemefuna, and to affiliate himself with his new mentors who have promised him individual fulfilment. In Ngugi's early novels, *Weep Not, Child* (1964) and *The River Between* (1965), Njoroge and Waiyaki paradoxically valorize colonial education into a redeeming ideology in which they play Messianic roles at the very moment when their communities are dispossessed and divided by the same European invasion (1993: x).

But the affiliation between writing and education goes beyond representation. Not only have many writers worked as teachers, continually or from time to time, but there has also been a certain confluence of the two positions, that is, many writers have seen themselves as teachers *in their capacity as writers*. The most famous and explicit instance is Chinua Achebe's paper 'The Novelist as Teacher' (1975: 42–45), but we could just as well refer to Ngugi wa Thiongo's politically motivated use of popular Kenyan forms and his mother-tongue Gikuyu – with the intention of educating the people and allow them to educate themselves in the workings of Kenyan society.

Furthermore, writers have not only bestowed a pedagogical duty upon their imaginative writing, but have also contributed to the theoretical reflection on education and knowledge. Among the more prominent examples, and one which has considerable bearing on our discussion of Ndebele, we find a South African, Ezekiel Mphahlele. In the first part of his seminal collection of essays, *The African Image*, much effort goes into envisioning what an African education might be.

As one option, and in the specifically South African context, Mphahlele proffers the notion of subversive teaching. Writing in exile, he tries to imagine how he might return to South Africa to tamper with the existing educational system so that it may serve emancipatory ends:

Go back and teach where you know you'll be contributing something real, something relevant for your people. Teach the youth what the government syllabus says and use it to sow the seeds of rebellion, and set on fire the passions that are already raging, waiting for articulation. Charge them up till they explode under the asses of white folks, subvert their crooked miserable lives (1974: 43).

This daydream – it is presented as such – is all the more striking when we consider Mphahlele's enduring resistance against Bantu education (1974: 43).[3] He counter-intuitively hopes to resist the educational system by being part of it. Such a desire lays bare the aporia facing the post-colonial pedagogue: either a person opts out of the educational system and is thereby restrained from contributing to its transformation, or else he or she will be restrained by the Eurocentric logic of the system. It might appear that the slogan 'liberation first, education later' of the post-1976 resistance movement in South Africa offered the only feasible escape from this aporia. What the slogan concealed, however, was that liberation does not of itself transform the education system. Apartheid merely offered the most extreme version of the educational dilemma; throughout the introductory essay of *The African Image*, Mphahlele remarks on the obduracy of colonial habits in schools all over independent Africa. In his attempt at prefiguring a way to resist this, he employs an undeclared totalising strategy which, to my mind, is characteristic of the post-colonial intellectual in Africa:

Our schools still structure courses in the French or British manner. Yes, some of the texts are being replaced by those that emphasize the African content. But food does not give shape to the pot. Our people still educate for the civil service. Little else. [. . .] Are we ever going to sit and contemplate a national philosophy of education that will establish and define national goals? A philosophy that will tie up education with other areas of life and give a new base to the national cultural institutions?

By and large African governments do not care for cultural

activities except during national festivals. Understandably, they see priorities in the people's economic life that cannot give way to what is popularly regarded as mere entertainment. [. . .] Such an idea is opposed to the traditional African idea of culture as a way of growing up, as fundamental to education. I see no reason why a ministry of education cannot at the same time be a ministry of culture. This way, an educational philosophy will also be a philosophy of culture. From elementary school, a child will be taught African music and dance as a part of his education. We ought to be writing history books for children in the form of entertaining stories about African civilizations, heroes and so on (1974: 21).

Here, Mphahlele allows several terms to merge and transform through a series of tacit rhetorical operations. Firstly, he opposes a potentially 'African' way of teaching to the 'European' manner. Secondly, he equates 'African' with 'national' – which is in keeping with the twin projects of Pan-Africanism and nationalism during the first period of African independence. The bending of these two words into one and the same signifier may seem questionable indeed – 'African' is obviously a *trans*national term – unless we accept that 'national' is defined in relation to Europe, to the historical fact of Empire, and not in relation to Africa. Thirdly, Mphahlele associates 'education' with 'culture' (by implication 'African culture'), an operation which prefigures how 'education' may be africanised. As a consequence, 'Africa', 'the nation', 'education' and 'culture' are made to occupy roughly the same semantic field within Mphahlele's vision.

Such linguistic manipulations testify to his predicament of having to imagine a post-colonial order by way of concepts and institutions that are part of a colonial heritage. The passage quoted above is shot through with a totalising desire: the obsessive splitting of any and all aspects of life into smaller compartments, not least the separation of 'education' from other activities of communal African life, Mphahlele would wish to replace with a new, holistic language. Unfortunately, Mphahlele's suggestive formulations merely beg the question. When he recommends writing history books for children, or teaching African dance – important endeavours in themselves – his holism is revealed as a screen of Africanism placed in front of the same old educational set-up. Once again, it is the dispersal rather than the production of knowledge that is viewed as the problem; the 'right' type of knowledge is already 'there', it just needs to be parcelled and distributed.

It is these assumptions that Njabulo Ndebele tries to disrupt; the ambition is explicit in his essays which are more theorised but no less locally grounded than those mentioned above. Rather than speak of education or teaching – as is done in his stories – this key passage from 'Redefining Relevance' (dated a few years after the publication of *Fools*) engages directly with the question of epistemology in the South African context:

For the oppressed, political knowledge came to be equated with the recognition of the blatant injustice which occurs in various forms throughout the country. To know has been to know how badly one has been treated. Every other thing is irrelevant unless it is perceived as contributing to the extension of this knowledge. Beyond that, having this knowledge implied that one either gave in to the bleak reality revealed, or committed oneself to removing this general condition of injustice. How this was to be actually carried out would depend on the means that are available to the oppressed at any particular moment.

On the other hand, for the ruling white racists, knowledge has been equated with the quest for mastery over the political and economic means of maintaining privilege and domination. To know has been to find ways of maintaining dominance. As a result, the white racists have, over the years, built a complex structure of government and an array of other social and economic institutions, all of which have diversified the sources and the means of acquiring information and knowledge for the preservation of political and economic domination (1991: 59).

These two forms of knowledge are antithetically locked in the same political and economical system. (The analysis refers to the apartheid era, but could in modified form be applied to South Africa post-1994.) Ndebele's great contribution to the South African literary debate has been to transcend this antithetical analysis and posit a third, more strictly post-colonial form of knowledge that could transgress the conceptual limits of colonial discourse – and thereby a new type of writing, since literature is seen as a specific kind of knowing, even a form of teaching. Literature is not only centrally implicated in the quest for liberation but it, too, needs to be liberated – not merely from the commercial and totalitarian co-option of the written word (leading to a sensationalist media scene on the one hand, and propagandist protest literature on the other), but from *all* varieties of 'white' hegemony. In the earlier and highly influential essay, 'Turkish Tales and Some Thoughts on South African Fiction', Ndebele explains that

> information produced, interpreted and disseminated by a variety of liberal institutions tends to be more readily accepted [by the African writer] because such institutions are perceived to be morally opposed to government policy on matters of race relations. This acceptance, in the evolution of African political resistance, has over the years, almost become dependence. [. . .] Furthermore, the liberal institutions' essentially anthropological approach gradually consolidated a picture of African society under South African oppression as a debased society. Studies and press reports on *tsotsi* violence, shebeens, convicts, sexual promiscuity, faction fighting, mine compound life, 'witchdoctors', 'strange' African customs and other instances of pathetic suffering have determined public (both black and white) perceptions of African suffering under apartheid. [. . .] Under such conditions it is easy for sloganeering, defined as superficial thinking, to develop. The psychology of the slogan in these circumstances is the psychology of intellectual powerlessness (1991: 24–25).

What Ndebele does here, in very concrete terms, is analyse the workings of the colonial stereotype and its capacity to permeate even oppositional ('liberal') layers of society. In such a way, he defines the specific aspect of alienation he must address as a writer. But more than that, Ndebele also approaches the basic issue of how knowledge is produced. The point continually made in his essays is that knowledge in South Africa cannot be looked upon independently of its agent.

Without reading his essays as simple statements of intention, and ticking off their realisation in his stories accordingly (which would reduce the literary text to a secondary function of a primary intention), these essays help us to pinpoint some of the more salient aspects of *Fools*. In none of the stories, for example, do we find 'spectacular' images of African suffering and debasement – debasement there is, primarily in caricatures of sell-outs such as the middle-class parents in 'The Music of the Violin' and in certain of Zamani's actions, but the text falls short of denying the characters any minimum of dignity. Even in the case of Zamani who, as we have already seen, can be laid bare 'like a frog' and occasionally roams the streets of Charterston location drunk and disgraced, the narrative saves him from ultimate objectification by placing him as narrator. (The main exception to this non-spectacular style – when the boer whips Zamani at the end of 'Fools' – is of course particularly significant for this very reason, and will be discussed in due course.)

But the absence of compromised 'information' does not in itself constitute a desirable model of knowledge. One authoritative description of this model is supplied by Vaughan, who interprets Ndebele as offering a Gramscian ideal of the 'organic' intellectual, but concludes that *Fools* is inconsistent in its articulation of such an ideal. It implies, again, two versions of knowledge, emancipatory this time (Vaughan, 1990: 189–191). Firstly, there is the self-identical, social knowledge of the community, condensed in the oral mode of 'storytelling'. Secondly, there is the alienated intellectual, the educated, middle-class individual who has been granted access to the centres of information and groomed as a leader, but is at the same time cut loose from the collective identity of the community, a description that fits both Zani and Zamani, albeit in slightly different ways. The 'organic intellectual' would then bridge the gap and regain an identity by immersing himself or herself in the community and function as a catalyst for the emancipatory potential of oral knowledge. Vaughan's critique of this ideal points to the frayed lines of communication obtaining between the subaltern majority and the intellectual. When Ndebele writes, he writes for readers – sophisticated, English-speaking readers at that. The rural life that Ndebele correctly observes is virtually absent from South African fiction is just as far removed from his own writing. According to Vaughan, the stories themselves 'have no *organic* connection with oral culture and oral narrative', and this culture 'does not "organically" give rise to an intelligentsia [. . .] It does not 'organically' give rise to a preoccupation with the problematic freedom, in the leader-protagonist, of the inner self' (1990: 194). In this respect, an 'organic' intellectual is a utopian concept that serves to disguise the heterogeneity of the subaltern population. Nevertheless, Vaughan's critique strikes me as somewhat beside the point. As I read them, rather than assume the existence of 'organic' connections between trained intellectuals and the rest of the subaltern, Ndebele's stories (and 'Fools' in particular) thematise the very lack of such connection. They then go on to investigate the feasibility of *constructing* such a quasi-organic relationship – a project which, as I argued earlier, has long been peculiarly imaginable in South Africa, due to the subaltern being defined by the arbitrary factor of pigmentation rather than economic status or cultural affinity. The wager in Ndebele's stories is that since oppression unifies an otherwise heterogeneous group, the intellectual can bridge the gap between the diverse cultural modalities of the subaltern population and overcome his/her own alienation without making excuses for being an intellectual.

I could provide many examples of this view. The protagonist in each story is invariably one of the literate minority, male, and often functions as a leader, but is surrounded by people with a different outlook on life. These features are condensed in the scene on the bus in 'The Prophetess', where the powers of the prophetess are under discussion (1983: 34–35). Feelings run high as various passengers tell of the horrors that haunt those that dare defy the prophetess. But there is some disagreement. A 'big woman', coded as 'one of the people', asks if anyone has actually seen these things happen. She gets support from 'an immaculately dressed man' – an intellectual – who restates the question and answers it himself: 'It's all superstition. And so much about this prophetess also. Some of us are tired of her stories' (1983: 35). A cut and dried issue, it would seem. The outcome of the story, however, appears to articulate what Vaughan calls a 'sophisticated scepticism' which 'does not [. . .] lead to outright rejection of custom, convention and traditional belief, but rather to a more complicated position whereby the 'resonance' of the practices is acknowledged, without being positively endorsed' (1990: 193). What happens in the story is that the little boy who goes to the prophetess to fetch 'holy water' for his mother drops the bottle on his way home. Distressed, he quickly finds another bottle and fills it with tap-water. He is afraid he will be caught out, but his mother gratefully accepts the water and is apparently healed by it. The story ends thus:

> 'As we drink the prophetess's water,' said MaShange, 'we want to say how grateful we are that we came to see for ourselves how you are.'
> 'I think I feel better already. This water, and you . . . I can feel a soothing coolness deep down.'
> As the boy slowly went out of the bedroom, he felt the pain in his leg, and felt grateful. He had healed his mother. He would heal her tomorrow, and always with all the water in the world. He had healed her (1983: 52).

'This water, and you'. The prophetess and her water, or what is taken to be her water, stand as signifiers for the self-respect and communal sharing that is the innermost value of subaltern culture in Ndebele's stories. Instead of deciding that the prophetess is a fraud, the boy feels proud. His mother's response confirms his sense of belonging in the greater whole of the community. The communal value of the prophetess exceeds, in other words, the simple positivistic dualism of true-or-false expounded by the young intellectual on the bus.

Interestingly, this respect for the various forms of knowledge to be found in the township is most often stated by women characters with a certain standing in the community. The mother in 'The Prophetess' says: 'take it from me, a trained nurse. Pills, medicines, and all those injections are not enough. I take herbs too, and then think of the wonders of the universe as our people have always done' (1983: 49). The prophetess herself, who apparently epitomises the oral, subaltern mode of knowledge, gives the boy who visits him two quite different pieces of advice on learning. Firstly, when speaking of his mother, she says:

> 'You are very fortunate, indeed, to have such a parent. Remember, when she says, "My boy, take this message to that house", go. When she says, "My boy, let me send you to the shop", go. And when she says, "My boy, pick up a book and read," pick up a book and read. In all this she is actually saying to you, learn and serve. Those two things, little man, are the greatest inheritance' (1983: 40).

But on the very same page, we read: '"You will not know this hymn, boy, so listen. Always listen to new things. Then try to create too. Just as I have learnt never to page through the dead leaves of hymn books"' (1983: 40). Her advice goes both ways. Reading is valuable – she even repeats 'pick up a book and read' beyond the imagined quote and makes the words her own – but reading isn't everything. She, for one, is proud of never paging through the 'dead leaves' of books.

This double sentiment, this levelling of orality's and literacy's relative positions, is echoed in 'Fools'. In conversation with Zani, Zamani's wife Nosipho explains: 'every day I say to myself: just as your ears hear something new every day, your mind must know something new every day. So I do what is unusual for most women of the township: I read all the time. But there are the likes of your mother, whose books are people, and who have amassed a wealth of wisdom the proportions of which I can never even imagine' (1983: 237). The gendered position of women in Ndebele's stories – involving above all a socially cohesive ideology of motherhood opposed to the 'irresponsibility' of men such as Lovington in 'Uncle' and Zamani – grants them easier access to that sense of cognitive ambivalence required to bridge the gap between 'elite' and 'subaltern' knowledge. Such ambivalence is, however, not quite synonymous with the 'sophisticated scepticism' mentioned by Vaughan, which would rather be an attitude external to the narrative, belonging above all to the position of the unseen but omniscient narrator. If 'scepticism' can be understood as an *exclusion* of certain possibilities, the attitudes of the women mentioned above are doubly *inclusive*. They know well the worth of medical and scholarly training, but also accept the 'traditional' knowledge of the subaltern on its own terms. (Or the other way round, which would be more adequate in the case of the prophetess: that is, she also accepts scholarly training.) The difference between these two attitudes – scepticism versus ambivalence – is slight but significant. Whereas scepticism, even 'sophisticated' scepticism, is predicated on an uncompromisable notion of singular truth (the sceptic will never 'say too much', lest he or she compromises this truth) ambivalence allows for the plurality, or should we say the provisional quality of every articulation of the truth. 'Western' and 'African' medicine say different things in different ways and thereby construct seemingly disjunctive dimensions of an ultimately unutterable 'truth' – ultimately, that is, because it cannot exist outside of any articulation, and no articulation can be sealed off, or completed, once and for all.

To my mind, such ambivalence comes close to Mphahlele's understated holism. In much the same way as he tries to rejoin concepts of knowledge that have been placed on opposite sides of the Manichean colonial divide – mainly 'African culture' and 'education' – so does Ndebele adumbrate an inclusivity that not only redeems the alienated intellectual, but, more importantly, allows the sham conflict between the scientific rationality of the 'West' and the psycho-social rationality of 'Africa' to dissolve. In fact, his stories admonish us readers to no longer think of scientific knowledge as Western or 'white' and incompatible with 'African culture'.

'Universal' science
A productive paradox is at work here.

Although universalism is explicitly referred to only in connection with the mystification of Western culture in 'The Music of the Violin' (1983: 130), there is no question that the fallacy of Western universalism is also a chief concern in 'Fools', and this time with regard to the 'objective' and 'disinterested' realm of science rather than culture. Zani's faith in science is absolute and universal.

It duplicates the faith in science the redeemer – the heroic version
of scientific rationality – that peaked in Europe during the heyday
of imperialism, that is, from the mid-nineteenth to the early
twentieth century, but which harks back to the Enlightenment
notion of universal reason. Zani, ever the eager eighteen-year old,
makes the grandiose claim that he will 'bring light where there has
been darkness' (1983: 164) and explains to Nosipho how he
gradually discovered the joys of scientific investigation at school in
Swaziland. Before long, he and two other pupils were conducting
systematic chemical experiments: '"We particularly loved making
gases. [. . .] And with each gas we made, it was like the world had
one big secret language and we were learning it more and more."'
(1983: 234) For Zani, at this moment, science and truth are
perfectly synonymous, and the singular scientific truth unveils the
singular 'language' of the world. Stated in these terms, such a credo
comes across as excessively naïve, but not only is such naïvety
credible (according to the demands of verisimilitude) coming from
a youngster, it also corresponds with the epistemic pretensions of
imperial Europe which, in analogy with the Christian monotheism
of the missionaries, privileged this form of rational knowledge and
marginalised or excluded all other forms. As I have claimed earlier,
such privileging was not merely the *result* of imperial domination,
but rather a chief mode of domination *per se* (interlocking with
other modes such as military force, economic exploitation,
etc.) – the consequence being that the universal claim of scientific
rationality was inseparable from its locus of articulation, that is, the
metropolitan centres of Europe, and therefore culture-specific, or
provincial.[4] Intriguingly, such a debunking of the universal claims of
science is ironically contained in Zani's statement. If I quote in full
what I just now foreshortened, we read:

> 'We particularly loved making gases. We were fascinated by
> our discovery that some army, I think it was the German
> army, used chlorine gas in the Second World War, I think it
> was. So we just made gas after gas. Our special achievements
> were methane, phosgene, and phosphine. Can you imagine?
> And with each gas we made, it was to us like the world had

one big secret language and we were learning it more and more' (1983: 234).

At first, the rhetorical structuring of 'boyish enthusiasm' (repetitive, unassuming syntax, the wide-eyed reference to military history) manages to naturalise this statement. The conclusion – how wonderful the world of natural science! – slips through unharmed. Yet, on re-examination, the mention of the Second World War and the German army is most unsettling. The use of gases in the Third Reich to exterminate Jews and other minorities is the ultimate and most horrifying example of how 'strong othering' – in the extreme case, outright biological racism and genocide – and seemingly neutral scientific methods can collude. The relation to colonial domination in South Africa through scientific discourse is indirect and inferential, yet undeniable. In both cases, 'universal' and 'objective' scientific knowledge furthered the interests of the very groups that claimed to be the originators and foremost producers of such knowledge. In Nazi Germany, 'Aryans'; in South Africa, 'whites' or 'Europeans', especially of British descent. As Michael Wade puts it, science in the colonial context is 'the new knowledge, proceeding from the infallible metropolis, proof of progress, rich in positive moral overtones. Through science the tribe [of colonisers] may be redeemed' (1993: 42).[5] It is therefore less than surprising that the rhetoric of positivistic science and measurement also became a foundational element of apartheid governance (Posel, 1996). Zani's apparently innocent statement thus leads to the familiar aporia of desiring entrance to that very world of knowledge that has actively produced, subjected and excluded the social grouping – the subaltern majority – with which he identifies.

The two typical post-colonial responses to this aporia have been either to ignore it – as exemplified by the liberation movements' pragmatic enthusiasm for education – or to invert it – Leopold Senghor's emblematic phrase 'L'émotion est nègre, comme la raison hellène' ('Emotion is Black, just as reason is Greek'), keeps the colonial stereotype intact by privileging feeling as a 'genuine' African trait (Gérard, 1986: 384). In both cases, reason, rationality, and scientific investigation remain the prerogative of Europe.

The strategy in Ndebele's writing is different. Rather than exclude the concept of scientific knowledge from the realm of the post-colonial, he limits its universal pretensions and incorporates it into a low-keyed emancipatory narrative of the subaltern community. To spell out the paradox: by making 'science' less universal along the vertical axis of cultural authority, it becomes more universal along the horizontal axis of inter-cultural exchange. The fallacy of European imperialism was to confuse the authority of scientific progress with cultural authority; to claim that since 'we' Europeans have harnessed enormous powers through science and technology, this is proof of 'our' cultural (and racial) superiority. Admittedly, the discursive situation within the metropolitan centres of Europe was more complex than such a statement would allow. Philosophers such as Kierkegaard, Schopenhauer and Nietzsche, a writer such as Dostoyevsky, a historical philosopher such as Dilthey all questioned the easy identification of scientific (and, by implication, technological) progress with cultural value. We should bear in mind Dilthey's distinction between *erklären* ('explanation': what the natural sciences should do) and *verstehen* ('understanding': the hermeneutic duty of the humanities) (*The Encyclopaedia of Philosophy*, 1967, vols.1 and 2: 403–406), as well as Wilhelm Windelband's corresponding distinction between 'nomothetic' and 'idiographic' disciplines (*The Encyclopaedia of Philosophy*, 1967, vols.7 and 8: 320–322). These attempts at limiting the progressivist arrogance of the undeniably successful natural sciences – despite the lack of any explicit analysis of the relation between power and the production of knowledge – would, ideally, have provided sufficient leverage for a deconstruction of scientific universalism in the European colonies and in latter-day South Africa. However, as we learn from post-colonial theory, in the imperial contact zones the progressivist discourse of nineteenth and twentieth century Europe was hegemonical and cut across all discursive spheres – scientific, aesthetic, religious, and historical. The evolutionary narrative of Darwinian biology, coupled with the 'objective' facts of scientific and technological progress in Europe, provided the paradigm by which anything and everything pertaining to Europe could be coded as 'more advanced' than what 'the rest' of the world had to offer (Brantlinger, 1986: 201–206).

The transformation of this paradigm in Ndebele's stories amounts to relativisation. Scientific knowledge is shown to represent a valuable aspect of rational knowledge, but not the only standard of rational knowledge as such. Suffused as the community is with an orally transmitted social and religious rationale, science need not automatically negate the collective identity of the subaltern. On the contrary, once its aggressive universalism is disarmed, science – and all that it would entail in Charterston location: systematic political analysis, raised standards of education, access to modern technology – shines forth as a prerequisite for the enfranchisement of the subaltern. Ndebele's stories function within the discourse of modernity in independent Africa, with its strong emphasis on education, but attempt to resolve one of its major contradictions by teasing out the universality of science from its iron cage of Eurocentric authority. In doing so, they also act on an ambivalent and inclusive understanding of 'knowledge' which, as is most clearly stated by certain educated women in the stories, makes possible the participation in two otherwise antagonistic forms of knowledge.

CHAPTER 7

Body Language

UNTIL NOW, my analysis has remained loyal to the dialectical, synthetic ambition of Ndebele's writing. The dialectical movement is traced in his essays as well as in the more explicit aspect of his stories, and accounts for the textual attempt to transgress the antithetically structured – or Manichean – closure of colonial/apartheid culture. The opposition between the 'alienated' intellectual and the 'people' is critical to these dialectics. Alienation can assume various forms ranging from self-hatred (Zamani) and middle-class arrogance (the parents in 'The Music of Violin') to the more insidious form of ineffectual protest that Ndebele finds in much South African writing and that is equally noticeable in the portrayal of Zani. However, alienation can always be understood as an effect of colonial/apartheid culture, on *whichever side* of the antithetical divide it is located (the middle-class 'sell-out' sides with apartheid; the ineffectual protester opposes apartheid but is overwhelmed by it and allows his or her thinking to be determined by it). The synthesis, the purportedly organic intellectual, is, paradoxically, locked inside this split concept of alienation. By implying a removal from an original state of integrity, alienation foreshadows its future negation, namely the closing of the gap between 'knowledges'.

'Black' bodies

By placing greater emphasis on a more submerged aspect of the text – its underbelly as it were – and on the issue of subjectivity, I shall attempt to register some significant disruptions in this dialectical schema. My argument engages at the most basic level the tension between literary form and historical response. Ironically, the mode of representation that facilitates the dialectical ambition obstructs its consummation. I shall presently identify the representational mode as the *Bildungsroman*, whereas I register the troubled response to 'history' in representations of *the body*.

My use of 'the body' as a concept is deliberately two-toned. On the one hand, I refer to 'the body' and 'bodies' in a literal sense since it is possible to read Ndebele's story cycle in such a way that it thematises bodily change and difference, and the political significance of the body in a colonial context. On the other hand, there is also a metaphoric level at which the body operates as an organising and synthesising principle. The corporeal metaphor, as I shall call it, establishes correspondences between the individual's body and the 'body' of the community. This sheds new light on our discussion of 'organic' relationships between various sectors of the community, and as we shall see, the link between these two aspects of the body is tight. The point is, of course, that while there can exist no literal, unrepresented body in the discursive context of imaginative writing, such a body proper is nevertheless assumed, ideologically naturalised, and made to guarantee the health and viability of its function as body symbolic.

I proceed from the assumption that the subaltern's body has been thoroughly troubled and circumscribed in the colonial context. This is not an innovative argument, initiated as it was by Fanon in the 1950s and carried through by the likes of Gayatri Spivak, Anne McClintock and Sander L. Gilman (1986: 223–261). A seldom-mentioned South African participant in this debate is N.C. Manganyi (1973).[1] His phenomenological analysis of the 'black' body image, based on clinical work, is a vivid account of pathologies that evolved under apartheid and reads easily in tandem with Ndebele's stories. A basic tenet of Manganyi's argument is that seemingly healthy 'black' individuals have 'diffuse body boundaries' (1973: 53). Since their bodies are defined as negations of the norm and patently non-desirable, this leads to a repression of those same bodies. A partial collapse of their life-world ensues, leading to a 'malignant sense of helplessness' (Manganyi, 1973: 53). In other words, the subaltern's cultural alienation returns in aggravated form as bodily alienation. (Which is in analogy with the feminist analysis of the female body being constituted by and for the masculine gaze.)

Manganyi's most important point, and my strongest motivation for using this particular perspective, is that existence and society, psychology and history, the ordinary and the spectacular, all converge on the body. Its alienated state has been caused by a 'sociological schema' that disrupts the early socialisation of the individual (1973: 51), and in what amounts to a move to historicise (albeit in purely androcentric terms) the claims of existentialism, Manganyi writes that

> there are quantitative and qualitative differences in the experience of existential stress. The fundamental difference [. . .] is that the slave does not or, better still, cannot experience the absurdity of his existence as being a condition of life. He rather experiences it as arising from the condition of being a slave. [This] means that one is too tied up with the actual business of living, of planning for tomorrow's supper, to be concerned about the so-called terrifying freedom of individual existence. For a man whose existential alternatives are so limited from birth, freedom, like eternal life, can only assume the status of a catch-word. [. . .] We find therefore, that while the white man is exploring the moon, the black man, deprived of all active participation in the history of man, is still suffering from the onslaughts on his body (1973: 53–54).

For the 'black' person, 'blackness' precedes existence, precedes humanity. This recalls Fanon's *Peau noire, masques blancs*. The neuroses that Fanon locates in 'black' Martinicans, the horror of being cast as a 'negro' in the quotidian epidermal drama of colonialism – these are essentially the same traumas dealt with by Manganyi (Fanon, 1952: 33–86, 108–134). Manganyi is not nearly as forceful a stylist as Fanon, but he is an important mediator between the specifically South African context and Fanon's analysis of the colonial condition. Fanon writes of his own experience in terms that prefigure Manganyi:

> In the white world the man of color encounters difficulties in the development of his bodily schema. Consciousness of

the body is solely a negating activity. It is a third-person consciousness. The body is surrounded by an atmosphere of certain uncertainty (1986: 110–111).[2]

I was responsible at the same time for my body, for my race, for my ancestors. I subjected myself to an objective examination, I discovered my blackness, my ethnic characteristics; and I was battered down by tom-toms, cannibalism, intellectual deficiency, fetishism, racial defects [. . .] I took myself far off from my own presence, far indeed, and made myself an object. What else could it be for me but an amputation, an excision, a hemorrhage that spattered my whole body with black blood? (1986: 112)[3]

Similarly, in *Fools* it is the onslaught on the body (and certainly not only 'his' but also 'hers') that is the vaster obstacle to overcome.

Bildungsroman
In 'The Test', the young Thoba measures his strength and freedom by running barefoot through the township and exposing his half-naked body to the cold rain. It is an act of defiance towards his mother and simultaneously an initiation into the fellowship of the 'other boys'. This introductory story sets the pattern for those that follow: Thoba, young as he may be, is already set apart from most people in the community by having parents that are formally educated and slightly better-off. Here, class difference is coded as a bodily difference. When playing soccer with his friends, he observes that their feet are cracked, whereas his are not:

> Thoba remembered that he had three pairs of shoes, and his mother had always told him to count his blessings because most boys had only one pair [. . .] Yet Thoba yearned to have cracked feet too. So whenever his mother and father were away from home, he would go out and play without his shoes (1983: 5).

The body is a marker of social identity and difference. Whether aged or young, whether it carries or lacks clothing, whether the feet are cracked or smooth or, as in the context of colonialism/apartheid, whether it bears light or dark skin: each detail determines the specific place of each body, sets it apart from its environment. This overdetermined apartness of the body is at odds with the collectivist thrust of the narratives, and hints at the contradictory ideological burden that the body is made to carry throughout Ndebele's collection of stories.

Following Michael Neill's suggestion, I read *Fools* as a 'loose *Bildungsroman*' (1990: 172). This is an unremarkable claim as such, in the light of Vaughan's observation that Ndebele's writing is easily 'read off' from a European realistic tradition (1990: 197). But the notion of the inevitability of European form needs qualification, and this is achieved by testing it against a generic concept such as the *Bildungsroman*.

My understanding of the genre relies on Franco Moretti's investigation (1987). In his view, the *Bildungsroman*, as it developed at the end of the eighteenth century and the beginning of the nineteenth, constituted the 'symbolic form' of modernity. By privileging youth, it tried to accommodate the rapid pace of change that 'the double revolution' (political and industrial) had brought about. The young male protagonist would, in his confrontation with a turbulent world, arrive at a harmonious synthesis called 'maturity', at which point (paradoxically) no further change was required and the novel could end (Moretti, 1987). The *Bildungsroman* allowed self and society to merge. The fulfilled individual was, by definition, fully integrated with society.

Fools is obviously not a novel, but neither is it a random collection of stories. Rather, it is a short story cycle with a formal tension between unity and diversity. In Forrest Ingram's analysis, the story cycle as a genre 'displays a double tendency of asserting the individuality of its components on the one hand and of highlighting, on the other, the bonds of unity which make the unity into a single whole' (1971: 19).[4] This is an apposite formal description of *Fools*, yet it also – strikingly – points to a thematic tension that runs through the narratives. The generic tendency to 'draw the co-protagonists of any story cycle into a single community' corresponds exactly to the thematic challenge of the narratives (Ingram, 1971: 22). Thus, in a consistent setting each story in *Fools* revolves around differences of culture, class and gender, and the imperative to achieve leadership and communal bonding despite these differences. But these consistencies are not static. To borrow a simile from Ingram, the stories function like a wheel:

> The rim of the wheel represents recurrent elements in a cycle which rotate around a thematic center. As these elements (motifs, symbols, characters, words) repeat themselves, turn in on themselves, recur, the whole wheel moves forward. The motion of a wheel is a single process. In a single process, too, the thematic core of a cycle expands and deepens as the elements of the cycle repeat themselves in varied contexts (1971: 20–21).

It is this progression in *Fools* that brings the *Bildungsroman*'s 'symbolic form' to mind. From 'The Test' onwards, the reader is invited to follow a middle-class-yet-subaltern boy's gradual passage into manhood. By whatever name – or nameless, as in 'The Prophetess' and 'Uncle' – the protagonist gets a little older in each consecutive story. In 'The Music of the Violin', he is a tormented teenager torn between his sell-out parents and his jeering peers, in a painful retake of Thoba's inner conflict in 'The Test'. In the two longest stories, the development is contracted in so far as Lovington in 'Uncle' functions as a future projection of the protagonist/narrator, and Zamani in 'Fools' can be read as an old, failed version of Zani, who stands on the verge of adulthood. This affinity with the *Bildungsroman* is, however, disrupted in a highly significant way. If the *Bildungsroman* deals with the emergence of the individual in society, Ndebele focuses on the difficulty for such an emergence to occur. The crisis in *Fools* is less about change than the lack of and desire for change. It is in this interruption of the *Bildungsroman*'s generic inertia that we may locate the historical, post-colonial specificity of *Fools*, of its treatment of the body, and of its utopian vision.

As we trace the fates of various bodies in *Fools*, their textual duties multiply. In 'The Test', things seem simple and straight-forward. As much as his smooth feet set him apart from his friends, it is through his body that Thoba can achieve an 'organic' connection with the community. When his more streetwise friends issue their challenge by running shirtless into the rain, Thoba hesitates at first, and is tempted by the other middle-class boy in the gang, Mpiyakhe, to chicken out. Then he decides to hurl himself into the rain and leave Mpiyakhe behind. It is an 'act' in the existentialist meaning of the word, a moment of choice that begets the self, and is construed in the following way:

> Slowly and deliberately, and with a gleam in his eye, Thoba unbuttoned his shirt, and as he pulled it over his head, he felt the warmth of his breath on his chest. And that gave him a momentary impression of dreaming, for he had a clear image of Vusi taking off his shirt. But the image did not last; it was shattered by the re-emergence of his head into the cold. He shivered as goose pimples literally sprang out on his skin before his eyes. But he would have to be reckless. That was bravery. Bravery meant forgetting about one's mother.
>
> Thoba threw his shirt on to the floor where it joined Vusi's and Simangele's. And the last thing he did before he burst into the rain was look at Nana [the smallest of the boys], as if pleading for approval. Their eyes met. Those were the eyes he would carry in his mind into the rain, as if the whole township was looking at him. Mpiyakhe? He did not even deserve a glance (1983: 20).

Bursting into the rain, Thoba wilfully exposes his body to a much greater force than he is able to control (not unlike Zamani's deliberate choice of being whipped in 'Fools' – there is even a phenomenological correspondence between the whipping and how 'the cold water of the rain hit him' [1983: 20]). The patterns of two ideological narratives typical of the *Bildungsroman* are traced on this act. One is the narrative of individuation and individual freedom in which 'forgetting about one's mother' is a crucial step towards becoming an autonomous subject. The other is the narrative of socialisation. For the subaltern middle-class boy Thoba, this entails a wilful forgetting of his class-position – he averts his gaze from

Mpiyakhe – and an attempt at being accepted by the subaltern community.

There is a palpable tension here. Whereas the *Bildungsroman*, in Europe, has epitomised the bourgeois understanding of subjectivity (an autonomous individual matures, attains a position in society, and reconciles this position with his – always *his* – private self), Ndebele's story cycle has a decidedly anti-bourgeois leaning. This means that although the two narratives of individuation and socialisation may, ultimately, be interpreted in the political terms of a post-colonial problematic – and correspond to the Enlightenment ideals of 'freedom' and 'brotherhood', respectively – they tend to displace one another. At first the narrative of individuation would appear to have the upper hand, but the social desire in *Fools* is strong enough to match its strength, and at times exceed it. The relative positions of these narratives fluctuate constantly – an instability which is borne out and masked by the body. Following the conventions of realistic representation, the existence of a body behind a name is simply assumed in Ndebele's stories and subsequently brought to attention, often through the use of synecdoche (the cracked feet, for example). The body thus assumed is equally 'realistic', that is, isolated, organic, integral, sealed off, and therefore perfectly suited for masking the tug and pull of disjunctive ideological desires.

If we follow 'The Test' to the end, we notice how the individualist narrative gains the upper hand. At first Thoba experiences an exhilarated, sensuous union with the rain and the street:

> There was something freeing in the tickling pressure of the soft needles of rain on his skin. And then he ran in spurts: running fast and slowing down, playing with the pressure of the rain on him. It was a pleasant sensation; a soft, pattering sensation. And the rain purred so delicately against his ears. And when he waded in and out of the puddles, savouring the recklessness, it was so enchanting to split the water, creating his own little thunder from the numerous splashes (1983: 21).

But then, immediately after this last sentence, we read that 'He was alone in the street' (1983: 21) He hopes that everyone will see him and acknowledge his bold feat, but the further we read, the lonelier he gets. The exhilaration wears off, he is cold, his legs ache. In an utter state of misery – 'shirtless; shoeless; a wet body in a dripping pair of pants that clung tightly and coldly to him' (1983: 26) – he encounters a group of women at a bus stop. The text emphasises that there are only women standing there, defined as 'mothers'. They are, in other words, non-isolated bodies. As mothers, they have literally carried the community within their own bodies.[5] In an ironic negation of Thoba's double ambition of 'forgetting mother' and being accepted by the community, these mothers reprimand him collectively for being out in the cold. Humiliated, he finally reaches home (nobody there) and goes to bed. His only victory consists in having endured the pain of humiliation and exhaustion, a victory of the individual against the world. By the end of the story, Thoba's body has traversed from isolation to communion to isolation again.

In the next story, 'The Prophetess', the question of the body takes on a new twist. For the first time, the issue of sexual difference is spelt out. Having been to the prophetess, the boy – he has no name, he is simply 'the boy' of approximately the same age as Thoba – meets a gang of teenagers where a certain Biza is trying to impress the others with a story of a sexual exploit. In an instance of juvenile grotesque, Biza claims he can prove it by showing off the mucous fluid on his penis. The protagonist, uninvited, happens to glimpse this in passing, but is chased off.

> The boy took to his heels wondering what Biza could have been doing with his penis under the street lamp. It was funny, whatever it was. It was silly too. Sinful. The boy was glad that he had got the holy water away from those boys and that none of them had touched the bottle.
>
> And the teachers were right, thought the boy. Silliness was all those boys knew. And then they would go to school and fail test after test. Silliness and school did not go to-gether.
>
> The boy felt strangely superior. He had the power of the

prophetess in him. And he was going to pass that power to his mother, and heal her. Those boys were not healing their mothers. They just left their mothers alone at home. The boy increased his speed. He had to get home quickly (1983: 47).

The influence of the mothers is pervasive, but here the logic of 'The Test' is reversed and the narrative of individuation suspended. Whereas the boys with the cracked feet in 'The Test' presented an entry into the community, these adolescents lead the way to the far more ambiguous world of sexual difference, which threatens to banish the body to a separate male or female community whose collective identity emerges only against their gendered others – as opposed to the inclusive, 'organic' community under the sign of mothers and children. Inevitably, the variously-named protagonist of this *Bildungsroman* must be confronted with his emergent sexuality, but it is still contained in 'The Prophetess'. The boy is young and he sides instead with the mothers, the prophetess, and through them with the holistic vision of African society. The very act of healing is a transgressive moment which allows the boy to believe he can affect the body of his mother. The barriers separating bodies are less than absolute. Rather, the cultural bonding of the subaltern community – represented in this story by the figure of the prophetess – creates a liminal space wherein a communal identity founded on a principle of sameness rather than difference permits the bodies to 'connect', as it were.

An 'imaginary' community

On the face of it, the reading above ties in with my earlier remarks on 'The Prophetess'. However, by intervening with the concept of the body we see that the reconciliation of differing modes of knowledge that I previously saw at work in this particular story requires an 'imaginary' sealing-off of the ideological conflict (individuation versus socialisation) inscribed on the body of the protagonist. It requires, in short, that the boy be young enough to be asexual in order to side with his mother and reject the disturbing allure of the renegade adolescents. By calling this solution 'imaginary', I appropriate Abdul JanMohamed's categorisation of colonialist literature via Lacan's concepts of the 'imaginary' and the 'symbolic' (JanMohamed, 1986: 84–85). But whereas Jan-Mohamed refers exclusively to *colonialist* representations and attempted dissolutions of the imperial structuring of 'white' and 'native', or 'white' and 'black' (Kipling, Forster, Gordimer, etc.), I find this terminology equally, if differently, applicable when reading texts from 'the other side' of the Manichean divide. I do not ascribe the aggressiveness of the 'imaginary' colonialist text to any of Ndebele's stories, but just as the 'writer of [colonialist] texts tends to fetishize a nondialectical, fixed opposition between the self and the native' and 'retreats to the homogeneity of his own group' when threatened by the metaphysical alterity that he has created, so do I detect a roughly equivalent retreat into homogeneity in 'The Prophetess', possibly conditioned by the fear that an emphasis on heterogeneity would put the possibility of political resistance at risk (JanMohamed, 1986: 84). There is an 'imaginary' solution in this story that harks back to the experience of plenitude achieved by identifying with a 'good object' (such as a mirror-image) and subsequently masks the difference between the self and the object of identification. The social/communal identity subsists only by evading the issue of post-pubertal sexuality and hypostasizing the libidinal economy of the symbiotic mother-child relationship.

> There was such a glow of warmth in the boy as he watched his mother, so much gladness in him that he forgave himself. What had the prophetess seen in him? Did she still feel him in her hands? Did she know what he had just done? Did holy water taste any differently from ordinary water? His mother didn't seem to find any difference. Would she be healed?
>
> 'As we drink the prophetess's water,' said MaShange [a visitor], 'we want to say how grateful we are that we came to see for ourselves how you are.'
>
> 'I think I feel better already. This water, and you . . . I can feel a soothing coolness deep down.'
>
> As the boy slowly went out of the bedroom, he felt the pain in his leg, and felt grateful. He had healed his mother. He would heal her tomorrow, and always with all the water in the world. He had healed her (1983: 52).

A communal/textual strategy of exclusion can be gleaned from this passage. The strategy is marked by anxiety; throughout the story the boy is anxious that he will not bring the bottle of water home soon enough. When he leaves the teenagers on the street we read that he 'increased his speed' because he 'had to get home quickly' (1983: 47), and even in the final paragraphs his love for his mother is disturbed by a lingering uncertainty. In other words, the boy's sense of belonging is circumscribed by a fear of not belonging. The community is not simply a given, but as the boy enters its core, it is *made to seem* increasingly 'organic'. The community of the prophetess, the boy's mother, the other mothers and, eventually, the boy himself, appears like a 'body' in the conventional metaphorical sense (conventional at least so far as Western tradition goes), an organic whole consisting of many parts. This corporeal metaphor is suggested in no uncertain terms by the dominant concern of the narrative: healing. The boy's final entrance into the community and the act of healing coincide, which mediates perfectly between the individual bodies of mother and son and the collective horizon of the corporeal metaphor. What is perceived as his ability to heal his mother is the ultimate proof that he belongs in the 'body' of the community: only a body can heal itself in this 'magical' way.

This version of organic community comes across as exceedingly gentle. The boy is, after all, bluffing, but feels accepted all the same. The water is an empty, universally accessible signifier that serves to mediate communal identity. This is concomitant with the 'inclusivity' and 'cognitive ambivalence' of which I spoke previously; a body can, after all, only be accepted in its entirety. This organic appearance relies, however, on the exclusion of its other. The anxiety that precedes the boy's sense of belonging shows how the notion of inclusivity co-exists problematically with a sharp distinction between being within and outside of 'the body'. To be outside of a body must be the equivalent of death: to the boy it would mean 'dying' into the pubertal world of bodily change and sexual difference. A development which, being inevitable, can only be fended off by 'imaginary' means. The clearly most 'imaginary' moment of the ending resides in the penultimate sentence – 'He would heal her tomorrow, and always' – which, through narrative closure, traps the boy indefinitely in a state of boyhood and ossifies his loyal, subservient relation to his mother.

This textual protection of the appearance of organic community is the second attempt within the *Bildungsroman* of *Fools* to resolve the tension between the narratives of individuation and social-isation. The interesting question is why this tension must be resolved, or, lacking a resolution, disguised. What does this attempt at *harmonising* the subject-position of the protagonist entail? A decentred view of the subject, one in which the tension between disjunctive ideological exigencies remains unresolved, translates of course as a risk in this context, a risk that must be contained. But why is it such a risk? The explanation that *Fools and Other Stories* simply duplicates the already written text of the realistic *Bildungs-roman*, manifesting as it does a typically 'bourgeois' desire for a fixed and harmonious subject, amounts to a dehistoricising re-duction of Ndebele's stories, a disregard for their synchronic worldliness – but neither can the formal aspect simply be dismissed. Once again we find ourselves at that troubled yet productive intersection of textual and historical reading which constitutes 'secular criticism', as far as I understand Edward Said's use of the term. In order once again to open up the historical dimension of our reading, I shall now focus on 'Uncle' and 'Fools'. In these longest stories of the collection, the body is inserted more directly in a political and historical frame of signification.

The nation as *Gemeinschaft*

'Uncle' is, arguably, Ndebele's most utopian tale. The storyteller's uncle, a non-conformist trumpet-player turned Muslim (not unlike the South African pianist Abdullah Ibrahim) comes to visit the storyteller and his mother one day. This man, sometimes called Uncle, sometimes Lovington, is chastised by his sister (the narrator's mother) for being careless and irresponsible. It appears that his major breach of confidence was to leave his mother and father.

> 'I was doing my last year of training when you were born. Exams were around the corner, yet every month end I would leave Bridgeman Hospital and take a train all the way home to Bloemfontein to help mother take care of you. And she used to say: "This is our last one, he will take care of us." And you were so weak. I don't know what would have

happened if it were not for my training. And then you disappear. Five years! And when my husband dies, we don't know where to get you. Fancy disappearing for five years and leaving Mother and Father all alone' (1983: 64–65).

Lovington's response marks him out as an Artist, a familiar figure in European literature: "'I've told you all I had to follow my calling. And everybody was saying I should have a teacher's certificate to fall back on in case something went wrong. A talent is a talent. I had to follow my talent'" (1983: 65). Leaving his parents and disappearing for five years could be seen as a less than surprising move, even a cliché, wholly typical of a young artist coming into his own. However, as soon as we consider 'The Prophetess', with its close ties between mother and son, as well as the cultural context of tightly regulated family relations in African societies, such a reading comes across as if not Eurocentric, then neither as unproblematic.[6] Within the context of the narrative, Lovington's act is just as startling as his sister makes it out to be, and stands in strong opposition to the close-knit community in 'The Prophetess'. The closure in which the boy in the previous story wished to reside now appears broken and open, and the narrative of individuation once again has the upper hand, albeit slightly displaced, since Lovington does not really 'belong' in Charterston and cannot threaten the community from within. Instead he projects a version of community that exceeds the physical boundaries of Charterston by far. To demonstrate this, I shall highlight three moments in the story which each in its own way intervenes in the narratives of the body. The first is a variation of that primal scene of post-colonial resistance, the drawing of a new map:

'Do you know that what comes out of that piano can take you places?' Uncle laughs and then says: 'Bring your atlas here and let me show you some of these places.'
    Uncle comes to sit next to me and we look at the map of South Africa. 'Show me Bloemfontein . . . yes . . . That is where your grandmother and grandfather are. Your uncles. Your younger mothers. They are all there. That is the centre of your life too. Your mother had to come home before you

were born because you were her first born. And that is where
I buried your umbilical cord. Right there in the yard.
Wherever you are in the world, you must return to that
yard. Now show me Johannesburg . . . yes . . . That is where
Uncle bought his trumpet. Now look at this: Ladysmith,
Pietermaritzburg, Durban, East London, Port Elizabeth,
Cape Town, Kimberley, Pietersburg, Middelburg, Witbank,
Pretoria, Springs, Germiston. All foreign names; but that
will change in time. This whole land, *mshana*, I have seen it
all. And I have given it music. You too must know this land.
The whole of it, and find out what you can give it. So you
must make a big map of the country, your own map. Put it
on the wall. Each time you hear of a new place, put it on the
map. Soon you will have a map full of places. And they will
be your places. And it will be your own country. And then
you must ask yourself: what can I give to all those places?
And when you have found the answer, you will know why
you want to visit those places' (1983: 66).

Nowhere else is Ndebele as explicit about *place*, that post-colonial
concern *par excellence*, and nowhere does a utopian vision of a new
nation take hold of the text quite so suggestively. The boy's uncle
evokes a land of the imagination – an 'imagined community', to use
Benedict Anderson's term – with manifold qualities. It is a land
at one with its people. The boy's extended family lives in
Bloemfontein, and since his umbilical cord was once buried there,
the soil of Bloemfontein is somehow *him*, the very centre of his life.
It is the traces of the body – the umbilical cord – that seals the
union between place and person. But from this traditional, 'African'
position – a limited geography of the familiar, so to speak –
Lovington naturalises the political construct of 'South Africa'. The
fact of the nation shown on the map – created as it was through a
series of colonial wars and political manipulations – is accepted
without further ado; all that remains is to appropriate the places
which make up 'South Africa' and eventually change their 'foreign
names'. The implied metaphor that governs this act of
appropriation is yet again biological. The inference might be glossed
like this: 'Just as you gave of your body to the soil of Bloemfontein,

so must you continue to give of yourself and, through giving, come to belong organically to each and every place in this country.' What is attempted is a transposition of the intimate and seemingly self-evident sense of home to be found in a more-or-less traditional African context to the political scale of nationalism. In the process, what until 'The Prophetess' was a relatively simple conflict between individuation and socialisation has become much more complex. Now the tension obtains between an intimate and a nationwide notion of community – between *Gemeinschaft* and *Gesellschaft*.[7] The uncle wishes the boy to be a citizen of a nation that functions as intimately as a *Gemeinschaft*, and this requires that the difference between levels be obscured. In order to solve this equation, a factor *x* is called upon, namely the individual body. Lovington stands before the boy as living, tangible proof that the *Gemeinschaft* of the nation is feasible: '"This whole land, *mshana*, I have seen it all. And I have given it music"'. It is as though by seeing it he has ingested the country and carries it within himself; by giving it music, it is as though he has spread himself all over the land. The unstated condition for such an all-encompassing interaction with a country is the mobility and materiality of the body. Time is not an issue here; it is not the duration of a person's connection to a place that counts, it is rather the material/spatial fact – however fleeting – of bodily presence.

The second moment in the story that I wish to highlight demonstrates a peculiar understanding of this 'presence'. The story-teller describes a drawing of his uncle playing the trumpet that an artist friend is making. The imperfect likeness disappoints him:

In the first place, the trumpet is too huge. The part that brings out the sound is so open that it is almost half the size of Uncle. And the rest of the trumpet is completely covered by Uncle's big hands and thick fingers. And Uncle's lips seem to have become part of the hands and seem to be swallowing the trumpet. And his blown up cheeks have become the whole face. And his eyes are a deep line across the cheeks. His nose is facing up as if when he breathes he will suck in everything (1983: 77).

The body is transformed in the creative act. The artist, brother Mandla, explains it in the following way:

> 'When you play you *are* exaggerated. You are bigger than what you normally are because you have become all those who are listening to you [. . .] We all go into you and swell you up as we cheer you and you take us all in, and you become stronger and stronger the more you play. And we all become powerfully one' (1983: 78).

We can read this in a number of ways. At the most obvious level, it celebrates the musicality of 'black' South Africa, music being one of its foremost cultural expressions, and jazz being the most successful form of 'black' modernism.[8] But more than that, the unity evoked between musician and audience echoes a common place in much writing on traditional African aesthetics. Chinua Achebe, when discussing an Igbo ceremony called *mbari*, concludes that there 'is no rigid barrier between makers of culture and its consumers. Art belongs to all, and is a 'function' of society' (1975: 22) For the *négritude* writers, as Achebe also points out, this was a fundamental characteristic of African culture. We may also recall how Ezekiel Mphahlele contrasts the 'capitalistic outlook' that 'a leisured class feels bored and requires amusement' to 'the traditional African idea of culture as a way of growing up', that is, a non-reified culture without any strict barriers and best understood as a process implicated in all aspects of life (1974: 21). An ur-text in this respect is Leo Frobenius's contribution to *Kulturgeschichte* at the beginning of this century. The image he constructed of Africa as a total, harmonious culture, an 'esthetocracy' where 'art is everything and everything is art' had a decisive influence on *négritude* and the paradigm of a 'culture without boundaries' (Miller, 1986: 290). In 'Uncle', we witness this idea at work in a typically urban setting. Lovington's jazz music is a purely urban phenomenon, it is innovative, it is not part of any 'unbroken' rural tradition but it is nonetheless assumed to express the very same cultural unity that is projected onto the African past: it reconciles 'blackness' with modernity and unifies the subaltern community of South Africa. The corporeal metaphor again – through the creative body of

Lovington 'we all become powerfully one' – but modified this time as a representation within the representation.

Whereas the 'imaginary' solution of 'The Prophetess' – with its insistence on a literal organic or bodily union, signified by the act of healing – required the repression of sexual difference and the hypostasis of the mother-and-child relationship, 'Uncle' has moved on to a 'symbolic' version of organicism.

Here we arrive at the third moment that I want to highlight. In accordance with the approximate schema of the *Bildungsroman*, the young protagonist/storyteller edges towards maturity and is confronted in 'Uncle', more directly than in the preceding story, with sexual difference when he gets a glimpse of a woman who has just made love to his uncle. At this point, ambivalent desire supersedes the puzzled repulsion of the boy in 'The Prophetess': 'And the skirt was gone now, and here were the thighs on my bed, and they are strangely joined together by hair that's a triangle. She is all so brown, all so moist, and I am looking. I've got to go now. I've got to go. But I can't. My heart is beating fast, and I am trembling, and I feel hot now, very hot. I don't know what to do' (1983: 82). It is worth noting that the woman is lying on the boy's bed, as though she were a premonition of his own entry into adult (hetero)-sexuality. The boy himself stands on the threshold between the symbiosis of mother-child intimacy (here, too, the relationship between the boy and his mother is depicted with great tenderness) and the more conflictual world of sexual intimacy, whereas Lovington stands as a model of manhood, someone who has successfully negotiated the sexual desire and gendered social relations of adult life. Such maturity necessitates a displacement of the organic/bodily metaphor and calls for its re-enactment within the symbolic order. It is no longer possible in 'Uncle' to ignore the heterogeneity of the various gendered positions within the community. Instead, the demonstration of unity is transferred to the realm of aesthetic expression. Brother Mandla's drawing stands as an emblem of the 'limitless body' of the community. Lovington's body is deformed for the simple reason that, as long as he plays his trumpet, it constitutes more than a mere individual. This is confirmed at the end of 'Uncle' by the carnivalesque celebration on the township streets brought about by dancing and singing miners, and additionally fuelled by Lovington's trumpet. It is a happy vision of togetherness that demonstrates how Lovington can 'belong' wherever he goes, and should be read as the ultimate response to his sister's censure. Nevertheless, and once again, I must remark that the harmonising urge tends to be so powerful in Ndebele's narratives that it obscures the issue of difference within the subaltern collective. The variously stated sameness of Lovington, the audience in Charterston, the nation, the *Gemeinschaft* 'back home' in Bloemfontein – a sameness which can be read as the political extension of the organic community which enfolds the boy in 'The Prophetess' – elides the fact that his project as jazz-musician and free-thinker is individualistic and departs from the 'body' of the community, even if this 'body' is contained by the 'symbolic' logic referred to above. The *sine qua non* of the 'symbolic' solution is, after all, those 'significant others' that choose or are forced to stay put instead of single-mindedly pursuing their talents across the face of an entire country; those workers and parents that ensure the existence of a *Gemeinschaft* in which the moment of aesthetic and cultural sharing can take place. The colloquialism 'significant others' distinguishes between the other of the Manichean divide, that is, the coloniser, and those that belong to the Same, but with a difference. They are the forgotten term within the Same and thus underscore the heterogeneity of the subaltern. This analysis is, moreover, validated by Anthony O'Brien's questioning of Ndebele's relationship (as critic and theorist) to African feminism. Although his thinking – and, as we can see, his narrative practice – is akin to feminist attentions to the local and everyday realm of being, he has remained strangely silent on the issue (O'Brien, 1992: 77–82). By underplaying the contentious aspects of 'ordinary' gender relations, Ndebele's stories ultimately occlude the tension between the disjunctive narratives of individuation and socialisation. This manifest homogenising desire is, to all appearances, determined not only by the strategic demands of unified political resistance – which, indeed, testifies to the historical urgency of the period when *Fools* was written – but also by the expectations of a 'resolution' that is a fundamental part of the realistic conventions employed by Ndebele.

CHAPTER 8

Disembodiment and Presence

O N THE ONE HAND, each story in *Fools* functions as a discrete entity, presenting a solution of some sort to a specific conflict. On the other hand, the stories are linked to each other and jointly form a story cycle reminiscent of the *Bildungsroman*. This makes the conclusion of each story more provisional than an isolated reading would allow. Instead, the consecutive resolutions of 'The Test', 'The Prophetess' and 'Uncle' describe a dialectical triangle: from the individuation of 'Thoba' in 'The Test' we move ahead to the total, 'imaginary' socialisation of 'The Prophetess', which is reworked 'symbolically' in 'Uncle' in order to negotiate a synthesis between the demands of the individual and the communal bodies. However, since each resolution produces a conflictual residue, the pressure mounts on each consecutive story. It is therefore perhaps logical that no resolution is offered in 'The Music of the Violin', the penultimate piece. Instead, it ends in bitter conflict between son and mother and depicts an absolute rupture in the respective cultural identifications of the 'people' and the middle class. This defers the conflict to 'Fools' which, ideally, must contain and/or cut through the complications that have accumulated throughout the book, however unreasonable such an expectation might seem.

Upon examination, 'Fools' can be shown to attempt this. The body is inserted afresh in this dominant piece of the collection; and the narrative does not echo 'Uncle', in the way that 'Uncle' and 'The Prophetess' complement each other. In general terms, 'Fools' hones the politico-historical edge of 'Uncle', but from a different angle.

Negating the body
What first calls our attention to the body in 'Fools' is its negation, a

95

direct reminder of Fanon's claim that '[consciousness] of the body is solely a negating activity' (1986: 110).[1] Two-thirds into the story, at the point where young Zani launches his quixotic crusade against the Day of the Covenant,[2] the word 'disembodied' starts to appear. When Zamani comments on Zani's failure to communicate with schoolchildren, it simply refers to the plight of the alienated intellectual: 'He had become his books, and when he moved out of them, he came out without a social language. [. . .] I wondered if he was not another instance of *disembodiment*: the *obscenity* of high seriousness' (1983: 217; emphases added here and in the following quotations in this paragraph). The last sentence refers to a previous situation, when a pupil of Zamani's comes carrying one of Zani's leaflets proclaiming 'DAY OF THE COVENANT: STAY HOME AND THINK'. On it, someone has made a drawing of a penis and a vagina, causing Zamani to lament that the young boy already thought sex was some '*disembodied obscenity*' (1983: 212). In a sentence referring to another boy in the class, one who was reciting a Zulu poem when the mischief-maker with the obscene drawing disturbed him, we again read: 'He still stood there where he had been torn away from his recollection of history, and thrown back into an *obscene disembodied* present which had no vital connection with the recollected glories; nothing in it to maintain the validity of the past' (1983: 212). Towards the end of the story, the word is used to denote Zani's disconnectedness – not from the community this time, but from his own words, his own potential: 'Whenever he spoke that way, it seemed as if there was something, some *disembodied* essence, speaking through him. He was grasping out to be part of it, but his arms were not long enough' (1983: 277).

All four examples indicate rupture. The subject is dissipated, body and voice are separated, the body itself is dismembered. This positioning of the body as a locus of absence is a highly significant textual move. It gestures towards 'embodiment' as the key metaphor of fulfilment, of organic totality, whereas 'disembodiment' is equated with 'obscenity'.

In the case of the obscene drawing, Zamani apparently deplores the fetishisation of the sexual act and the sexual organs, and implies that fulfilled sexuality concerns more than the sexual drive: it requires that the entire body and 'person' be part of it. My use of the word 'fetishisation' registers the challenge that such a reading issues, in an undercut way, to the Freudian tradition of privileging sexuality and the phallus as the main signifiers of subjective identity. Whereas Freud states that the fetish masks a lack, or rather the fear of a lack, of castration, by way of (a disembodying) substitution, the narrative apparently claims that the image of the phallus *as such*, of its sexual activity, is merely a fetish that masks the lack of a more 'embodied' sexuality which averts its gaze from the blunt fact of the genitals.

As for the boy reciting the epic poem, the fact of disembodiment is here assigned to the 'present', in opposition to what is perceived as the heroic past of indigenous Zulu culture. In the eyes of the narrator the present is obscene in that it does not allow the boy to be precisely that, namely 'present' in the present. Here, the compounded alienation of the subaltern is palpable, since the recitation invokes an irretrievable past within a present that is equally beyond reach.

Finally, the first and last examples of 'disembodiment' refer to the intellectual's place in the community. In the first case, the narrator frowns upon something called 'high seriousness' and hints at a more communicative attitude that would reduce Zani's alienation from the children. The other example contradicts the first in so far as Zani now seems to belong 'in reality' with the community, whereas his intellectual capacity has yet to arrive.

Following this exposition, two initial conclusions present themselves. Firstly, nowhere in *Fools* is the corporeal metaphor as explicitly stated as in the title story and, secondly, nowhere is it placed under such heavy attack. The latter conclusion is confirmed not only by Zamani's conflictual sexual relations but also by the very stylistic treatment of sex. The only time that sexual intercourse is depicted in 'Fools' – when Zamani seeks out Zani's sister – the reader is confronted with rape as well as unconvincing language. At this point, Ndebele's otherwise tempered metonymic prose breaks down into utterings dense with metaphor:

See, floating on the water, thousands of acorns, corn seeds, wheat and barley, eyeballs winking endlessly like the ever changing patterns on the surface of the water, and the rain of sour milk pelting the water with thick curds. I want to come into the water, but I can't. I am trapped behind thin screens of ice. I must break it down. I heave! And I heave! And there is a deafening scream of squawking geese. The pain of heaving! The frightening screams! And the ice cracks with the tearing sound of mutilation. And I break through with such a convulsion. And I'm in the water. It is so richly viscous. So thick. Like the sweetness of honey. And the acorns, and the corn seeds, wheat and barley sprout into living things. And I swim through eyes which look at me with enchantment and revulsion (1983: 195).

It might even be that the unconvincing attempt at poetic beauty in this paragraph *is precisely what makes it convincing*. For do we not see here what the term 'disembodied obscenity' might entail, rape being the ultimate obscenity and 'poetic' language being a prime example of disembodiment, the displacement of the signifier?

Much later in the story, when Zamani meets his mistress Candu, the text is also frank about their sexual encounter, only this time, Zamani is impotent and the style less flamboyant:

But nothing happens. Try as I may, nothing happens. I'm trying. I'm trying. I'm concentrating; but my concentration yields only an awareness of tortured consciousness: strength without power; desire without fulfilment. So much corn to eat! So much harvest, and the fire of hunger in the stomach, and the hand lifting the produce to my mouth, but the mouth is sealed. Everything is ready but for the indifferent limpness of the penis, so much without sensation that it seems not there any more (1983: 247–248).

This is a far cry from the easy-going confidence of Lovington and is a dismal projection of the youngster Zani's conceivable future. Zamani's brief affair, his act of infidelity, is at heart an attempt at achieving unbridled freedom, which makes his disgrace all the more devastating. 'Disembodiment' has settled within Zamani. In a grotesque dream in connection to this show of impotence he sees a saucer on a table filled with faeces. However much he tries to get rid of it he fails. He is captured in his self-debasement. It is no longer merely his actions but his own body that humiliates him utterly.

We might well ask *why* Zamani's indignity takes on such monumental proportions – we find nothing of the sort in the other stories. An obvious reason presents itself: whereas the earlier stories were allowed to function within and through the image of a largely self-sufficient subaltern community (which, strictly speaking, makes redundant the relationary term 'subaltern'), the post-colonial dilemma comes to the fore in 'Fools'. By comparison, the expansion of the historical and political horizon in 'Uncle' defiantly represents an individual – Lovington – whose freedom makes the 'white' society irrelevant. It is but a slight annoyance 'that will change in time' (1983: 66). Such a slight and easy dismissal of the apartheid state makes, however, the 'symbolic' ending of 'Uncle' dependent upon an 'imaginary' condition (the occlusion of the 'significant others'). It is therefore all the more significant that 'Fools' confronts the fact of colonial/apartheid power head-on.

This confrontation occurs at the level of the 'bodily schema' and the colonial stereotype, as discussed by Fanon and Bhabha. Nowhere does the ambivalence of the stereotype appear more starkly than here, since the body is always simultaneously inscribed in 'the economy of pleasure and desire and the economy of discourse, domination and power' (Bhabha, 1994: 214). As a case in point, Zamani's sexual desire is undercut by the determinations of colonial/apartheid power. These determinations were exacerbated during the apartheid era by a fantastical bureaucracy which ultimately aimed at rendering the body of the subaltern invisible and entirely visible at the same time.

In Deborah Posel's analysis, apartheid was largely a futile attempt to manage the influx of workers to the urban centres (1997 [1991]: 1–22). The economy demanded labour, but those who controlled the economy refused the labourers free access to the urban centres. This impossible equation resulted in the tangle of repressive legislation and the material patchwork of townships, homelands, hostels and migratory labour that we know as apartheid.

The body of the subaltern was thus constricted by a contradictory system. The Separate Areas Act, for example, was an attempt at keeping the 'black' population out of sight and yet accessible to the privileged minority, whereas the pass laws were a means of ensuring maximum visibility and thereby keeping the bodily mobility of 'blacks' in check.[3] The evidence of these power relations point toward the experience of 'disembodiment' expressed, or at least persistently invoked in Ndebele's novel: the subaltern is deprived of his or her own body; it is appropriated and defined by the combined forces of colonial discourse and state repression.

At this point, we see how our 'bodily' reading begins to merge with the earlier concern for 'knowledge', albeit with a difference. If the inclusive, ambivalent view of knowledge in 'The Prophetess' can be read as an answer to a dilemma, then 'Fools' rearticulates the dilemma as such and implies an analogy between the constrained body and the constrained knowledge, or 'consciousness', of the subaltern. On two occasions in the latter part of 'Fools' the prohibitions surrounding (and defining) the subaltern are directly alluded to. Firstly, surprisingly, in a letter written by the marginal figure Ntozakhe, Zani's girl-friend:

> Living in the townships, I tend to regard so many things as being impossibly out of reach, and then I realise that they can be done because someone else has done them and I'm so happy. I suppose because we do not have our lives in our hands, and endless prohibitions make the world so impenetrable, the achievements of others seem to lie beyond our understanding. And I am led to think that perhaps our ultimate liberty has much to do with our bringing as much of the world as possible into our active consciousness (1983: 252).

Later, in a sustained meditation on the physical appearance of Charterston location and the immediately neighbouring townships – the only time in the entire book, apart from the map-scene in 'Uncle', that the physical world beyond Charterston is brought to attention (and not just mentioned in passing) – the narratorial gaze of Zamani is fixed on two yew trees on top of a hill, an old landmark known as 'the eternal twins'. The object thus transfixed 'throws back' the gaze, and Zamani begins to wonder what these trees actually 'see':

[. . .] they saw division. They saw a township dominated by two buildings: a community hall, and a beer hall. The rest of the buildings, houses, were a flat mass of sameness. And there was the drab Coloured section just outside the township. There was no outstanding building there, only a mass of wooden or corrugated iron shacks. Here and there the brick houses of teachers or businessmen. The whole depressing sight accentuated the tragic illusion of people conditioned to draw their greatest inspiration from the little white blood in them. They lived in the perpetual uncertainty of not knowing whether they were loved or hated. The trees also saw the Indian section: surely the most enviable in the area, with big houses that were the fruits of commerce. It maintained an aloofness that had less to do with achievement than with compliant indifference. That's what the trees saw.

Yet how obvious the analysis ascribed to them. Zani was right. The obviousness of analysis! A mind given completely to a preoccupation with an unyieldingly powerful, unabating negation, is soon debased by the repeated sameness of its findings. And in the absence of any other engaging mental challenges, its perceptions of viable alternatives become hopelessly constricted. But the trees would remain there gazing, until a new day gave them a new voice (1983: 262).

This passage contains, as I read it, the narrative's desired interpretation of itself.[4] By imagining the view that the trees command with such indifference, Zamani tries to escape the restrictions imposed on his physical being, only to realise that his 'analysis' suffers from that very obviousness of which Zani has spoken. This 'repeated sameness' of the mind's findings, this return to the Same, is theorised by Bhabha (in reading Fanon) as the process of constant confirmation and reconfirmation – along the lines of the 'epidermal schema' – by which the precarious order of colonial discourse is kept in place (Bhabha, 1994: 80). By the same token, we might recall Manganyi's words that the slave can only experience the absurdity of his or her existence as being due to the condition of being a slave. He or she is stuck in a conceptual loop (absurdity being caused by the condition which is caused by the condition, etc.), without any freedom of existence to be frightened of in the first place. Ndebele's story hovers at this moment between the imperative to *think* itself into this freedom and to emancipate the body.

We might conceptualise this dualism in the following manner: the body cannot transgress the limits of historical possibility, and the relative freedom of the mind lacks substance so long as the body remains fettered. However, the mind is capable of *re-articulating* what is historically possible, which in turn allows the body to be reinvested with political agency. This is the wager of embodiment that operates throughout 'Fools', and nowhere so evidently as in the finale.

Repositioning the body

It is Zani who invites Zamani to the picnic: "'Just got word that there is a picnic in the wood at Rand Nigel. Please come and help me; I'm going to break it up. You'll find me there. Yours for the future, Zani'" (1983: 265). It is 16 December, Day of the Covenant or Dingane's Day, the Afrikaner holiday when Zani wants everyone in Charterston to 'stay home and think' – which is why he intends to break up the picnic. Zamani is hesitant, but eventually decides to go. Once there, he witnesses a heated argument about whether or not to enter the park between Zani and the principal of Zamani's school, Mr Lehamo. The principal is a caricature of the sell-out – like the parents in 'The Music of the Violin' – who is prepared to concede to all the demands of apartheid, and consequently defends those who wish to make merry on the Day of the Covenant.

The clash between Lehamo's treason of complacency and Zani's radical idealism is absolute and inevitable. Zamani gets involved when Mr Lehamo asks him to 'talk to this boy', but he refrains from doing anything. Mr Lehamo's frustration mounts, and eventually he and another picnicker start to advance menacingly towards Zani, who breaks into run. Mr Lehamo hurls a stone at Zani, but instead of reaching its intended goal, the stone hits a passing car:

It was an old, black, 1957 Ford driven by a white man. The stone hit its roof resoundingly.

Immediately, the principal clasped his hands at the back of his head like a woman mourning. Buti [the other picnicker] stopped in his tracks, and seemed undecided whether to remain where he was or to retreat. But the principal turned and walked back towards the gate, his face a mask of agony.

'Oh, my God, what have I done?' he cried. 'What have I done?'

The white man stopped his car some thirty yards away, and slowly reversed, carefully backing on to the side of the road, and stopping not far from Buti. He heaved himself out of his car, for he was huge, though he was short. [. . .] Calmly, he looked at all of us, and then walked towards the boot of his car and opened it. He took out a whip (1983: 272).

In this moment of terror, the power of the coloniser, the subaltern's other, comes into full view. The sell-out Lehamo grovels and pleads in a show of subservience – "'Please my great king, please'" (1983: 273) – whereas Zani is unrepentant and hurls an insult at the 'white' man. The Afrikaner starts to chase Zani but loses him and lashes out at Lehamo instead, who flees with the rest of the crowd at the entrance gate. Before long, Zamani is alone, a living provocation to the Boer:

'And you,' he sneered, 'why are you not running?'

I fixed my eyes on him, stared at him, challenging him to a contest of wills. He cracked his whip; I knew then that his whip was all there was to him. He had cracked it to help him look back at me. And then he appealed to his voice.

'Answer me, blinking eyes!' he shouted.

I merely stared back at him (1983: 275).

The Afrikaner is caught in the narcissistic economy of colonial discourse; his voice, his whip do not reach out to the other – instead they feed back to his ego in a closed loop. The other does not exist beyond the space of encounter delimited by his whip. Within that space, his control of the other (or his fantasy of the other) is precisely equivalent to his control of the whip; beyond, the other is irrelevant. Remarkably, however, Zamani reverses this self-contained logic, an achievement which demands to be quoted in full:

> I continued to look at him, and came to the decision that if he lashed out at me with his whip, I would have to fight back. But then he would be sure to beat me, for he was infinitely stronger than I. But he would have to beat me. It was not until he actually started lashing at me repeatedly, that I knew I would not give him the kind of victory he wanted. I felt sure that no amount of violence against me would give him any self-respect. He was of the same substance as his whip. I offered no resistance as he lashed at me. I just stared at him. I struggled hard to absorb the searing pain, trying to subject my body to the total control of my mind. I wanted to scream. It was as if my skin was peeling off and boiling water was being thrown over the exposed, lacerated inner flesh. But my silence was my salvation; the silence of years of trying to say something without much understanding; the silence of desperate action. This would be the first silence that would carry meaning.
>
> The Boer came at me again and again, his face so red that it seemed to have become the very blood he wanted to draw out of me. He did not look at me any more; he knew where I was. He looked only at the ground, at his feet, beating down the grass around him, to leave a small patch of clearing as a sign of the futility of his battleground. He seemed to grow smaller and smaller the more he came at me. Then I felt totally numb. My mind had shut out all the pain. And, for the third time in about two weeks, I felt in the depths of me, the beginning of the kind of laughter that seemed to explain everything. And when the sound of laughter came out, it filled my ears, shutting out the pain even further. It seemed to fill out the sky like a pounding

drum. And that is when the Boer started weeping. And he
seemed to weep louder, the fainter the power of his lashing
became.

The blows stopped; and I knew I had crushed him. I had
crushed him with the sheer force of my presence. I was
there, and would be there to the end of time: a perpetual
symbol of his failure to have a world without me (1983:
275–276).

As I have already mentioned, the ending of 'Fools' has caused some
controversy. Lewis Nkosi's condemnation of its 'sentimentality' has
been countered by critics who see it as a subtle inversion of power
relations in apartheid South Africa. Notably, Michael Neill argues
that 'it leaves the Boer effectually stripped of his identity' and
'signals a black man's determination to make his own meanings, to
refuse the closed circle of definitions that constitutes the system of
apartheid' (1990: 175). I agree with Neill, in that it displaces and
inverts the quotidian drama of apartheid, its spectacle. If, at the
beginning, all that existed was the Boer himself and that which his
whip inscribed, he is soon 'of the same substance as his whip', and
once the power of the whip is defeated, a non-being – instead, it is
Zamani who literally comes into being. He mobilises agency, resists,
through the 'fact' of his body. Or rather, he erects another body,
attains a dimension of historical possibility, other than that which is
defined by the rule of the whip.

The debased, subservient body is always already in place for the
subaltern to occupy. When the Afrikaner sets out to reconfirm the
fact of this subservient body – a body which is nothing more than a
mirror in which he may reflect his own image – Zamani cracks
open the ambivalence of colonial discourse. He offers what the Boer
ostensibly desires – a non-resisting, non-violent 'black' – but this
desire is fulfilled so insistently, so mockingly, that the Boer is
confronted with his utter powerlessness in relation to the other.
This gives us the image of the coloniser 'tethered to, *not* confronted
by, his dark reflection, the shadow of colonized man, that splits his
presence, distorts his outline, breaches his boundaries, [. . .] disturbs
and divides the very time of his being', as Bhabha writes with
reference to Fanon (1986: xiv). It also allows for a Levinasian

reading of the kind that I develop in Part 4. The totality of the Boer and his whip, although it inscribes itself incessantly on Zamani's body, is incapable of appropriating the infinity of Zamani. In a twin manoeuvre, this simultaneously inverts and rejects Zamani's *own* past as an oppressor, when he let his cane 'rain down' on his pupils (1983: 161). He is thus himself released from the closed circle of violence. Intriguingly, his release first results in silence (and later in laughter, which is also situated outside of language). This brings to mind Michael K's silence, or Friday's silence in Coetzee's *Foe* (1986): it is the blank mark of alterity, literally not possible to articulate within the narrative which still belongs to ipseity, to the order of the Same.

This repositioning of the subaltern's body may be viewed as an impressive consummation – but also, partly, a negation – of the earlier narratives. At this point, the individualist schema of the *Bildungsroman* is finally displaced, as well as the closed yet insufficient visions of 'organic community' in 'The Prophetess' and 'Uncle'. The confrontation with the ultimate manifestation of colonial power makes Zamani's freedom more credible, albeit slighter, than Lovington's. However, I have one last, lingering doubt concerning the issue of 'presence' and agency in relation to the aftermath of the whipping:

> I had crushed him with the sheer force of my presence. I was there, and would be there to the end of time: a perpetual symbol of his failure to have a world without me. And he walked away to his car, a man without a shadow. The sun couldn't see him. And the sound of his car when he drove away seemed so irrelevant. There he went: a member of a people whose sole gift to the world has been the perfection of hate. And because there was nothing much more in them, they will forever destroy, consuming us and themselves in a great fire. But the people of the north will come down and settle the land again, as they have done for thousands of years (1983: 276).

There is a vagueness about this passage that unsettles me. Firstly, and quite justifiably, it underlines the shift that has occurred in the relation between 'coloniser' and 'colonised' which renders these terms obsolete. Zamani has stepped out from the shadow of the Boer, who is now literally without a shadow (severed from his 'dark reflection'); the identities that were constituted in and through the logic of colonial discourse have been dissolved. But then, in a denial of the historically specific struggle that formed this 'presence', the text – in a unique instance of future projection – begins to employ millenarian rhetoric. The invocation of ancient and pre-colonial Africa ('the people of the north') – what some historians refer to as the *zamani* period (Lema, 1993: 15) – adds a suggestively symbolic dimension to Zamani's name, but forecloses the sophisticated analysis of subjectivity that has painstakingly been pieced together throughout 'Fools'. It is as though the depiction of the subaltern's alienation through the colonial discourse of apartheid – a narrative which provides a case in point of how subjectivity is constructed by the demands of ideology – loses its specific weight as soon as Zamani's act of resistance succeeds; as though an authentic, indigenous and non-ideological subject not only exists but is simply biding its time 'within' Zamani, poised to spring forth once conditions are favourable. In my reading, this negates the whipping scene where Zamani literally begets himself through struggle, by engaging with the opposition. The facile separation of the 'ideological' from the 'authentic' subject that is made immediately after the struggle is coterminous with the Marxist notions of ideology, 'false consciousness', and the fulfilled 'individual' that socialism is meant to bring about (Smith, 1988: 7). This causes an unfortunate lapse in 'Fools', a break between the high complexity of Zamani's emancipatory struggle and ahistorical mystifications such as 'the people of the north will come down' and 'I was there, and would be there until the end of time' (Zamani's 'I' suddenly includes an unchanging, all-encompassing notion of 'Africa'). Yes, I do hear the powerful anti-apartheid slogan *'Mayibuye Afrika!'* – 'Come back, Africa!' – in all this, and it comprises no more than a fleeting moment in Ndebele's narrative, but even so, the text is restrained at this point by the same shortcoming that has haunted Marxism: an inability mainly due to the strictly negative understanding of 'ideology' to convincingly envision an 'emancipated' subject. In the words of Paul Smith, 'the actual qualities of the post-revolutionary "individual" are adumbrated in terms which are disturbingly reminiscent of those older, humanist formulations in which the potentialities of "man" are mystified' (1988: 9). Substitute 'post-colonial' for 'post-revolutionary' and you will have described something of what happens in this particular passage in 'Fools'.

As opposed to this, I would suggest that Zamani's act of resistance and subsequent victory are profoundly 'ideological': it is only through the intense, 'bodily' experience of ideology, of colonial discourse, and the incommensurability between the various subject-positions demanded by ideology (on the one hand, one of the elite, a teacher, a leader of the community; on the other an invisible, subaltern 'black') that a crisis is eventually provoked and the 'new' Zamani made possible. This may have everything to do with the re-evaluation of orally based subaltern knowledge and reconstruction of African history (the boy in the class reading the poem about the Zulu king) which reinserts the agency of the subaltern in the historical narrative and makes the demands of colonial ideology all the more impossible to meet, but such a reconstruction seems best understood in terms of catachresis and is therefore hardly devoid of historically compromised elements.

PART 3

Trust Her?

Ambivalent Singularity in
Nadine Gordimer's
A Sport of Nature

Hybridity is heresy.
Homi Bhabha (The Location of Culture, *1994: 225*)

CHAPTER 9

Differing Interpretations of
A Sport of Nature

W HAT ARE WE to make of Nadine Gordimer's *A Sport of Nature*? The puzzlement expressed in this question has become a trope in its own right informing most critical readings of her ninth novel – readings which generally each claim to transcend that very puzzlement and resolve the complex equation of the 'white' protagonist Hillela (Johnson, 1987: 8–9 and cited instances below). Even so, I too will approach *A Sport of Nature* in a suspended state of perplexity, in order perhaps not to 'resolve' the novel's ambiguities as much as to explore how they are produced and what they imply from a post-colonial, meta-subjective point of view.

Roughly three different tendencies can be discerned in the attempts to understand and evaluate *A Sport of Nature*. Firstly, in the case of Jennifer Krauss (1987: 33–36) and Brenda Cooper (1990: 68–93), it is seen as a flawed, sensationalist, even cynical novel, one in which Gordimer's affiliation with the anti-apartheid struggle blocks out her sensitivity to aesthetic detail and political dimensions (feminism in particular) that lie beyond the single, spectacular cause of radical politics in South Africa in the 1980s. In a liberal version of this critique, Lionel Abrahams has complained that Hillela has 'no human unity, no heart [that] we can participate in'. Gordimer has betrayed her novelistic talent for the sake of revolutionary correctness, resulting in her 'poorest novel' (Abrahams, 1989: 28–29). In stark contrast to Abrahams's longing for more realism ('human unity'), but with a similarly negative assessment of the novel, Margaret Lenta has claimed that Gordimer's unwillingness to exceed the formal demands of realism makes Hillela incapable of bearing the allegorical weight laid upon her (1988: 133–145). This line of argument has been fleshed out by Michael Green who, in reference to Fredric Jameson, blames the all too 'overtly realised conception of the future' for the novel's failure to convince as a utopian text (1997: 263).

Secondly, a minority voice which we might identify with Susan Winnett (1993: 140–154) and Linda Weinhouse (1990: 91–100) suggests that the very irony and elusiveness of Hillela's position is the most enduring if not unproblematic quality of the novel. Weinhouse, employing a Lacanian frame of reference, sees Hillela as an empty signifier consistently displaced by the 'repetition automatism' inherent in what is taken to be political change. Thus, the novel can be said to question the very viability of the resistance and revolution that it ostensibly endorses. Winnett compares *A Sport of Nature* with *Burger's Daughter* and argues in favour of Hillela's capability to 'outgrow metaphors' and continually 'move on' rather than get stuck in the infinite regress of self-reflexivity. In Winnett's reading, the 'emptiness' of Hillela is definitely part of an emancipatory narrative 'in the service both of a new non-bourgeois subject and a yet unrealized form of the novel that will chronicle it' (1993: 153). The empty space anticipates that which will fill it.

Thirdly, there are redemptive readings by Rose Pettersson (1995: 108–132), Stephen Clingman (1993: 173–190) and Dominic Head (1994: 136–150) which insert *A Sport of Nature* squarely in the assemblage of Nadine Gordimer's *oeuvre*. The former two stress the continuity of Gordimer's writing and of those influences conventionally understood to be working upon the text. Clingman, in particular, makes a strong argument for how *A Sport of Nature* elaborates and recapitulates elements found throughout her work – both the fiction and the non-fiction – as well as her biography. Taking this a step further, Dominic Head claims that *A Sport of Nature* is a metafictional novel that comments on all of Gordimer's earlier novels: 'it is a book *about* her previous books' (1994: 136). Apart from these three, the more sceptical Kathrin Wagner also places the novel in the assumed continuum of Gordimer's literary efforts, noting her consistent use of stereotypes (political, racial) but also those moments when *A Sport of Nature* breaks free from the imperatives of the earlier writing (a prime example being when Hillela's daughter Nomzamo is allowed entry into the apolitical world of *haute couture*) (1994: 107, 136, 140–149, 151–154, 164–165).

Singularity
My own discussion – in full awareness of the objections raised by Cooper, Green et al. – will tend to the second alternative, emphasising the adventurous, incommensurable aspects of a novel whose generic status and narrative voice is just as elusive and resistant to appropriation (by politics, by academic discourse) as its protagonist Hillela is made out to be. Rather than Lacanian analysis, however, I shall take my cue from the post-colonial version of deconstruction elaborated by Gayatri Spivak. That is, I draw tangentially on some remarks – in yet another formulation of the post-colonial irony that we confronted in Ndebele's negotiation of differing modes of knowledge – on the barely classifiable position of the Bengali writer/politician Mahasweta Devi.

Spivak argues that Devi, as a *writer*, must persistently critique her own *political* engagement. Her commitment to the subaltern requires that she, in effect, deconstructs the very grounds on which she can claim to act in their favour. She cannot not [*sic*] be involved in the political struggle to 'implement the sanctions for the tribals and outcasts' written into the Indian Constitution, but this struggle is defined by the same imperial narrative that historically has excluded the narratives of those 'tribals and outcasts' (Spivak, 1993: 47). As Spivak points out, the

> political claims that are most urgent in decolonized space are tacitly recognized as coded within the legacy of imperialism: nationhood, constitutionality, citizenship, democracy, socialism, even culturalism [. . . These concepts] are thus being reclaimed, indeed claimed, as concept-metaphors for which no *historically* adequate referent may be advanced from postcolonial space. That does not make the claims less urgent. For the people who are making the claims, the history of the Enlightenment episteme is 'cited' even on an individual level, as the script is cited for an actor's interpretation (1993: 48).

It would be a misreading to take this as a claim for transparent agency on behalf of *European* subjects while refusing such agency to post-colonials in respect of the same set of political concepts. Constitutive of Spivak's thinking is the view that we all are 'scripted' by the epistemes imposed on us through history. The specificity of post-colonial subjectivity emerges rather in its peculiar split between value-systems. A crucial aspect of this 'epistemically fractured' condition, wherein the 'so-called private individual and the public citizen in a decolonized nation can inhabit widely different epistemes, violently at odds with each other yet yoked together by the everyday ruses of *pouvoir-savoir*' has already been demonstrated to us by Njabulo Ndebele (Spivak, 1993: 48). In Ndebele's case, however, *pouvoir-savoir* – the naturalising everyday capacity for enablement (if not empowerment) which negotiates the known and the possible, or the ordinary, as he would say – is proffered as an enabling instance, as that productive ambivalence which allows for opposing forms of understanding to co-exist and intermingle. Spivak's position, which I provisionally make mine, is rather more sceptical. It is of greater value to her that a sense of crisis between and within epistemes be upheld – as was attempted in the previous part's focus on the body in *Fools*. The strategy both to sustain crisis and gesture towards the non-imperial epistemes may be called *singularity*. In this way, Devi's narratives resist their inevitable appropriation by regulative discourses such as 'feminism' or 'theory of marginality'. Her characters are 'singular, paralogical figures for women (sometimes wild men, mad men) who spell out no model for imitation' but who rather mark out the limits of a political and/or academic discourse.

If we transpose this argument to South Africa and *A Sport of Nature*, we may first note that Nadine Gordimer's position is analogous yet different to Mahasweta Devi's. Both are politically active authors from the elite writing not on behalf of but with an acute awareness of the subaltern in their respective national contexts. Futhermore, Gordimer has often pleaded for her fiction to be read separately from her political interventions. She regards the act of writing fiction as potentially adverse to the demands of political necessity, not unlike the opposition Spivak constructs between these two spheres of Devi's activity (Gordimer,

1988: 104–110). The main difference between these writers' positions is that the reversal of imperial values which has been a constitutional reality in India since 1948 was deferred in South Africa until 1994, seven years after the publication of *A Sport of Nature*. But the point in appropriating Spivak's reading of Devi exceeds such a generalised comparison. Rather, I claim that Gordimer's writing of Hillela's subjectivity is an inverted instance of that very strategy of singularity which emerges from Devi's narratives. Hillela is an eminently paralogical character, defying assumptions of the 'proper' or 'correct' way to go about resisting oppression.

However, the issue at hand in *A Sport of Nature* is not so much the representation of the subaltern as a subversion of the 'white' elite position, transforming it so as to turn it against itself while at the same time this 'self' – implying the historical, racial and territorial assumptions, the techniques of knowledge and modes of gendering that construct it – is effectively dissolved, no longer 'there' to turn against. Thus the novel ventures to open the space of the colonial other for the 'white' elite, the very operation which Gordimer's more disenchanted novels such as *The Late Bourgeois World* (1966), *The Conservationist* (1974) and *July's People* (1981) deemed impossible.[1]

In order for singularity – Hillela's singularity – to function so paradoxically, the novel can be seen to employ a whole range of rhetorical and formal devices. These can be divided into three categories: the splitting and displacement of the sign 'Hillela'; the naturalisation of power and sexuality; and the tracing of the other ('Africa' and Hillela) onto the Same (the 'parent stock'/the West). In this instance *bricolage* and allegory are grafted onto realism, the world-map of 'struggle' onto the world-map of capitalism, factuality onto error, etc.

The strategy of singularity is thereby displaced onto manifold implicit strategies which work (and perhaps fail) differently towards enabling the political agency of Hillela. As this part unfolds, I shall assess the problematic generated by these strategies. I approach *A Sport of Nature* from three different angles which correspond to the categories just mentioned and which amount to a relay of readings which move from a more formal to a more historicising approach.

Firstly, I attempt a semiotic reading of Hillela (and Chiemeka) as linguistic sign and novelistic device; secondly, I consider the widely discussed utopian anchoring of the elusive Hillela in her body; and thirdly, I give the outlines of a reading against the grain which looks beyond the body and redeems the ethico-political project of the text in terms of a postmodern/post-colonial understanding of globality.

CHAPTER 10

Hillela as Sign

T HE STORY IN *A Sport of Nature* is of a girl first brought up in
Rhodesia and later in South Africa. She is known as Kim, but
takes on the name of Hillela. Regarded as something of a problem-
child, Hillela passes from the custody of her father in Rhodesia to
her aunts Olga and Pauline in Johannesburg, and eventually moves
out on her own at the age of seventeen. Her mother left her at the
age of two for a lover in Lourenço Marques. Each move is
precipitated by her transgression of some local taboo of a racial
and/or sexual nature. When she is in the care of the morally high-
minded Pauline, her breach of trust has nothing to do with
'race' – indeed cannot, since Pauline is a fervent non-racialist – but
with (what is taken to be) incest: she is found sleeping with her
cousin Sasha, Pauline's son.

Hillela is apparently not propelled by any political conviction or
moral fervour, but is described as intelligent beyond her years. She
drifts through young adulthood, takes on odd jobs and lands up in
Tanzania after fleeing from South Africa with her lover, a foreign
jounalist gathering subversive material on repression and apartheid.
In Tanzania she enters the local circle of South African exiles and
political refugees – mistrusted at first, but gradually accepted as
one of them – and starts working as a governess at the Belgian
ambassador's residence. She becomes the ambassador's mistress and
follows the family on their subsequent postings in West Africa. This
is how she meets Whaila Kgomani, an ANC-operative whom she
marries and with whom she has a daughter. When Whaila is
assassinated in front of her by South African agents, Hillela's own
political career begins, taking her to Eastern Europe, the United
States, and ultimately back to Africa as the Central African leader
Reuel's mistress and then wife. Along the way, a decision is made to

let her daughter attend boarding school in England. In a projection of the future, the closing chapter adumbrates elliptically the downfall of apartheid. Hillela, as would be expected, is in South Africa as a guest of honour (being the wife of OAU-president Reuel) on the day that the new order is pronounced.

As Linda Weinhouse has observed, Hillela's story is one of constant displacement (1990: 96). More than that, she is always on the outside of those contexts from which she is soon removed anyway. This separateness is contrasted, however, by that one place in which she is assumed to be absolutely present – her body. In a manner reminiscent of the Freudian radicalism of Wilhelm Reich, Hillela is uninhibited by the sexual mores and familial constraints of the society which fosters her.[1] This sets her apart. She 'knows' through her body in a manner conceivable but unattainable to her cousin Sasha, and utterly inconceivable to her aunts Olga and Pauline. Sexuality is her 'cache of trust' (1987: 283), her bodily presence an awe-inspiring force.[2] Consequently, critics tend to privilege the body as the touchstone of *A Sport of Nature*. It is here, it has been argued, that the displacements, sensual rapture and political passions of the novel are firmly secured. In the words of Stephen Clingman, 'Hillela is neither an overdetermined cypher of revolutionary wish-fulfilment nor an indeterminate signifier of pure absence; instead there are deeper issues at work through her constitution as a character, and she has a specific kind of presence which is far from insignificant: a *bodily* presence' (1993: 178).

I agree that the *projection* of bodily presence is of paramount importance in *A Sport of Nature*, but it seems to me here that Clingman et al., in their foregrounding of the socio-historical significance of the novel, elide Hillela's linguistic constitution. My point is obvious: Hillela can have no other body than that inscribed by the narrative process and subsequently imagined by the readers. Only by first asserting the textuality of Hillela (rather than taking her realistic status for granted) can we properly assess the novel's valorisation of instinct and body. My argument bears some affinity to Linda Weinhouse's in that I privilege Hillela as unstable signifier. However, I claim even this instability of the signifier to be indeterminate rather than definite. It is as though the text has generic difficulties to cope with ambivalence.

Naming

In the beginning, narrative names. Better yet, it gives what the slang of the digital age calls a 'handle', that which a reader can hold on to when exploring a story. The name collaborates with an expectation of consistency; a first rule in the game of narration is that a name at the start of a novel bears the same reference at the end. In other words, convention demands that the signifier and the signified stick together. This conventional integrity is so strong that the reader redeems multiple names (or, conversely, the non-name of a pronoun) whenever possible under the guise of an single, unique signified, regardless of whether it is assumed to be a person or (as in allegory) an abstract quality or function.

For Roland Barthes, the most salient quality of the name in writing is its resistance to wear. Unlike a common noun, which emits only one of its meanings in a syntagmatic burst, the proper noun is semantically dense. There is a potentially unending range of linguistically constructed signifieds that may be associated with it (Barthes, 1994: 1 370–1 372). Or rather, its very emptiness, its greater or lesser lack of foregone meaning, craves for it to be endlessly filled with meaning – an endeavour that can only fall short of achievement, since nothing prescribes when a name is 'full'. There is greater agreement on what a 'chair' may be then what a 'Hillela' is. Hence the *suppleness* of the name's perceived unity is predicated on its emptiness, and its insatiable thirst for realisation in language.

One way to describe the cleavage between realism and (post)modernism would be to point out how (post)modernist writers highlight rather than conceal the name. For Joyce, for Rushdie, for Coetzee, the name is an object to be foregrounded. Serious or playful, such writing freely admits the arbitrary nature of naming and therefore makes the most of it. Within realism, however, the name tends to be mystified. Its aim is not merely to fill a position in a language-game, but to suggest a feasible real-world referent. The reader is meant to believe in the name in the way that he or she believes in a person confronted face to face. If the name in realism has a symbolic meaning (as it often does) the symbolism adheres to notions of depth and concealed knowledge. It wants nothing to do with arbitrary signification; instead, it overdetermines the name, giving it the sheen of the inevitable.

Nadine Gordimer's later fiction, ambivalently poised between the ethical imperatives of critical realism and the *jouissance* of the free play of the signifier – between the demands of history and the potential freedom of writing – often employs names self-reflexively, but attempts to do so within an earnestly realistic framework. In a closely argued essay, Karen Ramsay Johnson suggests that it is precisely in her naming-strategy that Gordimer's radicalism reaches its fullest realisation (1995: 117–137). By weighing the anchor of the name, Gordimer lets adrift the essentialist ideology that pervades apartheid, and which still remains highly functional in contemporary South Africa (post-1994). This essentialist ideology could be dubbed pre-Saussurean: the meaning of a name is not an effect of difference; rather, it designates what individuals and groups *are* and always *will be*. Name is fate, Johnson contends, and Gordimer's characters – like Baasie/Zwelinzima in *Burger's Daughter* – challenge this fate. Although I find her assessment of apartheid (and, consequently, of Gordimer's resistance to it) to be simplistic, Johnson's textual observations are highly productive.[3]

At one point she observes that Gordimer's naming-strategy is nowhere so extensively deployed as in *A Sport of Nature*. But this is also – as a supplement to Johnson's analysis – where we might locate certain constraints to Gordimer's negotiation between realism and *écriture*. With the name 'Hillela' as its focal point, the novel repeatedly transgresses the limits of realistic conventions, but, wary of where to go from there, undercuts its own passage into a fully self-reflexive mode of narration. We are left not with a sense of a densely realised 'Hillela', nor of an untrammelled signifier, but of a curiously dissipated, even chronically postponed presence. I am suggesting, in other words, that there is a *formal* ambiguity in the naming and representation of Hillela that disrupts the overt *theme* of ambiguity inscribed in the character.

To understand the intratextual dynamics at work here, we must briefly reconsider the brand of realism normally associated with Nadine Gordimer. As stated in Part 1, her mode of realistic characterisation may be labelled 'typical' (Clingman, 1986: 9–10) or even 'stereotypical' (Wagner, 1994: 45–46). According to Clingman, types are 'highly individualized characters who engage in their fullest potential with the social and historical circumstances of their situation' (1986: 9), which fits in with Coetzee's definition of a 'supplementary' novel 'embodying contending forces in contending characters' (1988a: 3). We should add that if a type functions as an exploration and condensation of the said circumstances, then the humanist notion of individuality that the definition adheres to is heavily qualified. The type may be an individual, but he or she is not an autonomous individual. An illustrative case is the highly typical protagonist Mehring in Gordimer's *The Conservationist* who professes the ideology of individualism but is submerged under the historical conditions that he actively assists in creating.

This has immediate consequences for the significance of naming. If a name is understood to adhere to a type, then its arbitrary quality is contained. It is assumed that such a name not only exists in the space of the text, but refers in condensed form to a common social reality. As for Hillela, however, her non-typical quality is pronounced from the very beginning. The epigraph's *Oxford English Dictionary* definition of 'a sport of nature' even reads as a direct response to Clingman (whose monograph appeared a year before the novel) and above all to Lukács's theory of realism which Gordimer started to engage with as early as 1968 (Coetzee, 1988a: 10): '*A plant, animal, etc., which exhibits abnormal variation or a departure from the parent stock or type.*' At a later occasion we read that 'Hillela *could* have been like anybody else' (1987: 57, emphasis added) yet she is not. Hence the strategy of singularity: the sport of nature Hillela must *not* be a type, which affects in due measure our reading of the name, or names, rather.

As the book opens, we are told that 'the girl shed one name and emerged under the other [. . . S]he threw Kim up to the rack with her school panama and took on Hillela' (1987: 3) The name is, it would seem, released from its burden of suggesting reference and is played around with in a, by Gordimer's standards, rather frivolous manner. One signifier – which echoes that arch-imperial novel, Rudyard Kipling's *Kim* – leads on to another and eventually to a third, when 'Chiemeka' replaces 'Hillela', and we might even add a fourth name – 'Mrs Whaila Kgomani' – to this lot (Johnson, 1995: 129). But this impression is challenged even before the paragraph has come to an end:

[. . .] she was the only Hillela among Susans and Clares and Fionas. What sort of a name was that? Didn't know, couldn't tell them. What she did tell them, without a moment's hesitation, was that anyway she was always called by her second name, Kim. As the years passed, not even her teachers called her anything but Kim. No-one remarked when she went with the other Kims, Susans, Clares and Fionas to the Anglican Church on Sundays, although in her school record 'religious faith' was filled in as Jewish (1987: 3).

Here we have the first ambiguous moment in the novel's utterance of Hillela. If it began by demonstrating how the sign 'Hillela' begets itself through difference, it is now placed in a context of names and religions which serve to normalise not only 'Kim' but also 'Hillela' according to the demands of verisimilitude. In effect, the name 'Hillela' is typecast. This gives an odd twist to its status. The name may be different, but then again, it is Jewish – a classification which is ultimately subsumed in Gordimer's writing under the category of 'whiteness', as Michael Wade has shown (1993: 170–171). On all counts, it seems that the text releases 'Hillela' from its arbitrariness. The reader can *safely* assume that the protagonist's choice of name simply repeats the name that she 'actually' has carried throughout her life, as opposed to *taking the risk* of holding on to a name that has descended from nowhere. Upon re-examination, however, the remark that the girl 'Didn't know, couldn't tell them' what sort of a name it is, serves to separate the signified from its signifier. If at first it appears as though the character brashly cuts ties with her social context by effecting difference – pitting 'Hillela' against the world – now the girl effects a rupture between herself and the name Hillela which renders her unnameable, ushering 'her' (whoever she is) into silence.

Towards the end of the book, naming is foregrounded in a secular, African version of christening:

It was then that the General gave her her African name. She had forgotten the promise, taken as one of the kind offered her meaninglessly so often in the playfulness of sexual advances. —You'll be there on the register: Chiemeka Hillela.— Now she remembered. —What does it mean?— He took a smiling breath that expanded the muscles of his neck as well as his big chest. —It's not a name in my language, it comes from another country, but it means the same as my real name does. 'God has done very well'.—

[. . .]

—Why in another language? Because I'm a stranger?—

—Now, now. Wait a minute. It's an Igbo name, from Nigeria. I had a good friend there, I stayed with him and his mother, she treated me like her son. It's in her honour I call you. She fed me, she clothed me the first time I was in exile, as a youngster. And her name was the same as mine, a female version; a name that was fated . . . —

The name that was ready for her has been hers for official purposes ever since, but between the couple she remained Hillela, as he remained for her Reuel, his colonial baptismal name at the Catholic font. So that 'Hillela' has become the name of intimacy, withdrawn from the currency of general use and thereby confusing her identity and whereabouts, for others, further than these already had been (1987: 303–304).

Note how the withdrawal of 'Hillela' is said to confuse 'her identity and whereabouts'. Stated in positive terms, this indicates that 'Hillela' has become the site of relative stability for certain 'others'. In terms of the narrative – indeed, of the very next sentence – these 'others' are the likes of Olga and Pauline, all those who once knew the pre-political Hillela and from whom Hillela has freed herself. However, in terms of the act of narration, these 'others' should refer to readers. Readers are the others of the text: they are its non-present condition of possibility. On such an understanding, the passage concedes the indeterminate status of 'Hillela'. Already steeped in ambivalence, the transformation into 'Chiemeka' makes 'her' retreat further still from the readers. 'Chiemeka' marks a point of separation: the name is semantically thin rather than dense and is used on one occasion only in the remaining 35 pages of the novel. 'Hillela' occurs marginally more, while there is an abundance of other names such as Olga, Sasha, Pauline, Kgomani, Slovo, Tutu, Mbeki, etc. in the closing chapters. It is as though context – both familial and historical – prevails while the singular protagonist withdraws increasingly from the story. In this way, 'Hillela/ Chiemeka' evades closure; 'Chiemeka' gestures towards the limit-text, it is a name that is not properly elaborated within the narrative (as is 'Hillela') but indicates a continuation beyond its ending. Or, put differently, 'Chiemeka' marks the point where blankness is effected, where the protagonist departs from the conditions of possibility of literary representation and fuses with the unrepresentable ultimate horizon of history.

True to form, even the brief glossing of 'Chiemeka' in the passage above resists closure. By implication it is the protagonist's 'real' name, a feminine echo of the General's 'real' name. With the claim that it was 'a name that was fated' the notion of teleology is introduced, making it appear even more real. Interestingly, its authenticity is played out against the bourgeois/liberal understanding of the authentic as belonging to the intimate sphere. 'Official purposes' are thus posited as the proper site of authenticity. This is consistent with the challenge the narrative poses to liberal subjectivity, but what complicates this reading is that the implied meaning or authenticity of the name itself is an intimate and quasi-familial childhood memory of Reuel's. It pre-dates both his and Hillela/Chiemeka's era of 'official purposes'. In other words, 'Chiemeka' is displaced in a manner not unlike 'Nomzamo', the politically charged name that the protagonist gives her daughter. In the novel, 'Nomzamo' becomes 'Nomo' and is shot straight off from the political field into the heavily ideological but apolitical world of *haute couture*. In a similar way, the *intimate* authenticity of 'Chiemeka' (the myth of its origins) is contradicted when reserved for exclusive use in the public sphere. However, this is not presented ironically in the same way as 'Nomzamo's' transformation. The public status of 'Chiemeka' is offered with a straight face, despite its intimate origins. One could perhaps suggest that the name dissolves the private/public dyad, but this is not allowed for by the text, which in fact upholds precisely such an opposition by distinguishing between 'Hillela' and 'Chiemeka'. The text works at cross purposes.

These two moments of naming are not unlike holographic fragments, containing patterns found throughout the entire novel. First and foremost, the oscillation between risk and safety, between textual daring and realistic confirmation, is a defining feature of *A Sport of Nature*. In this play between textual modes, the position of the sign 'Hillela' (and even more so of 'Chiemeka') is seldom stable and often runs counter to the current mode. The text is caught in a double bind between uttering Hillela's singularity and representing it; between the performative and the pedagogical, to use one of Homi Bhabha's conceptual binaries (1994: 145). At the performative moment of utterance (which opens a space in language for her singularity) the pedagogy of representation contradicts it; and as language attempts to represent her singularity, then utterance, naming, is withheld. In the case of 'Chiemeka', authenticity is offered and called upon in the act of naming, only to reveal authenticity as split and disjunctive; and once uttered, 'Chiemeka' simply retreats into silence.

Narrative perspective on the margins
The formal instability of the text is clearly observable at the level of narrative perspective. I shall first demonstrate how this instability operates on the margins of the narrative, namely in the italicised passages that sporadically break the flow of narration. In *A Sport of Nature* there are ten of them – not counting the italicised excerpts from letters (Ruth's, Hillela's, Sasha's) – ranging in length from a few lines to two full pages. Brian Macaskill values this stylistic device as a sower of confusion and dialogic tension, and points to its indeterminate status in *A Sport of Nature*: 'To whom should we attribute the italicized utterance that sometimes constitutes a chapter or an interchapter all of its own? Sometimes these interchapters embody Hillela's point of view; more frequently, however, they do not' (Macaskill, 1993: 68–69). We can only say for certain that their place apart from the greater portion of the text endows these passages with an intensity to match their meditative mood. We may read them as the associative, free flow of images common to the brief moment between sleep and waking. They are reflexive and at odds with the very *progression* of a narrative which otherwise has formal properties in common with such directional

genres as the picaresque and the *Bildungsroman*. They turn the gaze of the narrative upon the narrative itself or, more appropriately, they self-consciously echo elements that have previously been introduced in the narrative and, in so doing, distort or transform these elements.

In the first of these italicised interstices, the indeterminacy of perspective (and of Hillela) is striking:

> *Hillela no longer falls asleep at the hairdresser's.*
>
> *A jaw with a well-turned angle on either side, a slightly prognathous mouth and the full lips that cover with a tender twitch the uneven front tooth; it has defied an orthodontist who made conform perfectly the smiles of Clive and Mark. The cheekbones lift against the eyes at the outer corner, underlining them, aslant. All right so far. But it's difficult to meet the eyes. They are darkness; there is a film to it like the film of colours that swims on a puddle of dark oil she has seen spilled on the earth at a garage. They react under their own regard as pupils do under an oculist's light; but doubly: the change observed is also experienced as a change of focus. Nothing can be more exact than an image perceived by itself.*
>
> *The face is small and thin for the depth from the cup at the base of the collar-bones to the wide set breasts. In the trance of women gazing at themselves in the mirrors they face, she is seeing herself. The mirror ends her there* (1987: 7).

Hillela as a displaced mirror-image. Bodily features are easily registered whereas the eyes, conventionally 'mirrors of the soul', resist reflecting anything, let alone the soul of Hillela. The only hint at internality is the curious mention of the change of focus which transfers the narcissistic economy of the gaze and the mirror-image to a sub-psychological level: it is not so much Hillela seeing herself as her eyes that perceive themselves seeing.

The moment of the eyes is pivotal. The combination of an external description of their appearance and a registering of their act of focusing positions Hillela in a liminal space which challenges the very notions of inside and outside, subject and object. Hillela is indeed a *lusus naturae* (sport of nature) seen only by itself, unlike the parent stock and therefore unknowable to the parent – which at a literal level should be understood as the narrative voice. Her eyes are opaque, elusive, not merely a barrier separating inside from outside, but a third space in their own right, not susceptible to control by the knowing gaze, including her own, reminiscent of Merleau-Ponty's theorising of the body as that which unsettles the subject-object divide (1945: 81–86).

More than that, the emphasis on the focusing of the gaze disrupts the status of the narrative voice. Who is observing Hillela here? The third-person narrator/parent? Or should we read it as Hillela's voice, as yet another example of how Hillela begets herself, objectifying in the present tense the moment of perception which she herself is experiencing? The latter reading would place her at an immense remove from herself – in keeping with the promise to make her singular – but would also, paradoxically, serve to wedge her more firmly in a received realistic context. It is, after all, more 'reasonable' that she herself, rather than an external narrator taking pains not to 'enter' the mind of the character, should register a change of focus from within. The former reading, by contrast, would normalise the characterisation of Hillela – deprive her of some of her otherness – but would have greater difficulty in accounting for the observation on the eyes.

Thus the sign 'Hillela' oscillates and splits between the formal possibilities of textual free play and realistic verisimilitude. The italicised sections that follow on the first one often resemble streams of consciousness. We might assume (a bit more often than Brian Macaskill allows) that the consciousness represented is Hillela's. This is the closest we get to a conventional understanding of internal subjectivity in the novel – but to complicate things, not only is the signifier 'Hillela' left out of these passages, but so is the first person singular. The subjective signifier is displaced at the same instant that its signified appears, and this in a most ironic fashion. A third of the way, we find the shortest of the italic insertions:

I, me.
Time, now. They had always, they went on fitting that self into their conjugations, leaving out the first person singular. Except one of the cousins, poor boy; he didn't.

> *It's not possible to move about in the house of their lives.*
> *A china cat survived two centuries and was broken. Awful*
> (1987: 124).

The elliptical syntax is closer to poetry than prose; there is nothing that makes us necessarily read this as Hillela's thoughts, but the implication is that Hillela is not like 'them' (her aunts and their families) which she at this point has left behind in South Africa. 'They' lack something, a self-presence achieved by using the first person singular, by joining the 'I' with the 'now'. It is represented as a formal linguistic lack but is really about putting the self at risk, literally to put it in motion, join it with the flux of the historical present. Hence the irony of the final exclamation: the bone of contention is not the breaking of the cat, but the fact that it had survived in suspended animation for two centuries.

However, if we read this statement programmatically, in the sense that the 'first person singular' will no longer be left out from the subsequent italicised margins of the text, we are mistaken. Quite to the contrary, the *omission* of the first person singular persists precisely at moments where we are closest to the intimate, emotional life of Hillela. After Whaila's death, when she is in Eastern Europe experiencing the 'burial' of winter (his death is her death), emotions are particularly severe:

> *Happiness dancing in a shop window behind glass, while*
> *outside there are hungry crowds in the street, looking on. Not for*
> *long. The glass explodes; their arms reach up to drag, to claim.*
> *The only love that counts is owed to them. Waves of resentment*
> *towards him, for not firing first, for not saving himself for the*
> *rainbow family, the only love made flesh, man gloved inside*
> *woman, child emerging to suck the breast the man caressed: the*
> *perfect circle, cycle. But he never belonged to it, the beloved—*
> *the bastard!—he belonged to the crowd outside and he died for*
> *them. The other wife, whom he left behind in Krugersdorp*
> *location, would not be lying in bed alone reproaching him.*
> *She was one of the crowd, she knew what belonged to them*
> (1987: 232).

What contradicts these emotions is the refusal to put the 'I' at risk, to place it firmly in relation to that which is being expressed. *'Happiness dancing in a shop window'* or *'Waves of resentment'* objectify feelings that only by implication reside in Hillela. There is an attempt here to escape the taint of language, its definiteness, by ushering the 'I' into silence, even though this weakens the tension between the 'luxury' of individual ('white') emotion and the harsh demands of collective sacrifice that motivate the paragraph. The 'white', naïve, sentimental 'I' retreats prematurely from those emotions that it locates in itself and denounces.

On those few occasions that the 'I' (or 'me', as the case may be) does appear in italics, it immediately readjusts to third person-narrative once the moment of intimacy is over. When Hillela is in bed with Arnold, one of the exiled leaders in Tanzania, there is a meditation on her credibility, on what she might amount to in her association with *bona fide* freedom fighters. Throughout the passage there is a studied disregard for coherence; direct speech merges with free indirect speech, the perspective is spectral, without any strict boundaries separating the narrator from Arnold, and these two from Hillela. On two occasions the third person singular abruptly switches to first person singular, and then back again. The first instance might feasibly be read as direct speech, the second cannot be. Both are connected to meditations on where Hillela 'belongs'. Firstly:

> *What credibility has she to show for herself, now, but the protection of yet another man?*
>
> *Without a cause is without a home; lying here. I've learned that. Without a cause is without a reason to be. That's all decreed by others, as elsewhere everything was decreed by the absence of one sister, the decisions made by two more, and the long-distance authority of a putative father on the road* (1987: 162).

This seems relatively straightforward. The 'I' stands separate from the cause/home. It is at large, home to itself but outside of every home, and stands apart even from its current context. The second instance is, however, harder to account for:

> *This one won't accept to be a humble apprentice to the only objective worth living for. Who does she think she is? Unreliable: and this judgment tantalizes him to come back into the flesh again, to find that just consolation, that peace and freedom that is certain, and lasts only minutes.*
>
> *The glisten of black eyes opening again.*
>
> *[. . .] But he is nibbling, kissing, feeding on me, his face wet with me, exasperated. Because if she isn't the right material, she isn't one of that kind either* (1987: 163).

In the last example, the first person singular is used in a purely descriptive sentence, coding sexual intimacy as textual intimacy. The effect is startling – it implies that Hillela is nowhere as subjectively present as at a moment of sexual proximity – and can be read either as evidence of a reductive, patriarchal gendering of Hillela or (perhaps less convincingly) as an assertion of Hillela's autonomous sexuality.[4] There is, however, also a third, ironic possibility which would tie in with the homelessness of the 'I' in the first quote. If, as Barthes writes, *jouissance* (in the sense of ecstasy, eroticism, excess) is unutterable, is that which effaces speech, then the text subverts and empties *jouissance* by allowing the 'inner' subject to utter itself at precisely that point when it cannot do so with any credibility – and this in a paragraph which thematises 'credibility'![5] The 'me' is not one of plenitude but of emptiness, of prattle, an excess of the excess, the one cancelling the other. It is a formally unreliable subject, as Arnold concludes in this very passage.

It should be clear by now that the italicised margins of the text repeatedly refuse to utter the subject, particularly in those moments when they represent it. The representation of 'Hillela' (the semantic layering of the name) is at odds with its signifier. We are left with an absent, nameless subject speaking out of nowhere, or being spoken to, adressed by a grammatically unstable narrative voice, a disembodied voice, or embodied at the moment that it most credibly would be blocked out.

Progressive narrative perspective
The bulk of the narrative contrasts strongly to its meditative,

italicised margins. Here, progression is the order of the day. Hillela moves inexorably forward and outward. But although her movements are at times barely believable, the narrative effects a bias towards the common-sense assumptions of realism by containing and displacing her singularity.

The most striking device used to negotiate plausibility and deferral is the biographical mode. Many critics have remarked on this, and Richard Peck even simply calls the narrator 'the biographer', but this precludes its inconsistency (1988: 75–93). The distanced tone of the biographer is, in fact, sparingly used and introduced mainly at the beginning or end of specific sections. Only on rare occasions does it inform an entire passage (for example, 1987: 169–171). Even so, its sporadic interventions are clearly meant to indicate provisionality. What constructs the 'biographer' is not what it knows but what it claims not to know. In a move diametrically opposed to the obfuscation of subject-positions in the italicised margins, it openly professes imperfect knowledge. Unsurprisingly, these gaps – which introduce the possibility of a disjunction between Hillela and the narrator – are at the centre of much critical attention. There is, however, no consensus on how to read this biographical rhetoric. Richard Peck stresses the 'biographer's' disapproval of Hillela. The incompleteness of knowledge serves merely to underscore the distance, or even the antagonism between the two, and leads in his view to a damaging ambivalence. With a different emphasis, Susan Winnett argues that the narrator is diffident and simply 'seems content to represent what it knows and claim ignorance of what it doesn't' (1993: 151). The biographer is complacent rather than antagonistic. Judie Newman, for her part, stresses *both* the 'fervour' and 'irony' of the narrative. In the biographical lacunae she detects the presence of myth: they mystify and heroicise Hillela, associating her (explicitly on page 100) with other 'greats' such as Christ and Shakespeare, thereby appropriating a male heroic paradigm on behalf of a heroine. On the narrative technique as such, Newman emphasises its externality, claiming that it 'registers the crisis of the Liberal view of the individual subject, with its accompanying assumptions of the organic coherence of the individual, transcending social conditions' (1988: 94–95). She, too, reads the story in general terms as a piecing together of 'the biography of a public figure' (1988: 94–95).

What does this tell us? 'The biographer's' structural function is generally described as 'mystification' and 'externality'. It does indeed place the authority of the text in doubt and foregrounds the limits to its knowledge of Hillela – 'It must have been in June 1963, exact date unknown, she left South Africa' (1987: 117), '[. . .] she is difficult to keep track of once the Ambassador's extended family moved' (1987: 169) – or the conditions of possibility of that knowledge:

> Everything is known about her movements. Americans are such industrious documenters: the proof of her presence among them, like that of their own existence, is ensured by reports of symposia and conferences, prospectuses of institutes and foundations, *curricula vitae*, group photographs, videos, tapes, transcripts of television interviews (1987: 237).

At other moments, the mode is conjecture:

> She does appear to have left the ambassadorial employ at some point before or not long after she began to be seen with the black South African revolutionary envoy; and she must have had to earn a living somehow (1987: 171).

> One version of her departure was that she had left in a fit of temperament because she had quarrelled with a Russian lover she expected to marry her. This seems gossip's inversion of the other, political theory, that the Africanists in the organization wanted to oust the influence of white communists, and, somehow, because she was white and was too close to the Russians living in the country that was hosting her, she had got swept up (1987: 235–236).

> It became evident afterwards that Hillela went on several missions for the General (1987: 282).

The attitude is that of a biographer who pragmatically assumes the continuous existence of the subject in question and fleshes her out only so much as judicious ('external') research will allow. In narratological terms, these moments confront us with an extradiegetic narrator (outside of diegesis, the 'telling') and a hypodiegetic, embedded narrative.[6] The preferred interpretation is, as we have seen, that Hillela eludes all but factual discourse. She is not possible to represent save for the observable, retrievable documentation of her 'life'. The 'real' Hillela is to be found elsewhere, perhaps in the gulf of silence separating the biographical from the italicised narrative.

If, however, we are more literal-minded, the biographical mode seems designed somewhat haphazardly to convince sceptics of realism. It suggests that Hillela ultimately dissolves into a confetti of hearsay, news reports, letters, recordings, snapshots, etc. There *is* no Hillela save for these material and verbal traces. Paradoxically, such a splintered view of subjectivity actually makes her more acceptable in a postmodern age which cannot accept the mystification of a 'real' Hillela that would somehow reside beyond the text (as flesh residing beyond the word). By making her purely discursive, by de-realising the sign, the text makes Hillela *more* realistic. Far from being singular, she is wholly appropriated by a discourse of factuality, as would any individual whose life was charted publicly.

But is this ruse of factuality credible? Does it, in fact, convince? Not entirely. The contradiction is that the narrative voice wants it both ways. Save for the interventions of the italicised passages, the voice itself will not splinter; save for the letters quoted *in extenso* (mainly Sasha's) it will not supply the reader directly with uncommented citations or images out of its presumed archive. Instead, the narrator jealously guards his or her privilege as the interpreter of the 'facts' and – more importantly – does not allow the biographical de-realisation of Hillela to have any effect on the exquisite but conventional narrative mode that dominates the story.[7] We can see this in the same chapter that reminds us at length how little is known for certain about Hillela's sojourn in West Africa.

The Ambassor saw her as he was passing the market; her profile with the light catching the cheekbone, her breasts swinging forward as she bent to test the ripeness of some fruit; her old poverty diet she had told him about in the sweet, light confidences of bed. He put a hand on his driver's shoulder, the car drew up in the swill of the gutter.— Get in.—She paid for her mangoes, first. She sat angled towards him, knees neatly together, presenting herself, smiling as if she had been at the Embassy only yesterday.

—Where are you living?—

They spoke behind the driver's ears open to them under his braided cap.

—There's a house where we all live.—

—So you're with him.—

—We're all together.—

—Tell me. Hillela? . . . Well if it hasn't happened yet, it will. You're like me. You'll try . . . It's quite a novelty, isn't it. I've had a few of his kind, myself. I always was attracted. And of course where I come from, it's no crime. No, to be fair, it's still (he made a familiar damping-down signal with his fine caresser's hand)—not done . . . —

She took the hand. Her own was sticky with the juice and dirt that had dried on the fruit in her lap, her cheeks were the colour and smoothness of the rose-brown mango skin, the black eyes were those that had opened under him many times, holding for his reassurance the depth of pleasure he could plumb (1987: 174).

Further down on the same page they part, and then – without any obvious rupture – we read of the marriage between Hillela and Whaila, the 'black' man that is alluded to above:

He gave her the mimed kiss, small sharp blows on either cheek, that marked both farewells and felicitations among people of his own kind.

Funerals and weddings are identical occasions when it comes to disguising in a generally-accepted façade of sorrow or celebration any previous state of relations between those taking part. *If there was what can be called a wedding party at all when the black man married her (and there is no doubt that they were legally married, whatever the status of her other alliances) it was given by the Ambassador and his wife at their Residence* (1987: 174, emphasis added).

What we see here is a shift, literally from one sentence to another, from carefully crafted deixis to the conjectural mode of the biographer which transforms Hillela into pure surface-text. Up until the mimesis of the ambassador's 'mimed kiss' the narrative flow is securely lodged in realistic representation-as-presentation. The textual attitude is condensed in the line 'She sat angled towards him, knees neatly together, presenting herself.' Hillela's own story is angled towards us readers in much the same way. Her poise indicates the terse prose which, through a controlled abundance of detail, hopes simply to *present* itself, be *real*. It is diegesis under erasure, so to speak, and clearly at odds with the extradiegetic biographical voice, since no biographer could legitimately assume such authority (down to the 'damping-down signal', the sticky hands, the elliptical, casual dialogue) except in ironic and explicit awareness of the formal transgression, *the move towards literariness*, involved in staging such an intimacy of the moment. Note how it contrasts with 'If there was what one can call a wedding party', etc., as well as with my previous examples of biographical discourse. Now it is the *feasible* story, rather than the story-as-such, that is presented. The biographer may, and indeed does, establish circumstances and determine the likelihood of specific versions, but must stop short of embellishments that are unaccounted for. The biographical voice – in order to be read as such – must always in some measure address its discursive context. It inserts a filter of provisionality between the reading of the story and the story-as-such. By saying that there is *no* doubt that Hillela and Whaila were 'legally married', the possibility of doubt is introduced. In other words, factuality opens a space for its other, for error, and thus for the indeterminacy of the sign Hillela, whereas the conventional realistic mode will not concede that error is possible.

What I want to stress is that 'the biographer' is less significant in the telling of Hillela's story than has been claimed by critics employing the external/internal opposition. It is easy to associate the 'external' portrayal of Hillela – its lack of conventional psychology – with 'the biographer'. If instead we focus on the relative rhetorical weighting of the literary and the factual, the former clearly dominates the latter and tends therefore to elide the discursivity of Hillela. But even so, I do not see this as a clean split. The two modes are presented as one (no italics or spacing to set them apart), and both employ the rhetoric of real-world reference and type in order to make their statements credible. The 'mimed kiss' of the ambassador is used 'among people of his kind', much as he himself in world-weary fashion claims to have 'had a few of his kind', that is, 'black' women. People are continuously placed, sorted into categories. Although a category can only dissolve into its specific instances, the mere mention of the category puts the stamp of the real on the characters. In the overtly biographical sections we see the same rhetoric in use. 'Funerals and weddings' are not only 'identical occasions' but are of a kind, in the same way as – in a previous quote – 'Americans' are of a kind, namely 'industrious documenters' (1987: 237).

This leaves us not with a unified nor with a purely splintered voice in the dominant strain of narrative. Rather, albeit differently from the italicised margins, the novel maintains a state of representational ambivalence over and through which the sign of Hillela hovers. At one moment, the text desires clarity and depth and wants to overcome the abyss between world and word by suspending the reader's disbelief and presenting fiction as truth. At the next moment, the glass of representation is clouded over and Hillela is transformed into a surface-text, an agglommeration of probabilities. And yet, throughout, there is a recurring attempt (which is more scandalous in moments of 'pure' fiction than in 'biography') to anchor Hillela's context through means of real-world reference.

CHAPTER 11

Hillela as Realistic Character

IN SO FAR as *A Sport of Nature* is a perplexing novel, the discussion in Chapter 10 shows that there is cause for confusion already at the semiotic level. There is a formal instability in the text that apparently functions at cross purposes. The question must be asked, however, if this ambivalence is productive in a hermeneutic reading, despite the problems that arise at the formal level. If, in a reading of Hillela as a 'character' (not a sign) that conveys meaning and challenges the determinations of colonial discourse, ambivalence enables rather than disables the strategy of singularity. In this chapter I therefore treat Hillela more or less as given, and direct my critical impetus towards what is said 'about' her. I shall pay specific attention to what is projected as the one point of stability in the text: Hillela's body, and the power that is taken to emanate from this body.

Trickster

When describing Hillela's ambivalence, Susan Winnett compares her with Rosa Burger in *Burger's Daughter*:

> If *Burger's Daughter* is about positioning and repositioning – making metaphors about the process of making metaphors, *A Sport of Nature* is about change as it becomes revolution-in-progress and its incompatibility with the metaphor-making that gives the white liberal subject the luxury of figuring out ever anew who she is and where she stands. Hillela, the novel's protagonist, is uncannily able to outgrow metaphors; she is, as the novel puts it, someone who can 'move on'. [. . .] She honors neither conventional taboos nor sentimental ties for their own sake. What she

carries with her of the past is that which speaks to the demands of the current situation (1993: 149).

Yes, Hillela moves on, moves out, moves beyond the spaces delimited by the *pouvoir-savoir* of her contingent contexts. She is constantly buffeted about by circumstance (material, political) but never fully determined – underdetermined rather than overdetermined – by the sum total of circumstance. This also means that she never fully *opposes* her present context: instead, her engagements are oblique, perhaps touching on her immediate situation but directed towards something else, generally that which she has just left behind her. Such a lack of direct resistance reads initially as a response to that pervasive contradiction of post-colonial resistance: its complicity with the forms and values established by Empire. Instead of resisting through catachresis, by appropriating and re-inscribing imperialistically coded values, Hillela would supposedly embody the possibility of a radically other, non-compromised form of resistance.

The character who most forcefully contrasts with Hillela is Pauline, who consistently opposes the racial state-system and tries to bring up Hillela in her own image. Pauline, as type, is the epitome of the engaged liberal (in Gordimer's novels) who tragically fails to discard the very assumption of cultural authority which brings the force of assertion and organisational skill to her commitment.[1] Her exasperated patronising of the 'black' youth Jethro is the prime example (1987: 57). She is, through and through, intensely engaged with the immediate. When she and her husband Joe burst in on Hillela and Sasha and discover their quasi-incestuous relationship, it is upon rushing home from a holiday 'because of a crisis they knew how to deal with, in an anxiety not unexpected in the context of their lives', namely the arrest of Joe's colleague (1987: 90). Hillela strikes them from an angle they hadn't even imagined would need guarding; she operates in a different register than Pauline. Had she functioned in the same register, there would have been opposition or adherence. Instead, she moves laterally across spaces which her aunt keeps strictly separate. Hedonism and politics do not mix in Pauline's world. Upon hearing that Hillela has left the country, Pauline reacts with both bitterness and concern:

—That's a laugh! Hillela, 'having to flee the country'! That's
how my sister puts it, I could feel her trembling in her
boots, at the other end of the phone . . . What could Hillela
have done, she didn't even have any interest in helping black
schoolchildren on Saturday mornings! Smoking pot in a
coffee bar, that was more in that little girl's line. [. . .] She
has no political sense, no convictions, not the faintest idea,
that child! Hillela a political refugee—from what, I'd like to
know (1987: 121–122).

Over time, irony prevails. Hillela's 'response' to Pauline's political
desire is deferred until later when she becomes involved at the very
heart of the struggle, far superseding any of her aunt's achievements.
But even then she is engaged at a remove: as a final postponement,
Hillela later takes part of the independence ceremony not as a
South African but as the wife of an African president. In the terms
of the novel, the country belongs to (the dead) Whaila, not (the
living) Hillela (1987: 325).

The way in which Hillela confounds her surroundings
makes her into something of a trickster. Like the arch-trickster
Esu-Elegbara, she is a sower of confusion (Gates, 1988: 3–44).[2]
That her third and final name Chiemeka is Igbo, that is, from the
same part of Africa as the tradition of Esu-Elegbara, seems
appropriate in this context (1987: 303). Like Esu, she unsettles
the received categorisation of her surroundings. Not merely the
pouvoir-savoir of everyday taboos and survival strategies but also the
puissance-connaissance of institutionally sanctioned 'truth'. With
Pauline, Hillela's odd relation to 'politics' and 'morality' is brought
to the fore. At other defining moments, the discursive regimes of
'literacy', 'aesthetics' and 'psychoanalysis' are either rejected by
Hillela or indirectly represented as alien to her.

Allow me to elaborate. A recurring intertextual reference in the
novel is Dostoyevsky's *The Brothers Karamazov*. It inscribes, not
inappropriately, *A Sport of Nature* in the grand tradition of pre-
revolutionary literature in Russia. Not only does Gordimer – a
professed admirer of Russian realism[3] – emulate the high ethical
tone of such writing, but there is also a structural pattern in
her story that echoes Dostoyevsky's novel. Just as *The Brothers*

Karamazov tells the story of three brothers who each represent different life-choices that broadly correspond to Kierkegaard's three stages in life – the aesthetic, the ethical and the religious – so do we find three sisters in Gordimer's novel (which also hints at the unmentioned Chekov's *Three Sisters*) who follow divergent paths in life. The religious stage is missing here, but instead we find two versions of the aesthetic: Ruth's primitivistic sexual hedonism as opposed to Olga's reificatory adulation of *objets d'art*, whereas Pauline represents the ethical option.

This is not quite as blunt as I make it out to be. The first time that Dostoyevsky is mentioned is just before Hillela and Sasha enter their liaison. Sasha has heard a teacher at school mention the incident when Dostoyevsky stands before a firing squad and is reprieved at the last moment, the hideous intensity of which attracts Sasha. He enters the novel 'as millions had done before him, although to him it seemed its knowledge of all he needed to know, that nobody ever told him – even though everything was discussed, talk never stopped – was part of the possession of the house boarded this silent weekend when it was lit-up and empty' (1987: 86). It is a reading scene of a Proustian calibre:

> As he read his absorption deepened like the stages of sleep; and he was aware of his companion [Hillela] only the way the cat, actually asleep, showed awareness of the comfort of human presence and the fire's warmth by now and then flexing thorns through the white fur of a paw. Then he fell into a passage that semed to surround and isolate him. 'I am that insect, brother, and it is said of me specially. All we Karamazovs are such insects, and, angel as you are, that insect lives in you, too, and will stir up a tempest in your blood. Tempests, because sensual lust is a tempest! Beauty is a terrible and awful thing! It is terrible because it has not been fathomed and never can be fathomed, for God sets us nothing but riddles. Here the boundaries meet and all contradictions exist side by side. I am not a cultivated man, brother, but I've thought a lot about this. It's terrible what mysteries there are!' (1987: 86).

Much is displaced and substituted here in a swirl of tropes. Reading resembles sleep; the cat, asleep, resembles Sasha; the hypnotic intensity of reading is matched by the fervour of Ivan Karamazov's exclamations, which, in turn, anticipate what is about to happen between Sasha and Hillela, particularly since the name 'Sasha' refers both to the character in Gordimer's novel and the 'angel-brother' Alyosha/Sasha to whom Ivan is speaking.[4] Added to that, the quotation could be read as a more far-reaching comment on the 'terrible beauty' of political struggle – the Yeatsian overtones are not to be ignored.[5] In short, it is an eminently suggestive piece of writing, as is the entire chapter. Even so, it does not of itself suffice to posit *The Brothers Karamazov* as anything other than a fleeting intertext, merely indicating the intensity of Sasha's emotional life. Only as we encounter two more references to Dostoyevsky does the older novel's intertextual and narratorial function become evident.

Despite the all-consuming significance of Sasha's encounter with Dostoyevsky – it is described as a moment of transformation, a coming of age – Hillela, the main character and Sasha's companion, *does not read the novel*. In fact, she is never represented as a reader, nor as someone who writes. It is even said that 'Hillela had never been known to write' (1987: 96), and on the only occasion that she *is* shown to write – a letter to her father Len – it is a baldly inept piece (1987: 111). This, to me, is the first and necessary condition for Hillela's apparent departures from the Eurocentric regimes of colonialism/apartheid. She is simply not meant to be part of the language games of the Western episteme, not even of Dostoyevsky, the imposing critic of Western modernity as it was evolving in the heyday of racial imperialism.[6]

The following two occasions when Dostoyevsky is mentioned are likewise emblematic moments of departure from the West. At one level, the mention of Dostoyevsky is purely incidental, but it also functions as a *leitmotif* signalling a shift in, or addition to, the construction of Hillela. Firstly, during a brief spate of work at a psychiatrist's office she confounds her employer's assumptions about cultured conversation: 'So she read Dostoevksy? What a pleasure to talk with her about Dostoevsky, to give her some psychoanalytic insights into the irrationality of his characters' (1987: 105). But Dostoyevsky does not trigger the literary/intellectual discourse he expects from her. The psychiatrist, a synechdoche for psycho-analysis, is simply unable to subsume Hillela in his regime of *puissance-connaissance*. Her view of the patients undergoing psycho-therapy is stated clearly enough:

> And there's nothing wrong with them! Any of them! It's all made up, imagination? Isn't it? Those kids go to nice schools, they have toys and bicycles. Those girls can have as much food as they want, they're not starving, they just don't eat. Those men who talk to you for hours about sex—they never even take a glance at any woman who happens to be in the waitingroom . . . just sit there looking at the same old ratty magazines Rawdon arranges every morning (1987: 105–106).

To this thoroughly *materialist* rejection of the claims of psychotherapy, which at the same time is Hillela's farewell, the psychiatrist can only respond jokingly: 'Oh my God, Hillela, you are so healthy it appals me! It's wonderful. I don't know where they got you from!' (1987: 106). His mock-horror and playful admiration reads as a thin disguise for the dread of discursive disavowal. In his eyes, she remains an enigma, 'without a past before yesterday and a future beyond tomorrow' (1987: 106), and as she leaves, she is described rather too obviously as 'the one who was not a beauty but completely desirable to him, the one who was not an intellectual but whose intelligence was a wonderful mystery to him' (1987: 106).

The brazen refusal of Hillela to acknowledge the value of psychoanalysis – let alone be a suitable object for its ruses – obstructs one of the most powerful, Western-derived theories of subjectivity, a 'subversive' one at that.[7] Hillela cannot be psychoanalytically reduced; her alterity is emphatically not the alterity of neurosis or schizophrenia, neither does the transgressive element of the novel have anything to do with the 'madness' that the early Foucault tried to retrieve through writers such as Artaud (During, 1992: 41–42).[8] These various pathologies are historically specific and Western, attributable to those warped and warping relations of the bourgeois nuclear family that Hillela has escaped

(Cooke, 1993: 26–29). She represents instead the scandal of epistemically pristine health.

The final occasion when Dostoyevsky is mentioned is, perhaps, the most programmatic one. The scene is set in Tanzania and Hillela is together with her German acquaintance Udi who, during a discussion on the difference between being lonely and alone, happens to draw on Dostoyevsky: 'One can love one's neighbours at a distance, but at close quarters it's almost impossible. D'you know who said that true thing? Said it for me. A man named Ivan to his brother Alyosha, in a book called *The Brothers Karamazov*' (1987: 146). It is consistent with the depiction of Udi as an exceptionally well-read person and is glossed in the following manner: 'Again that novel. He didn't have to explain about that! —I've read it, long ago.— She wouldn't be expected to remember the whole of such a long book, even if she had' (1987: 146). Hillela's white lie is in this context quite striking, since *The Brothers Karamazov* is referred to as a touchstone not only of literary but also of ethical value. It embodies the beauty of truth, truth which Hillela formally controverts by claiming to have read the book.

Her exteriority to the institutionalised value-structures embedded in the references to Dostoyevsky is elaborated further down. As Udi takes Hillela on a trip through Tanzania with the intention of showing her Bagamoyo, 'where Livingstone started out to cross Africa from east to west' – a simple diversion sanctioned by the Eurocentric version of history – Hillela of course confounds this plan:

But when they got as far as the new hotel where he had intended that they should return to spend the night on the near side of the historical destination he had in mind, she hung back irresistibly. She ran to marvel at it from all perspectives, from sand so hot she danced across it as a fakir over the white ash of a bed of coals, to the cool of palms, remnants of the oil plantation the site once had been, now reified by a Scandinavian landscape gardener into his idea of a tropical garden. Her benefactor took his first photograph of Hillela there; the shadow of a palm tree falling before her. [. . .] He didn't insist on continuing the drive according to schedule; was content to study, as one standing back in a museum from a canvas whose conception he could not share but was fascinated by, her greedy pleasure in the post-colonial kitsch of the place—a Holiday Inn pervasion of piped music over poolside bars and buffets composed of a German-Swiss chef's attempt at reproducing his kind of food out of unidentifiable flesh and fowl decked with hibiscus flowers—all housed within a facsimile, as Udi informed her, of the 13th-century palace of Sultan al-Hassam Ibn Sulaiman (1987: 147).

'Kitsch' is a keyword here. Kitsch is heresy, it is the other of 'truth' and 'taste' which Udi supposedly possesses and which the narrator appears to endorse, albeit not in so many words. The entire resort is represented as an ersatz, a failed attempt at fulfilling a colonising Western desire for the exotic. The metaphor of the canvas underscores the distance between kitsch and taste. Hillela's 'greedy pleasure' is diametrically opposed to Udi's detached gesture of 'standing back [. . .] from a canvas'. This opposition applies in equal measure to the relationship between the narrator and Hillela, as to that between Udi and Hillela. It reiterates, in fact, the subtle split within the narrative in so far as it stands away from that which it represents. As it is this time articulated in aesthetic terms, the tension is brought to crisis. The text is clearly biased towards the aristocratic 'standing back' of high culture – how else should we understand condescending descriptions such as 'a Holiday Inn pervasion of piped music'? – and is, in itself, a manifest attempt to attain the status of high culture. At the same time, the utopian thrust of the novel is, as ever, located in the counter-aesthetic figure of Hillela, she-who-revels-in-kitsch.

Stated in theoretical terms, the contradiction obtains between a modernistic resistance to reification and commodification and the desire, codified through Hillela, to take the leap into a different emancipatory register, one that is inclusive rather than exclusive. (In spirit, this is not dissimilar to Ndebele's resolution of epistemic conflict.) There are two feasible solutions to this dilemma, neither of them quite satisfactory. The first, namely the investment of Hillela's body as nature, as a pre-cultural-yet-ethical space, results paradoxically in an appropriation of Hillela on behalf of the Western high-cultural project and undermines the ethical project in its strong version. The other, which will require that we reconsider the cross-cultural ersatz nature of the holiday resort, could perhaps enable an ethical leap beyond the colonising discursivity of high culture, but only at the cost of entering into dialogue with the reificatory forces of global capitalism and thereby jostling the aesthetic foundation of the novel. We are thus compelled to choose between two forms of complicity.

The virtue of the body erotic

As previously stated, Stephen Clingman suggests that a strong reading of *A Sport of Nature* must focus on Hillela's 'bodily presence' (1993: 178). If the trickster Hillela circumvents the very Western regimes of power (juridico-political resistance), knowledge (psychoanalysis), beauty and truth (Dostoyevsky, cultured taste) which are constitutive of the text, the rhetoric of body and instinct is what enables her nevertheless to reside immanently in that same text. In such a reading, the body anchors Hillela in history and circumstance whilst allowing her to elude discourse continually. In accordance with the strong Lawrentian undercurrent of Gordimer's writing, the body thus understood is a primitive, mystical, but also ethical force, which offers a release from the labyrinth of false consciousness erected by bourgeois civilisation (Wagner, 1994: 89–90). The body cannot lie, liberated sex is truth:

> *It is there, you feel it, it happens all over and inside you and there is no difference between you and the one you're doing it with, you don't have to try to reach him, help him, teach him— you can't lie, or spy or kill, so what could ever be wrong about it? Left behind by my mother, they say, because of it; because they told her it was wrong. The man they call a double-dealer, who lied about Sweden and Germany: the place he told the truth was in bed, with his lovely body, the feelings he gave me were not his fantasies or his boasts* (1987: 141).

And truth, in turn, is associated with presence and place: '*and inside each other, that's the only place we can make, here*' (1987: 141). Later we find the same association between body and presence:

> Pregnancy did not blunt but made more powerful the
> physical presence that had once drawn him [Arnold]
> after her into the sea. On the bare boards of this no-place,
> no-time, she was an assertion of *here* and *now* in the
> provisionality of exile, whose inhabitants are strung between
> the rejected past and a future fashioned like a paper aero-
> plane out of manifestos and declarations (1987: 181).

If indeed Hillela's body plays the same role in *A Sport of Nature* as
the African landscape does in many of Gordimer's previous
novels – as Susan Winnett has suggested (1993: 151) – then this is
as good a confirmation as any. Rather than constructing home out
of landscape, rather than imagining Africa as home on behalf of any
ethical subject prepared to accept it as such, we find here home in
the body.

In Hillela's relationship with the Belgian ambassador, the truth
facilitated by sex is supplemented by simplicity and wholeness: 'It
was a great sweetness to him; it brought the two halves of his life
together as they had never been before. An annealment, wholeness;
a new eroticism.—You have simplified everything' (1987: 167).
Finally, added to this list of virtues, we encounter the most redeeming one of all, trust:

> Everyone has some cache of trust, while everything else—
> family love, love of fellow man—takes on suspect
> interpretations. In her, it seemed to be sexuality. However
> devious she might have to be (he [General Reuel] realized he
> did not know why she should have wanted to be chosen by
> him) and however she had to accept deviousness in others,
> in himself—she drew upon the surety of her sexuality as the
> bread of her being (1987: 283).

The insistence on the self-presence of the body erotic ultimately,
indeed necessarily, falls short of success. Presence can only be represented through mediation and approximation, which defers it in
time and transforms into non-presence. The utterance of physical
presence does not actualise it; instead, it tends to be *abstract*
qualities and metaphors, 'an annealment', a 'cache of trust', '*here*

and *now'*, that refer back to the uncanny body, a body that is supposedly so concrete as to be independent of any language or pre-conceived signification.

What confronts us here, I believe, is an aporia located in the very concept of a sport of *nature*. The text places a heavy utopian burden on the body-as-nature and its ability to break free from the strictures of Empire and apartheid, but as Spivak has pointed out, the body as such cannot be thought:

> As a text, the inside of the body (imbricated with the outside) is mysterious and unreadable except by way of thinking of the systematicity of the body, value coding of the body. It is through the *significance* of my body and others' bodies that cultures become gendered, economicopolitic, selved, substantive (1993: 20).

In other words, it is through its very use of nature (metonymically coded as body) that the text most candidly reveals its *cultural* affiliation – more specifically, its romantic and primitivist bent. Nature, unrepresentable as such, takes recourse to a compromised Western discourse of self and other.[9] To be precise, it is not the actual employment of 'nature' and 'body' that is the issue here, but the refusal within *A Sport of Nature* to foreground the discursive inscription of these concepts. This, I believe, is what has caused the ire of feminist critics. Certain patriarchal modes of gendering are, in effect, given carte blanche in the portrayal of Hillela. Nature is what is seen to be uninterrupted, therefore must neither Hillela's eroticism be perceived as a challenge to established patterns of (hetero-) sexual desire. She is a fulfilment of male fantasy, a 'small, generous, urging, inventive body' (1987: 283) that manages to console some seven or eight men and rouse the lust in innumerable others before the novel has run its course.[10] Hence, it is stated that 'Hillela's field was, surely, men' (1987: 279). The utopian rationale behind this is that Hillela, as always, does it on her own terms. When placed as first among wives in General Reuel's polygynous context, an oft-quoted sequence of negations try to assert that Hillela is as independent and elusive as ever: 'Hers is the non-matrineal centre that no-one resents because no-one has known it

could exist. She has invented it. This is not the rainbow family'
(1987: 309). However, what makes it impossible to accept such a
contention, particularly on behalf of the silenced 'no-ones' who out
of meekness or surprise are deemed incapable of resenting this
newcomer, is that at this stage in the narrative Hillela *commands
power*. No longer does she elude the world and escape the framing
devices of its discourses – she confronts it head-on. She has come
into her own. If ever she is *present* as subject it is in her marriage
with Reuel, but instead the text marks her out, more explicitly than
before, as a negation of anything that can be affirmed in language.
Hillela's power is thus naturalised, and her patriarchally complicit
body is instrumental both in attaining that power and naturalising
it.

The association of power with body is explicit, so much so that
the text announces when this relation is disrupted. During Hillela's
sojourn in the United States, the narrator remarks that

> Of course Hillela had the body. The old, like Leonie, have
> no body except in its necessities for food, drink and shelter,
> and its creakings of pain. The body quickly knows—is the
> first to know—it has not been shot. It is still alive, alive in
> the Eastern European snow as in the tropical sand-bed. But
> it also knows when it is being ignored. Neglect of the body
> doesn't mean not washing or cutting toe-nails. It's a turning
> away from its powers. It's using it like a briefcase, to carry
> oneself around, instead of living through it (1987: 245).

And yet, even during this period of bodily neglect, Hillela is so
successful in raising funds for aid to Africa that it prompts an
American politician candidly to concede that 'Lust is the best aid
raiser' (1987: 245), thereby confirming a previous italicised reflection on Hillela's 'flirtatiousness': '*One can offer, without giving. It's a
form of power*' (1987: 198).

Power is clearly a defining factor in the writing of the body. But
even so, the *mediation* between the intimate powers of the body and
power at a historico-political level is mystified throughout. If we
juxtapose Ndebele and Gordimer, we encounter two different
means of transposing bodily power into political power: resistance

and acquiescence. Zamani's act of defiance at the end of Ndebele's 'Fools' is an exemplary moment of bodily resistance. He chooses his own means of resistance rather than the one symmetrically prefigured by the dominant force. He does not, within the scope of the novella, gain political power proper, but his action is the credible starting point for the slow construction of such power. By contrast, Hillela, in so far as she attains political power through her body – power which, to be sure, is used to resist the consequences of a colonial/racist history – does so by acquiescing, by playing *with* rather than *against* the demands of various patriarchal gender-systems. Her 'cache of trust' is thus shown to be by no means incapable of *de facto* deviousness. This is not simply a matter of the feminine body having fewer options under patriarchy, since Zamani's masculine body is also objectified and foreclosed – by racism – to a degree fully comparable with the gendered objectification of women. Rather, the difference between Zamani and Hillela spans the ethical distance between tempered idealism and pragmatism.

CHAPTER 12

Hillela as Allegory

IF WE READ Hillela-as-body in the terms set out by the novel – the body as nature and bearer of virtue – these terms are shown to self-destruct and produce their opposites. Nature encodes culture, virtue facilitates opportunism. This is a result of the novel's impossible ethical wager to combine, in the image of Hillela, full transcendence (from historical and discursive constraints) with full immanence (in the historical process). The fleeting comparison between Hillela and Christ points precisely to such an ambition (1987: 100). Just as Christian dogma will claim that Christ is 'all God and all man', so is Hillela meant to square the circle by being both within and outside of history. Her ambivalence proves therefore to be equally problematic in the hermeneutic reading (Hillela as character) as in the semiotic reading (Hillela as sign).

This confirms one of the criticisms levelled against *A Sport of Nature*, namely the argument that the insistent realistic ambition of the novel, the attempt to close the gap between Hillela as transcendent, utopian idea and the gritty sociohistorical reality of Africa, makes it a failure (Lenta, 1988: 133–145; Green, 1997: 263).

If, however, we go against the grain of the novel, if we do away with the earnest longing for the Absolute and accept the in-authenticity of the sign, a different story can be told. Rather than place our bets on the unlikely innocence and authenticity of Nature and body, we should reconsider the significance of the ersatz. We must see how Hillela, as the other of a compromised world order, is traced allegorically upon this order of which she is in excess, and is substituted for it. Only then, in such a differently construed hermeneutic reading, can we properly determine whether Hillela's displacements make way for any utopian re-placements; indeed, whether the ambivalence of *A Sport of Nature* may be read as a productive instance of post-colonial catachresis.

The clutter of contemporaneity

In order to clarify just how I claim that 'the world' enters or resides in *A Sport of Nature*, I shall start at the opposing end: the diachronic 'literary' reading which places Gordimer's novels in a temporal sequence of textual influences and shuns any 'flat' readings which isolate the novel in a synchronic now. The strongest exponent of the diachronic reading is Kathrin Wagner. In her view, the feminist critique of Gordimer's novels is misdirected. The frustrated search for a feminist bias in Gordimer's fiction does not take into account that '[feminist] awareness is an entirely contemporary, mainstream Western phenomenon, and was simply not part of Gordimer's early *Weltanschauung*' (Lenta, 1988: 133–145; Green, 1997: 263).

Instead, we should read the topos of sensual liberation in Lawrentian rather than feminist terms. The implication that Lawrence, being a primary influence, also offers the most enduring truth of Gordimer's later work is, however, not unproblematic. By privileging this continuist understanding of Gordimer, as does not only Wagner but also Pettersson, we undercut her consistent engagement with contemporary matters. I am not primarily referring to the obvious political concerns of southern Africa but rather to the broad canvas of social change. Fashion, music, colloquialisms, interior decorating, political strategy, changing sexual mores: the desire for the contemporary to be 'all there' – named or implied – is an intrinsic part of her realist project. (We have yet to read a historical novel by Nadine Gordimer.[1]) However, since it so easily gets written down as just an aspect of realism, as that excess of detail which produces an *effect* of the real but has no purchase on the real *issues* that are at stake, it is easily underplayed.

The political and ethical coding of the narrative are assumed beforehand, transforming its texture of contemporaneity into so much incidental clutter. The extent to which the clutter is deemed relevant is judged from the already established political content of the text. Brenda Cooper's claim that '[t]he repressive laws, the bannings, the bombings, the torture, underground activity and guerilla warfare, encompass Gordimer's South African history entirely, rather than constituting one aspect of it' (1990: 79) is an obvious example. Another is Stephen Clingman's discussion of fact and fiction in *A Sport of Nature* (1993: 173–177). Such a reading requires that we have already defined 'history' in Gordimer's novels as 'political history', in which case her portrayal of 'the struggle' can certainly be accused of being superficial and clichéd.

What are the alternatives? How else may we interrogate the status of historicity and fact in *A Sport of Nature*? Of what use, other than for the complex forms of illusion-making which I have discussed earlier in this part, are these verbal cut-outs and time-markers from verifiable extra-fictional contexts? Neither the seductiveness of the 'all there' – merely a form of impressionism which ignores the specific inclusions and exclusions that go into its construction – nor the reductiveness of the imposed political interpretation appear to account properly for their significance. Previously I criticised the ambiguous use of factuality as a narrative mode; I now intend to explore two recurrent factual faultlines in the light of their historical implications. The first concerns the disparity between local politics and a commodified, globalised culture. The second, as these disjunctive phenomena gradually conjoin and transform in the figure of Hillela, leads into the grafting of a global 'map of struggle' onto a map of capitalism.

Hedonism and factuality
In the third chapter of *A Sport of Nature* we read:

> GO-GO DANCERS LIVEN SATURDAY STREETS: a Sunday paper publishes a photograph of two young girls, flying legs and hair, dancing in a shop window. So this is what Hillela is doing with her Saturday mornings, now (1987: 35).

The incident is the first, and perhaps most significant conflict between Pauline and her niece. It is never stated, merely assumed that the transgression is horrendous:

> But Pauline must have decided, with the wise counsel of Joe, to take it tolerantly, carefully, considering the girl's

background.—What on earth is go-go dancing, darling?
And whose idea was the shop window?— [. . .]
    There would be no second time for the proud young
wage-earners of the new currency just introduced [. . .] (The
headmistress must have been grateful that the girls' names
were not published; there was no summons to her study.)
(1987: 35).

In the ensuing chapters, this image of unabashed, commodified
hedonism – the novel prompts us to read it in this way – is alluded
to several times, most notably in the vison of '*Happiness dancing in
a shop window behind glass, while outside there are hungry crowds in
the street, looking on*' (1987: 232). The immediate contrast, at the
time of the incident, is Pauline's Saturday school for black
children – a philanthropic venture in which Hillela does not
participate. Hillela will simply not do what her morally demanding
friends and family would prefer. We might expect the text to remain
neutral on this issue, given Hillela's gradual and ultimate as-
cendancy in the narrative. Upon closer scrutiny, however, the
deployment of factuality in the first third of the novel (before
Hillela leaves South Africa) evinces a stern attitude towards her
hedonism.
    'Other than go-go dancing, there are a few specific references
to consumerism and pop-culture in connection with Hillela's
teenage years. The moment of the 'coffee bar songs' such as 'We
Shall Overcome' and 'House of the Rising Sun' sung by Hillela
at Nick's Café is one (1987: 53). The mention of cassette-tapes
(1987: 19, 89) and a hi-fi (1987: 83) is another. We should also
note the cumulative enumeration of adolescent consumer articles
such as hairbrushes, deodorants, tampons, etc. in Carole's room
(1987: 19, 34). A fourth example is the advertising agency where
Hillela endures a brief stint of secretarial work (1987: 108,
111–112).
    All told, this forms a subtext. It inserts Hillela and her peers into
an emergent globalised culture, apparently ephemeral but buttressed
by the permeation of various 'affordable' technologies and media.
(Not yet television in the South African context, however.) The
swiftness and scope of its spreading makes it less constricted to

specific places or contexts than any previous cultural form. It is best described in temporal terms, as a specific 'time' – Nick's Café is renamed Arrivederci Roma 'to keep up with somebody's times, somewhere' (1987: 53). Its accessibility is diametrically opposed to Olga's bourgeois reification of *objets d'art*. The difference is stated clearly enough in a comment on the copywriters at the advertising agency: 'They believe they're writers and artists. The muse of consumerism is the new Apollo. [. . .] They're all neither one thing or another. Not workers, not artists'(1987: 108). Distinctions between commodified labour and supposedly autonomous art, between low and high, collapse when applied to advertising, the exemplary representational form of consumer capitalism.

This brings us close to the Jamesonian definition of the cultural condition of postmodernism, according to which the demise of high-modernism leads to a dissolution of depth, unified space and authenticity, as well as of distinctions between commodities and art (Jameson, 1992: 22–23). The emergence of such a culture on a global scale has everything to do with the internationalisation of English and, consequently, the history of Empire. Its independence of place must therefore not be confused with any freedom from geopolitical power relations. The metropolis (Western Europe and, increasingly, America) is still perceived as an Origin which posits Hillela's Johannesburg as periphery and a 'second world'.[2] It is also precisely because of this second-world status, with the intense local political conflict that it entails, that the 'global' facts of hedonism take on such specific meaning in the first third of the novel.

Moving on to the contrasting, disjunctive time of local politics, factual details of resistance history form a subnarrative of their own, sometimes contrapuntally, sometimes in full integration with the main narrative. Still restricting ourselves to the early part of the novel, they coincide largely with Pauline's political engagement. Particular emphasis is placed on the All-In African Conference in Pietermaritzburg, where Nelson Mandela spoke freely and in public for the last time until his release in 1990. Pauline attends the conference and returns with 'Nelson Mandela's words in my ears, something you can't stop hearing' (1987: 59). The conference is represented as a final, failed attempt to ward off the option of armed resistance which increasingly radical resistance movements demand in the wake of the Sharpeville massacre. It is noted that Mandela went underground after the conference (1987: 65), and later we are told of the first acts of sabotage (1987: 101).

Hillela, we are constantly reminded, is no part of these volatile developments.

> To kill or not to kill: her urgent choices are not these, could not even conceive of these. Indecision is between which group of friends she should choose to 'go with' more steadily than the other; whether to enjoy being swayed by some dominating personality in the one, or to enjoy being herself the boldest, brightest, the most magnetic, in the other (1987: 70).

In similar fashion, a rhetorical question highlights the separation between the collective, political narrative and Hillela's individualised trajectory: 'Where was the seventeen-year-old on the Day of the Covenant, 16th December 1961, when bombs exploded in a post office, the Resettlement Board Headquarters, and the Bantu Affairs Commissioner's offices?' (1987: 101). Of course, the syntagmatically unified enunciation of this disparity implies proximity. In the same chapter, the bodily exhilaration of Hillela in her first love-affair with the elusive journalist Rey is juxtaposed with the extremes of oppression: 'That year when Hillela was living in the city with some man was the same year when torture began to be used by the police' (1987: 112). The conflation of discrete events approaches the absurd, demonstrating the simultaneous horror and domesticity of South African society – 'While electric currents were passing through the reproductive organs of others, Hillela had an abortion' (1987: 114) – but the important point is that she is never far removed from those currents: 'It happened inside her; her body, her life: and the torture was one of the things he—Rey—had ways of knowing about, outside' (1987: 114).

Only at the time of Hillela's departure from South Africa, when she flees with Rey, do the two strains of narrative properly clash for the first time; only now is the hedonist Hillela directly affected by local political conflict. From this point onwards there is a shift in the use and historicising significance of factuality.

Political facts tend to be precise with regard to space or time, or both: '16ᵗʰ December 1961', 'Maritzburg', 'the same year' (referring to 1961). When not specified in such a way, references to bus boycotts or the debate on armed resistance and the formation of the Pan-Africanist Congress are easily identified and accord perfectly with authoritative accounts of recent South African history. We can place our trust in these facts – a trust which ironically betrays its opposite, the need to overcome a sense of suspicion towards the claims of the text.

In the case of the emergent globalised culture which is also alluded to in a specific, factual way, no such easy recourse is offered to verifiable *events*. Rather, it is repeatable or repetitive phenomena such as the go-go dancer, American coffee bar songs, advertising or mass-produced commodities such as music cassettes that form the 'real-world' reference. The non-specific nature of these facts is exacerbated by tiny slips and slides into anachronism. A glaring instance is 'go-go dancer', a term elevated to the status of chapter heading (1987: 34), and used in connection with the year 1961, four years before the first recorded use of the phrase 'go-go' in association with dancing girls.[3] Another is the reference to music cassettes, in 1960 to 1961, some few years before that form of audio recording was readily available on the market (*Oxford English Dictionary*, 1989). The coffeehouse songs make their casual appearance somewhat prior to their global breakthrough: Hillela sings Joan Baez songs the same year (1960) that Joan Baez started recording (1987: 23), which is not impossible, but certainly predates the singer's greater fame some two or three years later (*Nationalencyklopedin*, 1992).

What intrigues me is how these minute details are brought to my attention simply because they are anachronistic; they are like a tic in the face of the text, deceiving me into staring where I shouldn't.[4] They are probably simple mistakes, but are also readable as literary devices. To present as a given fact, as 'real', that which is an error, merely extends the scope of signification. It invests Hillela's teenage life with a lingering sense of unreality and underscores a Marxist view of consumerism and globalised mass culture as nothing more than a manipulative trafficking in *false* consciousness (albeit with a slightly privileged place for 'political art' such as protest songs of the 1960s); the time of global pop culture is literally the *wrong* time for South Africa (Jameson, 1992: 22–23). Consequently, contrasted as it is with error, the veracity of the political facts brings about a sense of the real, that very reality which at the time of her flight overtakes Hillela and catapults her, along with her hedonistic, mass-cultural affiliation, into a synthetic third position bristling with the allure of newness. There is an intriguing complexity about this movement that inverts and restates the significance of *anachronism* as the mode of error, since Hillela's escape does not 'restore' time to some pristine wholeness. It achieves the exact opposite and brings about an ever greater fragmentation of the temporal mosaic.

Mapping the ersatz
Hillela's departure from South Africa is represented as gratuitous. Those left behind struggle to make sense of it. Pauline eventually decides that she simply 'Attached herself to some man—that's what it was all about. *He* was the one who had to go' (1987: 123). Ostensibly, yes, but in terms of a broader socio-historical reading, Hillela's exodus is overdetermined. Until then, nothing has placed her 'authentically' in South Africa. She does not partake in the locally grounded politics of Pauline, neither is she susceptible to the South African 'morality' of race, class and gender. Furthermore, her own parents, whose very absence emphasise Hillela's heritage of placelessness, are separated and live outside of the country. Add to this the teleological overtones of the story and it seems clear that Hillela's departure is 'merely' a question of time. Rather than her acting as a selfless appendix to Rey, it is Rey who unwittingly functions as her temporary vessel of escape.

The move marks a paradigmatic shift in the narrative. Tamarisk Beach in Tanzania, where Hillela is first sighted after leaving South Africa, is referred to as 'the place of resurrection' (1987: 125). Hillela is reborn as she wanders unknown among exiles who gradually accept her as one of them. At the level of historicity – at the level where agency is constituted in the conflict between divergent historical and ideological forces – Hillela begins to fuse radical politics and globalisation. Her transnational mobility and the displacement (or deracination) of politics in exile, are the conditions of possibility for such a fusion or conjuncture, and the change from a national to a transnational context instantly diminishes the realistic gravity of place in the narrative (hopping from country to country and continent to continent rather than exploring one place – Johannesburg – in ever greater detail), and endows the multiple places, as well as their internal connections, with more of an allegorical significance. Place-names as well as entire continents or countries, 'Africa', 'Europe', 'America', 'South Africa', attain through Hillela's picaresque movements a near-mythical, but also curiously blank status. We read that Hillela and Reuel 'were in the familiar territory of exile, that knows no hemispheres; a globe of blank spaces between those areas where one has been allowed in' (1987: 270).

I am not claiming that the narrative's dominant realistic mode is abruptly discarded when Hillela begins to travel, but the relative difference in the deployment of place between the pre- and post-exile parts of the novel begs to be read.

I argue that Hillela, in exile, enters a fully postmodern condition, with all the difficulties in retaining a coherent vision of 'progression' that this entails. Through an act of 'cognitive mapping' – a quasi-allegorical representation of a world-system (Jameson, 1991: 51–54) – the novel then entertains Hillela's position as a utopian option of refashioning the postmodern world-order in the desired image of Pan-African post-coloniality. However, as I said earlier, this is only at the cost of undoing the novel's own aesthetic prejudice. In this way Hillela is transformed into an allegorical figure who represents the 'new Africa' negotiating the contradictions of contemporary world history.

This shift requires that we refine our understanding of what the 'world' might be in the narrative, since it now extends beyond the metonymy of transnational pop culture and becomes more distinctly geographical. Already in the first third of the novel the 'world' functions as a disjunctive yet dominant concept vis-à-vis the local political turmoil of South Africa, not only through the mass-cultural and consumerist fragments that gesture beyond the local, but also as an imagined space (already half-mythical) of its own. At seventeen, Hillela would be seeing herself—where?—anywhere she has never been, some apartment in a city never seen, Los Angeles or Paris, as comfortable as Olga's house but of course not at all like Olga's, or Pauline's or anybody's, with good-time friends (but not like the friends she makes do with now) or just one person, a man older than herself who adores her and makes love to her and takes her all over the world (1987: 70).

This is a teenager's daydream, qualitatively equivalent to the phantasms of pop culture. But daydreams are not only imagined: they must also be imaginable. In Hillela's case the limits of the imaginable are determined at an immediate level by those very friends and relatives that the daydream tries to exclude. At a historical level, it is determined by the agency of 'white' South African privilege constructed by the dual forces of imperialism and late capitalism. This is adequately demonstrated as Olga and Arthur entertain business acquaintances, and the 'world' is reduced to a showcase of so many buying options:

—There's a delightful place on the market, not far from ours. I think the position's even better than ours. Why don't you buy a little pied-à-terre in Italy? It'd be lovely to have you as neighbours now and then.—
—The way things are going, it might have to be more than that!— Olga laughed when she said it, and the butterfly lady did not pause to take in the inference: —Though I can understand, if I lived in this beautiful country, with those wonderful vineyard estates at the Cape, and those marvellous beaches, so clean—not like Europe—uncrowded, I wouldn't see much reason to go anywhere else— (1987: 64).

The consumerist imagining of the world is articulated in equal measure, although with greater enthusiasm, by Hillela's peers. In conversation with Sasha, her cousin explains that

—All you need is enough for a cheap one-way ticket. If you can get that together, then you can work your way around

Europe. There must be people we know we could stay
with . . . connections.—
    —Billie—she's got family in London. You know—my
step-mother.—
    —I want to keep away from youth hostels. I've had
enough of living in dormitories. They say in France, if you
go to the South where so many rich people are, you can get
taken on as crew for a yacht. Girls too. There's someone at
school, his brother went all the way to the Bahamas—
fantastic (1987: 88).

The geopolitical reduction of the world to South Africa, Western
Europe and the United States should, of course, be read
symptomatically, as a self-reproducing image of the parts of the
world that 'matter' from the horizon of 'white' South Africa in the
heyday of the Cold War. It is not to be mistaken as simply a 'false'
image, but rather as an accurate assessment of a geography of
influence produced by the world-system (which, by the 1960s, has
touched every last pocket of the globe in the guise of an East–West
dualism). Western capital, as well as Western media representations,
that flow through the privileged 'white' South Africa constitute the
historical time in which these particular parts of the world are *made*
to matter.[5]

In the meantime – or rather, in other times that coincide with
this privileged Western time – the locally or nationally defined
struggles of South Africa and other parts of the colonial or
post-colonial world continue, each according to its specific
historical dynamics, in the shadow of this imaginary geography. By
describing their incommensurability as a temporal rather than
spatial disjunction, as sheer difference between modes of contemporaneity rather than between more and less 'advanced'
histories, I draw on Homi Bhabha's influential addendum to the
thinking on globality. In a studied critique of Fredric Jameson's
theoretical exposition of the baffling, untotalisable global space of
postmodernity, Bhabha insists on conceptualising it in terms of
time: 'What is manifestly new about this version of international
space and its social (in)visibility, is its temporal measure [. . .] The
non-synchronous temporality of global and national cultures opens

up a cultural space – a third space – where the negotiation of incommensurable differences creates a tension peculiar to borderline existences' (Bhabha, 1994: 218).

In *A Sport of Nature*, the text's spatialisation of Hillela's 'moving on' occludes temporality and colludes with an all-too-easy validation of the 'here and now' of her body. In a certain sense, the exclusive spatialisation of the body forecloses the possibility of change and transformation since the body is always 'here', no matter how it may be displaced. This is precisely where the temporal aspect – focusing on the 'now' rather than the 'here' – can re-open *A Sport of Nature*, since the 'now' is not as easily contained by the body, but determined, fractured, jostled by circumstance. This being so, the incommensurability of the various 'nows' does not preclude contact or change. What occurs when Hillela leaves South Africa is, crucially, a switch from static geographical fantasy to actual movement, leading to a deformation (or re-formation) of her time. And not only *her* time: likewise are the exiled freedom fighters she meets temporally disjunct in relation to the ongoing struggle in South Africa. Their South African time is, so to speak, both arrested and susceptible to change under the influence of other temporalities. Gathered on Tamarisk Beach, graphically representing the hyper-conventional Western image of the easy life, upholding incongruous political enmities, taking and dropping casual acquaintances and hangers-on (1987: 126), the exiles are in fact 'neither one thing or another', not wholly unlike the apostles of consumerism at the advertising agency, whose postmodern predicament could be said to ironically prefigure the interstitial existence of exile – the irony being underlined by the fact that it is Rey who not only passes judgement on the copy-writers but also flees the country with Hillela. The exiles' split position in between various temporalities – simultaneously 'in' and 'between' – presents us as readers with 'the anxiety of enjoining the global and the local', of signifying 'the temporal break-up that weaves the "global" text' and therefore of conceptualising the potentialities inherent in that temporal break-up, the tatters of history as it were, of (re)constructing a post-colonial agency (Bhabha, 1994: 216, 217).

The point is that the exiles, and Hillela in particular, although *not unlike* the advertising agents, must not be the same as them, or else the entire ethical project implodes. The post-colonial must be distinguishable from the postmodern, and *A Sport of Nature* invites us to spot the difference.

Such an allegorical reading of singularity, it must be stressed, is quite different from taking recourse to the 'natural instinct' of the body, or positing Hillela as a sign beyond all signs. Instead, it reinscribes the imperfect and compromised materials of various contemporaneities, in order to see how – to appropriate a formulation from Judith Butler – singularity can be established 'not *outside* or *beyond* that reinscription or reiteration, but in the very modality and effects of that reinscription' (quoted in Bhabha, 1994: 219). This requires of course a sense of potential, not merely of loss, in the fractured global 'text'. It is along these lines that Hillela's enthusiastic response to the hotel in Tanzania – already quoted on pages 143 and 144 – should be understood.

The hotel is the epitome of inauthenticity, a postmodern amalgam of pastiche. Nothing here is 'truly' African, it is all set up according to European standards of exoticism and facile luxury which are themselves degraded repetitions of orientalist and imperialist fantasies, copies of inauthentic originals, that is, simulacra. And yet Hillela, the Pan-Africanist-to-be, *marvels* at it. Perhaps she does not take the kitsch to be real, as is despairingly said of her own mother's descent into the nightclubs of Lourenço Marques (1987: 46), but she does *sense its potential*. The resort, notwithstanding its visual allegorisation of late capitalism's fragmented cultural visage and of the same era's representational and economic power-relations, defines a mode of hybridity in which the ersatz can work towards emancipatory ends. The emphasis of my reading lies therefore on its residue of trans-formative utopianism, not its manipulative features. It is as though Hillela's enthusiasm, with hindsight, can be glossed as 'two can play at this game'.

The disjunction and linkage of various temporalities brings about the need for cultural translation, or – better yet – *causes* translation. As we follow Hillela after her departure from South Africa, her travels multiply and become uncountable. From Tanzania she joins the Belgian ambassador's family on two different postings in West Africa. There she joins Whaila Kgomani and follows him to Zambia. After Whaila's death she spends time in Eastern Europe, moves on to the United Kingdom, then to the United States and eventually back to Central Africa. On top of this, the periods in between the actual moves become increasingly transient. Hillela is less and less a resident of any particular place. During her period in America she not only criss-crosses the country to raise funds, but also travels repeatedly to different parts of Africa on various aid missions. When she 'settles in' as the wife of President Reuel, her position is merely a base for a busy official life of travelling (1987: 307). She becomes a privileged nomad with an emotional attachment to the non-places of Hilton and Inter-continental hotels (1987: 305) and lives a life ever more distant from the '*hungry crowds in the street*' (1987: 232), those in whose name she acts and who, generally speaking, are bound all their lives to one and the same place. Yet we are to understand that she, chameleon-like, is never a stranger to the poor and the suffering.

The immediate rejoinder would be to say that of course Hillela is attached to a place. Page by page, her energies are increasingly focused on the African continent. But this is precisely our dilemma: how do we credibly articulate such an involvement, such agency, under the conditions of quasi-global fragmentation represented in the novel? Hillela's 'Africa' is after all not a place – we would be hard pressed to think of the second largest continent as one specific 'place' – and it is not even an imagined community but a patchwork of disjunctive, transitional temporalities that straddle, tautologically, the position 'between Africa and the world' (1987: 333).

To close in on just how the novel works its way through this dilemma, I wish to focus on three specific moments of temporal and cultural *bricolage* that help to delimit Hillela's post-colonial transfiguration of postmodernity.[6] The first is a spatial rep-resentation that refers back to the hotel in Tanzania. Here we find Hillela moving through the capital of a former French colony in West Africa, on her way to see the Belgian ambassador, her lover:

> Boutique, bistro, bar, nightclub—these were the marked routes of the diplomatic and expatriate community. There was a path of her own drawn through the grass; the grass

closed it away behind her. It led across one of those stretches of ground that are called vacant lots in the cities of other continents; here it was a vacant patch in history, a place where once manioc had been grown and goats had wandered, now appearing on some urban development plan as a sports or cultural centre that would never be built. A tiny scratching of planted maize was hidden in the grass, like a memory. Her path crossed those made by the feet of fishermen, and servants moving from and to where she was going, the enormous hotel that multiplied itself, up and up, storey by storey, shelf by shelf of identically-jutting balconies and windows that eventually had nothing to reflect but sky. There was no other structure to give it scale, nothing to dissimulate its giant intrusion on the low horizons of islands and water, that drew the eye laterally. Even the great silk cotton tree and the palms left as a sign of its acculturation when the site was cleared were reduced to the level of undergrowth beside its concrete trunk.

Inside, the scale of unrelation, of disjuncture continued; through ceremonial purplish corridors she walked, past buried bars outlined like burning eyelids with neon, reception rooms named for African political heroes holding a silent assembly of stacked gilt chairs, crates of empty bottles and abandoned mattresses, sudden encounters with restaurant stage-props – plastic palm-trees and stuffed monkeys from some Tropicana Room, rolled-up carpets from the Persian Garden. At the white grand piano outside a locked entrance where photographs of girls whom gilt text dated the previous year announced as direct from the Crazy Horse in Paris, she turned to a bank of elevator doors like the reredos of some cathedral. Her path was always the same; through the grass, through the carpeted tunnels of corridors, the soughing ascent to the same floor. She had her key to the room; the bed was as big as the one in Sultan al-Hassam Sulaiman's fake palace. The Ambassador came by some path of his own through this dark ziggurat, pyramid, Eiffel Tower, Empire State Building raised to the gods of development (1987: 166).

This remarkable passage elaborates in much greater detail the ersatz mode of the Sultan's fake palace, only this time it is not so easily rejected as pure imperialist fantasy. Now 'Africa' has a stake in the inauthenticity of the postmodern. Its political heroes are reduced to interchangeable signifiers in the naming game of style, atmosphere and marketable exotica, but also deliberately placed as symbols of locally rooted power in this most concrete monument to the powers of transnational capital. The hotel is, in both a literal and figural sense, a 'structure' that looms over all else in the environment, supposedly acculturated but in fact subsuming everything in its vicinity as well as those 'foreign' cultural markers of an international lifestyle. The point is of course that nothing is really foreign in this context, and neither is Hillela. If we compare this passage with the previous hotel scene, we find that Hillela is no longer the enchanted onlooker, but an integral part of the whole. She has a 'path of her own' through the grass, walks on the same ground as the local fishermen and servants, finds her way unobtrusively through the labyrinthian 'ziggurat, pyramid' and eventually produces her own key to a room within the structure. She does not respond to the place other than by accepting it as a given fact: in itself a notable response, considering the oddness of the hotel.

Hillela's walk through the grass and up to the hotel room is a passage through extremes of temporal disjunction, of a collage of incommensurable yet simultaneous time-fragments. The dominance of the hotel over the landscape is due to a lack of equivalent or opposing structures. It is juxtaposed not with any 'local' struggle or entity, since the hotel contains the local through its transnational form (both materially by employing servants and symbolically by naming rooms after political heroes), but with the 'vacant patch in history', that conspicuous space across which Hillela moves with the same ease that she enters the hotel, the erstwhile farming land evacuated to make room for some public building that will never be built. Note how different this opposition is from the more conventional one between commodified false consciousness and the 'authenticity' of national struggle. There is no way of knowing what will become of this patch, or indeed if it is a true opposition (considering Hillela's seamless transition from grassland to hotel). We can only assume that this is the utopian space that will figuratively be occupied by Hillela, the space in which she will resituate the degraded, political *promesse de bonheur* of the hotel.

In our second moment of *bricolage* the narrator's ambivalent fascination with the details of an affluent, globalised life-style surfaces once more. It is a passage which tells the story of Hillela's daughter, Nomzamo, and which edges us closer to Hillela's utopian space, only to invert it:

> The namesake grew up very black. This has been an advantage for Nomzamo although she does not live in Africa, since the vogue for black models, which had begun esoterically in Paris when Ruthie, Olga and Pauline were playing with golden-haired Shirley Temple dolls in Johannesburg, spread to the United States and Britain during African decolonisation and coincided with the period in which she took up modelling at sixteen. She also grew as beautiful as the woman she was named for. [. . .] The girl, described in an agency's portfolio as exotic, is known as all the most successful models are simply by a single name— hers is Nomo—easily pronounceable by French, Italian, German, American and English couturiers and readers of fashion journals. An international model does not hamper her image with national politics; to the rich people who buy the clothes she displays or the luxuries her face and body promote, she is a symbol of Africa, anyway; one preferable to those children in the advertisements of aid organizations begging money to keep them from starving. She has not made use of the origin of her diminutive except, during a certain period, on occasions when she was hired by a committee giving a fashion show benefit for a cause such as aid for South African political prisoners—then she had a byline in the sponsored programme: 'Appropriately, top model Nomo is named for the black leader, Mrs Nomzamo Winnie Mandela, wife of Nelson Mandela' (1987: 195).

At first this seems like a mere duplication of the well-worn opposition between authenticity (struggle, Winnie Mandela) and compromised or 'false' consciousness (bourgeois culture). But the irony runs much deeper. Consider first Hillela's *success* in bearing the 'perfectly black' (1987: 195) Nomzamo: 'not to have reproduced herself, not to have produced a third generation of the mother who danced away into the dark of a nightclub' (1987: 195). Her satisfaction is unequivocal and validates the analyses by Pettersson (1995: 55–63) and John Cooke (1993: 21–32) of filial relationships in Gordimer's novels, according to which the circle of reproduction is always vicious and must somehow be broken. Wagner confirms that Nomzamo is unique in Gordimer's work, in so far as she is allowed a non-political life without being morally condemned for it (1994: 165).

But this peculiar success in (re)producing alterity, the not-self, is fraught with contradiction. Firstly, to stretch the metaphor of the reproductive circle, we should add that Hillela's ambition is not to break the circle so much as to fold it in half, in the shape of an arc: the only utopian idea attributed to her is 'the rainbow family' which would harness historical and social differences in a harmonious private form. Hence her satisfaction, since the birth of Nomzamo inaugurates her rainbow family. The dream of private happiness detached from the imperative of political change is brought to an abrupt end by the assassination of Whaila (1987: 212–213) and for the remainder of the novel 'the rainbow family' is negated or used ironically. Our understanding of Nomzamo must nevertheless take into account that she carries with her this utopian residue which is subsequently transformed in her specific reassemblage of incommensurable temporalities. Because of this, and by dint of her very detachment from her mother, she actually resembles Hillela all the more closely.

Secondly, to interpret Nomzamo's blackness as a 'success', we must accept as given the racial mode of thinking, albeit in inverted form. The joy that Nomzamo brings is assumed to be directly proportionate to the darkness of her skin. Also, the emphasis on the epidermal difference between mother and daughter elides the uncanny proximity of their relative positions in the global temporal text. So close are their positions that they are rather like the negative and print of the same image. We see this at first in how they both benefit from the attractiveness of their bodies and become international celebrities. Both of them enter – as names, as images, as figures of relative power within their discrete fields – a global circulation of symbolic capital. It may seem obvious enough that Hillela lends herself to the public sphere and gives up any pretensions of having a 'private life', but the same can be said of Nomzamo. Her 'private life' is a misnomer, since it is precisely by visually exploiting her body – the physical limit of private individuality – that the model earns her public and professional currency. The distinction between public and private applies as poorly to Nomzamo as it does to her mother.

Besides these similarities, it is even more striking to note how the smaller positional differences between Hillela and Nomzamo also merely reverse one another, as black reverses white. If Hillela incongruously benefits from her sex appeal when raising funds for Africa, then Nomzamo, just as incongruously, represents 'Africa' and happens to be associated with the South African political struggle when this helps to raise her marketable 'credibility'. A moralising gaze, unprepared to accommodate the radical complicities of globalised culture, would renounce the transgressions of both.

The enduring point is that even as both women move in the 'unimaginable' space of a marketable globe, that postmodern space where incommensurable bits and tatters of disparate temporalities get jumbled, reassembled and reified in the overriding interest of creating ever greater returns on capital, Nomzamo's trajectory mirrors, and *reverses* by mirroring, Hillela's. She transplants the sign and image of struggle in the privileged world of *haute couture*. Hillela transplants the sign and image of 'white' privilege in the world of struggle.

A politics of style
However, the mere claim that Hillela transplants the sign of privilege does not in any way explain how this might be ethically tenable. That is, we have still not properly discussed whether Hillela's ambivalence disables or facilitates the construction of a post-colonial agency (the filling of the 'vacant patch in history'). To do so, and as a way of approaching the conclusion of the novel, I look at the chapter 'State Houses'. This provides us with a third instance of *bricolage*. The title is a pun on the disjunctive content of the chapter itself. At an obvious level, it indicates that the chapter is

'about' State House – Hillela's and President Reuel's official residence. The latter half of the chapter, however, consists of a letter written by Hillela's cousin Sasha when incarcerated in a maximum security prison in South Africa – a 'state house' of a different kind. The pun causes a clean split in the notion of a unified history and makes it necessary once again to distinguish between a South African and a transnational 'moment' (as was done in the first third of the novel). This time around, however, the relation between the local and the global is disjunctive or parallel rather than antithetical. Moreover, the title's split signification is also a marker of equivalence between the relative positions of Hillela and Sasha. Absurd though this may seem – one is a president's powerful wife, the other an isolated prisoner – the text provides an argument for the ethical proximity of the two cousins or, should we say, of their integrity, an argument which works against the political valorisation of the position of the oppressed.

'State Houses' calls for a re-assessment of some specificities of the period in which *A Sport of Nature* was written – that is, the mid-1980s, described by Stephen Clingman as a time of 'fantastic cynicism' (1993: 188). Although a form of historical reading is what I argue for generally in this work – and in the context of Gordimer studies the argument may indeed seem unremarkable – such an imperative is reiterated at a *formal* level in *A Sport of Nature*. This is because, as I discussed earlier, a narrative of contemporary history constantly seeps into the fictional narrative through factuality, and requires by implication that (the reading of) the fiction reflects back on history.

In 'State Houses' this formal dialectic is brought to a head by Sasha's letter which, on the one hand, gives the outlines of a fully historical narrative and, on the other, is such an eminently fictional device, an unlikely letter produced inside the belly of the beast, which Hillela never receives.

What Sasha writes is a version of the South African or local 'now' of the writing of the novel:

> *When the United Democratic Front was launched* [historically, in 1983], *and the unions I was working for affiliated, I got drawn in along with them; by then, blacks had sufficient*

confidence to invite whites to join the liberation struggle with them, again. They have no fear it'll ever be on the old terms. Those've gone for good. So you're not the only one who's spoken on public platforms. I was up there, too. [. . .] Our unions don't see their responsibility for the worker ending when he leaves the factory gates every day. Their demands aren't only for the baas, they're addressed to the government, black worker power confronting white economic power, and they're for an end to the South African way of life.

There've been a great many funerals. The law can stop the public meetings but not always the rallies at funerals of riot dead – although the law tries. Sometimes the police Casspirs and the army follow people back to the washing of the hands at the family's house, and the crowd gathered there is angry at the intrusion on this custom and throws stones, and the army or police fire. Then there is another funeral. This has become a country where the dead breed more dead (1987: 321).

This view of intense repression and resurgent resistance is confirmed as we turn to 'properly' historical narratives. In Davenport's description, the 1980s were largely defined by the rule of P.W. Botha and his 'total strategy' against the 'total onslaught' of so-called communist forces on South Africa. The brutality of the state apparatus had, of course, been graphically apparent at the pivotal moments of Sharpeville in 1960 and Soweto in 1976, but the protracted states of emergency of the 1980s, beginning in 1985, turned a genre of raids and clamp-downs into daily fare. As Davenport puts it, '[t]he resources of the state were more severely extended during the crisis of 1985–7 than they had been in 1976–7', and '[t]he glare of international publicity was also greater' (1991: 440–441). However, the dominant popular response to this was not resignation but defiance. As Davenport goes on to say, the

emergency revealed an organising capacity in the black townships which had not been evident a decade earlier. Protests against the Black Local Government Act, not in itself, but because it had been offered as a sop in place of parliamentary representation, led in one township after another to the resignation of councillors [. . .] and to the *de facto* but not *de jure* collapse of the system (1991: 441).

It is not enough to speak of the 'fantastic cynicism' of the 1980s in South Africa. Rather, the cynicism of the state brought forth an enduring, idealistic political response, a view which is corroborated in Nadine Gordimer's essay 'Letter from Johannesburg, 1985', where, even as she decries the cynical satisfaction many whites find in the Emergency, she lauds the courage and 'genuine cheerfulness' of an activist (1988: 307). Pauline's moral paradigm seems unharmed, even considering that blacks rather than whites are leading the struggle now. This is still a spatially coded Manichean world, divided between Good and Evil; a world in which 'authenticity' (as opposed to cynicism and false consciousness) still functions as a marker of ethical legitimacy.

As a fictional device, the allegory of Sasha's letter reflects back on this historical understanding of the period and adds that it is more isolated from a global historical process than ever – for better or worse. If we understand the letter as a chain of signifiers that represent (in a colloquial rather than a literary sense) the historical moment, we must also take into consideration its containment inside the prison-house of the repressive state (which, moreover, includes censorship of the press and television, etc.). The letter, which was to be smuggled out of prison, is intercepted by the authorities and produced at Sasha's trial as evidence of his subversive inclinations (1987: 325). The double move of simultaneously withholding and exposing the letter marks out, allegorically, the hubris of the state: it believes it has the power both to arrest the very historical process with which it is imbricated and to study it, penetrate it from a detached juridical position that lies on supposedly neutral ground. Such hubris necessarily foreshadows a peripateia, since the very degree of state violence needed to aggravate the global/local divide – wherein a privileged 'white' such as Sasha transgresses the limits of the global (or globalised West, rather) at his own peril, and 'blacks' are confined to the local – prefigures the state's ultimate failure in upholding this division. Its attempt to prevent the global and the local from leaking into each other is almost by definition self-defeating, as indeed is assumed by the transitional-cum-apocalyptic mode of Gordimer's 'interregnum'- writings.[7]

This reading of the letter as foreboding a different historical condition could also be reinscribed metafictionally: the letter – along with those other letters that Sasha writes to Hillela but return '[u]nwanted, unopened' (1987: 300) – could be seen as a metaphor for the act of writing the very novel that we are reading. Through writing, the author attempts to express herself, bridge the gap of experience between her isolated position in South Africa and the 'world outside'. But the world will not be reached in this expressivist mode. The dispersal and (mis)interpration of the text that we call reading only occurs within the same conditions of disablement that define the author's predicament (the courtroom and those present in the courtroom). The radically disjunctive world – so the implication goes – requires instead the ironical mode of writing that dominates (or struggles to dominate) so much of the novel.

The writing of Hillela's State House – as opposed to Sasha's letter – articulates this other, worldly condition that, despite its global reach, does not correspond to the global/local dichotomy. What we find at State House is not the hedonism of pop culture but rather the high-powered politics of Hillela and Reuel, wherein the spatial metaphor of global and local is displaced by an ongoing translational act between disjunctive times.

The transnational moment in which we locate Hillela merits perhaps better Clingman's designation of 'fantastic cynicism'. Its resurgent Cold War-rhetoric was exceptionally ill-suited to tackle the increasing class-differentiation of the globe as well as the various forms of political oppression of the period. Dominated politically as it was by Ronald Reagan, Margaret Thatcher and Pope John Paul II, with their respective monetarist and neo-conservative ideologies, and philosophically/aesthetically by nihilistic brands of poststructuralism and postmodernism, the chances for an 'authentic' political response comparable to the one in South Africa seemed rather slim. Both Reagan and Thatcher, for example, advocated the 'constructive' approach to the apartheid regime, which meant no sanctions (Davenport, 1991: 462). This is precisely the motivation for my reading of Hillela – as an attempt at re-articulating 'commitment' in a moment which has abandoned the 'naïvety' of activism.

In 'State Houses', what immediately confronts the reader is a convergence of the previous moments of *bricolage*. The detailed description of the residence, which reverberates with the fetishistic eroticism of texture and taste, not only reinscribes the spatial mode of the earlier hotel passages, but also incorporates the upper-class transnationalism of Nomzamo's modelling circles. It begins by juxtaposing Nomo ('Nomzamo' is now completely subsumed by the brand-name) and a stuffed leopard standing at the entrance of State House. 'When Nomo has a week to spare between seasonal haute couture presentations in Paris, Rome, New York and London, and flies out to Africa, the moment of arrival for her is when she passes an elongated hand over the creature's head' (1987: 305). This leads to a comparison with a softer version of leopard, a fur-coat designed for her by a Japanese couturier. Thus, the first four sentences of the chapter offer a double image of reified African 'wilderness' and an invocation of three continents and six countries. As we enter State House, we enter in other words an imperialist phantasmagoria or, to be more precise, its refurbished shell, altered but not destroyed, appropriated but not evacuated. Significantly, the leopard is said to stand for 'black independence' (1987: 306). This inverts the meaning of the 'heroic animals' in paintings mentioned a page later – which reproduce 'the white man's yearning for Africa to be a picture-book bestiary instead of the continent of black humans ruling themselves' (1987: 306) – as much as Hillela and Reuel invert the architectural coding of the residence itself:

> State House was originally Government House and built to the standard design of one of the sovereignties of hot climates in the imperial era [. . .] The President has wanted to brick up walls and extend to the whole place the airconditioning system he long ago installed in the public and private rooms, but Hillela's early exposure to the stylistic graces and charms of the past, spending school holidays with a collector aunt, left latent in her an appreciation that has emerged in the mistress of Presidential residence. She has insisted that State House appropriate Government House,

not destroy its architectural character. She has been in charge of all extensions and structural alterations. A style of living commensurate with the dignity of the State, she persuaded the President, is not expressed in the idiom of the Hilton and Intercontinental [. . .]. As for luxury—a measure of which every Head of State, even one determined to live as close to his people as Nyerere was, must have in order to symbolize some estate now attainable to the people, since every head of a black state was once one of its oppressed people—real luxury is expressed in gardens and the indulgence of individual notions of comfort, idiosyncratic possessions. Behind the leopard of black independence, the atrium opens across the reception area from which official visitors waiting to be received by the President can watch, in the park, peacocks from the last governor's tenancy trailing worn tails (1987: 305–306).

Note first of all how Hillela's response to the phantasm has gradually changed from enchantment (at the fake palace) to indifferent acceptance (of the hotel in West Africa) to cool mastery of each stylistic and emotional nuance of the unlikely spectrum of idioms in State House. There is ambivalence in this mastery: it demands that the mistress submits to that which she will control. In what reads like a return of the repressed, Olga's bourgeois influence resurfaces and becomes 'useful'. It determines for Hillela just how to define 'the dignity of the State' and submit to the architectural style of the residence. And in a game of tit for tat, President Reuel returns her argument about 'dignity' by making it clear 'that his companion could not go about with him in cotton shifts, jeans, and sandals made by street cobblers' (1987: 307). But the reader understands that this is not a problem, since 'she knew fine fabric and good cut; as a child performed the equinoctial rites of storage, carrying silk and suède garments against her cheek' (1987: 307). At this moment, Hillela no longer eludes her personal past or the categories of her present context. On the contrary, she revels in them.

Her utopian moment is one of submission, and there are other implications to this than patriarchal subjection. Regardless of gender, the text seems to say, constructive engagement requires submission. Or, which is a more controversial way of putting it, political agency can emerge only when the subject *chooses* its subjection. This is, interestingly, the same understanding that emerges from the 'local' context of Rosa in *Burger's Daughter* as well as of Sasha, both of whom are otherwise read in opposition to Hillela. In the penultimate sentence of his prison letter, Sasha explicitly claims a paradoxical freedom: '*From jail, from here I'm free to say everything*' (1987: 324). Rosa's and Sasha's choice of subjection is, of course, particularly drastic, but it is structurally concomitant with Hillela's self-imposed stylistic and social discipline, which means that she incorporates, rather than quixotically resists, the absurd levels of incommensurability between the various temporalities that state power negotiates in a globalised age. (This is an incommensurability which is exacerbated precisely by the combination of social elevation and ethical ambition.) This also leads to a vision of Africa in which there is nothing 'purely African' in the contemporary context except that which is historically and culturally impure, hybrid, appropriated, refurbished. Following the shock and devastation of colonial modernity, the novel seems to demonstrate that there is no going back, there is only the possibility of reassembling the tatters of a compromised history. In so far as any claims are made specifically for 'Africa', they are to be found in Reuel's ultra-pragmatic credo on the first occasion that he and Hillela meet:

—I was going to train for the priesthood, at one time. That's a fact! But once in this world, you have to decide what you are doing here. I became an African nationalist; but it wasn't the church, it was Marx who told me why that was. So I'm a Marxist. My own kind. A Catholic Nationalist Marxist— African-made—
—Like the nightclubs in West Africa.—
—No, don't laugh—it's part of the same thing. Whether I'm inside, in our bush headquarters, or outside, making deals with our brothers (oh of course, Arab brothers, too) or in bed with a woman, it's all part of my African-made— work, love-making, politics, economics. We've taken all the

things the world keeps in compartments, boxes, and brought them together. A new combination, that's us. That's why the world doesn't understand. We don't please the West and we don't please the East. We never will. We don't keep things separate. Isn't that what orthodoxy is—separation? We make our own mess of things. They interfere; we ask them to interfere—what else am I doing? What else were you doing in Europe? (1987: 266).

Reuel's inside/outside corresponds to the local/global split – but the split is not there, for him. Both aspects form part of a seamless continuum. To claim that only the world – and never Africa – keeps things in boxes is an overstatement, but in this happy embracement of heretical hybridity I see a point of convergence with Ndebele's inclusive ambivalence. Africa thus defined is not a place or a cultural essence, but an attitude, a way of relating to and translating between disjunctive pockets of time. It is defined, we might say, as a *style*, not essentially different from other globalised versions of the world, only more successful at reconciling the irreconcilable.

There is a lot of wishful thinking at work here. State House is no longer a promise of happiness, but its consummation. Its exceptionally well-oiled domestic and public machinery, the unquestioned economic and political success of President Reuel, and the final chapter which describes the ANC's takeover of power in South Africa underscore the allegorical aspect of *A Sport of Nature*: Hillela is more a principle and precursor of human fulfilment than anything else. Given this conclusion, it is certainly in its place to ask: how come this is emphatically *not* the rainbow family (1987: 310)? What other utopian element is at work here?

There are two ways of answering this. Firstly, State House by far transcends the private closure of the rainbow family. Secondly, the mode of reconciliation of State House does not abolish conflict *per se*. It is directed towards catachrestically negotiating contradictions and ironies rather than transcending them, or retreating into the comfort of essentialising certainties. Thus, the rearticulation of 'Africa' into manipulations of style and attitude causes a *double* articulation that is ultimately directed towards the erasure of 'Africa' (not least since Hillela out-Africanises most 'blacks'), or its un-invention, to paraphrase V.Y. Mudimbe, but nonetheless places its solidarity among those whose subjectivity is projected as the other of Europeans, or Americans, or even Arabs (1987: 266). This double articulation of 'Africa' also becomes a transposition of modernity and postmodernity, since both these concepts, notwithstanding their global reach, are still so firmly grounded in a Western metanarrative.

Hillela, as a utopian, allegorical figure, thus does not 'change' the world in the strong sense – she does not remake its contents – but her displacement as political subject is at the same time a manifestation of solidarity. This solidarity functions as the minimum requirement for Hillela's redemption from the ethical vacuum of sheer pragmatism. By claiming centre-stage for modernity's and postmodernity's other – Africa as the Dark Continent in the first case, as the barely modernised continent still marked by authenticity and depth in the second – precisely within a version of the postmodern, *A Sport of Nature* foregrounds the trace of the other, the excluded term, and releases it from the conceptual stasis of otherness.

This reading also affects our understanding of the ending. What is most obviously read as a self-consciously hyperbolic vision of what came to pass seven years later, namely, the ANC's ascension to power and the consolidation of 'South Africa' as nation – as a 'local' entity – in 1994, can also be understood as a precursor to the dissolution of 'South Africa' in its self-enclosed form. Through its reinsertion into a global circulation of signs and commodities, the specificity of the local struggle is all of a sudden muddled, squandered, displaced. The ironical asides are legion. Whereas Olga's sons remain in the 'new African state that used to be South Africa' (1987: 337), with one of them – Brian – negotiating 'trade alliances with the world from which the old white regime was excluded, in particular the Afro-Asian and Eastern blocs' (1987: 340), Sasha lives in the Netherlands. When the local struggle is consummated, most emblematically in the image of the old South African flag that is hauled down and ripped to shreds at the stadium where the celebration will take place, the moment is instantly globalised by 'television crews from all over the world' who, according to the simulacral logic of the media, are first of all concerned about making good 'coverage', never mind the specific, irreducible quality of the moment (1987: 339). The contrast with Sasha's prison-letter is clear whereas the intense authenticity of the letter could not reach beyond its local context, unable to wilfully foreground its own status as representation, the televised image cuts through the authentic moment of the flag, transforms it into simulacra reproduced endlessly in its transmission across the globe.

It is to this new global logic that Hillela and Reuel present a solution of sorts, with their ability – which mirrors Brian's business negotiations – to move themselves as effortlessly as televised images among 'the American Assistant Secretary of State for African Affairs, the director for Africa from the French Foreign Office, the East German Ambassador or the heads of African states' (1987: 332), as well as among exhausted 'exiles, flying from country to country with the responsibility of arguments, strategies, methods of presentation and persuasion to be carried from offices up rickety stairs to State anterooms, from bush camps to Intercontinental Hotels' (1987: 332). Hillela and Reuel are mimic people. Through mimicry, they unsettle the master discourse, but they also grant themselves a place among the living in the current world, the same world that seems, pessimistically, to ensure that the new 'South Africa' will not be the same country that was dreamt of in struggle.

> Hillela is watching a flag slowly climb, still in its pupa folds,
> a crumpled wing emerging, and—now!—it writhes one last
> time and flares wide in the wind, is smoothed taut by the fist
> of the wind, the flag of Whaila's country (1987: 341).

The final words of the novel could also be read: the flag of the dead man's country. The country of those alive has a host of other flags. They flap mutely as we turn the pages of *A Sport of Nature*.

PART 4

'. . . a wrong story, always wrong'

Reading the Ethically Sublime in J.M. Coetzee's
Life & Times of Michael K

Art then lets go of the prey for the shadow.

Emmanuel Lévinas ('Reality and Its Shadow' in
The Lévinas Reader, *1989: 141)*

CHAPTER 13

Critical Responses to *Life & Times of Michael K*

THE MEDICAL OFFICER at Kenilworth Rehabilitation Camp stands as a warning to any reader who dares to approach J.M. Coetzee's novel *Life & Times of Michael K* with a hermeneutic ambition. The officer narrates the second part of the novel in a manner that harks back to other troubled first-person narrators in Coetzee's fiction, namely Eugene Dawn in *Dusklands* (1974), Magda in *In the Heart of the Country* (1978), and the Magistrate in *Waiting for the Barbarians* (1981). The medical officer's voice is reflective, self-denigrating, subdued. He is the generic frustrated liberal, side-stepped by history yet destined – as master, as a site of privilege – to suffer the consequences of this history. Hence, he is a profoundly ambivalent character, a figure of authority whose authority is dissipating. When confronted with the prisoner Michael K he demands to hear K's *story*, but K tells him next to nothing. We could perhaps ask if this is due to a failure of authority or to the fact that K actually has nothing to tell. There is, after all, a certain barrenness about *Life & Times of Michael K* and its narration of the travails of a 30-something gardener struggling to live through the turbulence of a civil war.

The country experiencing this upheaval is understood to be South Africa. Towns, regions, beaches and sports stadiums have names that correspond exactly to South Africa's known contemporary topography, and 'place' is thus easily identified in realistic terms. As for 'time', it is generally agreed that *Life & Times* depicts the 'future of the present', which means that it extrapolates political tendencies in the South Africa of circa 1980 (Attwell, 1993: 90–91). The 'signs' of the times are, briefly, curfews, raids, roadblocks, internment camps and mass displacements of people.

The narrative begins when Michael K's mother, who suffers from dropsy, wants to leave the Cape Peninsula for her childhood home in Prince Albert. Amidst great difficulties, Michael K tries to take her there on a wheelbarrow. She dies halfway, after which K continues the journey alone with his mother's ashes in a box. He reaches an abandoned farm, begins to settle there, but leaves when the proprietor's grandson – a conscript on the run – arrives. K spends time alone in the mountains, lands in a labour camp, escapes, spends time on the farm and nearly dies of illness and starvation, is captured again for a longer period, but escapes once more with the ambition to go back to the farm. Upon each return (or prefigured return, as at the end) to the land that he cultivates, K's presence is exceedingly subdued.

Hence, the external facts of K's life are indeed quite bare. Not much happens in his world, particularly when compared with the historical drama that is unfolding around him. If the 'times' are unbearably full, K's 'life' appears empty. This is thematised in the novel, and Michael K himself reflects on what a 'paltry' story he has to tell (1983: 240). The emptiness of Michael K as subject alludes, moreover, to the more famous K in Kafka's novels, also adrift in times that he cannot fathom (Merivale, 1996: 152–167; Penner, 1989: 91–93). Yet, for the medical officer, this empty story is reduced even further, as though it were his very attempt to extract the story by decree that denies him of it. Standing firmly in a world of binary oppositions, he decides instead that there is no story. To his superior he implores: '*There is nothing there*, I'm telling you, and if you hand him over to the police they would come to the same conclusion: there is nothing there' (1983: 194).[1]

Whether there is a story or not, the novel associates me, the reader/critic, with the medical officer, places me alongside the scouts, interrogators, diagnosticians and cartographers of Empire as I focus my gaze on Michael K to determine what order of meaning can be extracted from him. I cannot hide from this fact, only concede my daunting privilege as an agent of reading.[2]

Reception and controversy

The hermeneutic challenge of *Life & Times* tends to cripple the authority of both reader and writer. Accordingly, Coetzee's refusal to 'give voice' to the subaltern figure of Michael K and affirm his agency in the contested political field of South Africa has provoked a wide range of responses since the novel was first published in 1983. On the side of the critical field that insisted upon literature's mimetic and (as a political consequence of mimesis) utopian role, Coetzee was praised for 'finally', after three dire experiments in allegory and derealisation, depicting a recognisable South Africa – but at the same time censured for his lack of political affect. The most often discussed instance of this critique has been Nadine Gordimer's review, where she derided the 'revulsion against all political and revolutionary solutions' that apparently emanates from the novel (1984).[3]

Less critical, but still intent on retrieving the ethico-political potential of literary representation, Stephen Watson and Stephen Clingman have each commented on *Life & Times*. In 1985, as one of the first to appreciate the importance of positionality to Coetzee's writing-practice – Watson invokes Albert Memmi's phrase 'the coloniser who refuses' to describe Coetzee's dilemma – and prove himself equal to the philosophical challenges of the fiction, Watson remains frustrated by Michael K's retreat from history and the 'failed dialectic' in Coetzee's fiction (Watson, 1990: 54).

Clingman's resolution of a similar frustration leads to the Adornian notion of a 'negative dialectic':

> Rather than constructing an antithesis to colonial or imperial power, it rejects that temptation at the same time as it does the dominant term, and this becomes a different kind of antithesis (hence in Coetzee's latest novel, *Foe* (1986), it is Friday's *silence* which is his ultimate resistance). In this scheme of things perhaps it would be the refusal in turn of that negative antithesis at some future stage which would introduce a synthesis of yet again a very different kind: a history which at present is literally unthinkable (1990: 49).

This makes considerably more of Coetzee's oblique relationship to the main current of literary/political resistance in South Africa. Even so, Clingman makes two assumptions that elide much of the critical potential of the novel. The first is that *Life & Times* relates to history in an ontological sense rather than 'history' as a discursive category. The second is that the novel must be read in terms of representation rather than performativity and/or metafictionality. It is, as we shall see, in opposition to these assumptions that the most productive readings of *Life & Times* have emerged.

The two remaining attempts at 'making sense' of the novel within the representational paradigm are those of Dick Penner and Susan VanZanten Gallagher. Penner's cautious comparative readings amount mostly to an accumulation of paraphrase and conventional aesthetic observations (1989: 89–112).[4] His perspective is internalistic: the literary artefact is taken as given, as is the status of the author as intending originator of the text. This cuts against the main thrust of Coetzee's *oeuvre*, which simultaneously highlights its own position as 'literature' and places it under erasure.

Gallagher's approach is, by comparison, strongly externalistic. Driven by a sense of conflict and the imperative of resistance in the South Africa of the 1980s, Gallagher places the novel lengthwise along this historical moment. Her implication that the novel 'reflects' the increase in political violence fails however to account for Coetzee's re-inscription of and departure from the spectacular mode of representing South Africa (1991: 136–146).[5]

A properly metafictional (and more adequate) understanding of *Life & Times* was first elaborated by three different critics, more or less independently of each other, namely, Teresa Dovey (1988), Arnim Mennecke (1991) and David Attwell (1993).[6] Dovey sees *Life & Times* – a bit too restrictively – as a response to a particular genre, the story about the subaltern, as exemplified by Elsa Joubert's *The Long Journey of Poppie Nongena*. It is a genre that 'claims to give a voice to the voiceless victim' and hopes to 'create the impression that a life is unfolding itself before the reader with no intervention by the writer' (Dovey, 1988: 368). By effacing its own discursive status, the genre's most consequential implication is that the subaltern is a free agent, unaffected by the controlling desire of writer and reader.

Coetzee's subversion of this genre takes the form of 'text construction' as opposed to realistic narrative. This is where Dovey locates the emancipatory potential of Michael K himself:

if, in the mode of realism, the obscurity and mute presence of this type of protagonist offer the possibility of a story, of exposing to view what has up until now remained concealed, in the mode of text construction this same obscurity allows the writer to construct a figure of so little substance that s/he is able, in some measure at least, to elude this hierarchy of authorities (1988: 267–268).

Dovey then demonstrates how *Life & Times* inhabits the structures of the genre, and succeeds in doing so – only to show how Coetzee turns these generic expectations about face and victimises the reader, as it were.

In order to pinpoint just how the genre is abandoned after its resurrection, Dovey borrows the term *atopia* from Barthes (Dovey, 1988: 289).[7] The word is defined in opposition to 'Utopia' and signifies 'drifting habitation'. It refers to K's ability to move laterally across the structures that inscribe him without *reacting* against them. When we arrive, therefore, at K's (as it seems) only affirmative act, that of cultivating a garden, Dovey insists on its proximity to the act of writing and, more significantly, to that of Derridean dissemination, a process which enables the text by castrating the phallic authority of the author. Thus, K, having first emerged from the generic image of an appropriated victim, now stands for 'a mode of writing that would relinquish control over meaning' (Dovey, 1988: 296).

The aporia hinted at here – between articulable genre, narrative and meaning on the one hand, and the inarticulable freedom from determination on the other – finds its resolution in K's release from time, which, simultaneously, is the writer's freedom from having to 'bring the self into being in the narrative present' (Dovey, 1988: 323). At this stage, Dovey's argument becomes susceptible to the same type of critique against closure and 'ultimate' meaning that she reads from *Life & Times*. Cast as critic, Dovey falls prey to the imperative to chase out every last unclarity, even when these verge on the unutterable.

In the only German monograph on Coetzee – and as such largely ignored – Arnim Mennecke pushes one ironical possibility of *Life & Times* to the limit. He concludes, like Dovey, that the novel problematises the liberal appropriation of the subaltern, and he decides that the entire first part of the novel is the medical officer's redemptive fantasy of Michael K's life. The actual start of the novel would therefore be the moment of K's capture at the end of Part I. Frustrated in his desire to know what preceded that moment, the medical officer invents a life for Michael K that relieves his own angst and delivers him from the stasis of history (Mennecke, 1991: 129–173). This is a bold and intriguing interpretation that fulfils (one aspect of) the internal logic of Part II, but it remains unsatisfactory precisely because it allows the second part to subsume the novel in its entirety. Rather than destabilise the already fractured hermeneutic regime of the medical officer, Mennecke's reading consolidates it.

David Attwell's reading of *Life & Times* reinscribes the textual slant of Dovey's analysis in a historicising mode. He contextualises the novel at three different levels: firstly, with regard to political developments in South Africa when *Life & Times* was written; secondly, in relation to Coetzee's *oeuvre* (up until *Age of Iron*); and thirdly, in view of the aesthetic and philosophical challenges that Coetzee addresses (Attwell, 1993: 88–103).

At the first of these levels, Attwell underlines the political stasis of the period. Coetzee's rendition of a near future points above all to 'the *consequences* of the state's spectacular failure to address the essentials of the crisis it was facing' (1993: 91). I agree with, and shall eventually elaborate, Attwell's contention that the scenario of *Life & Times* is not apocalyptic, but depicts instead increased surveillance, militarisation and anomie (1993: 91).

At the next level, Attwell argues that *Life & Times* (along with *Foe*) constitutes a third phase in the *oeuvre*. If the first two novels, *Dusklands* and *In the Heart of the Country*, constitute an attack on 'the rationalist, dominating self of colonialism and imperialism', *Waiting for the Barbarians* is a pivotal work which uses rather than displays formal conventions with an end to representing History as such as a product of Empire (Attwell, 1993: 5, 70). (In the early work, 'history' was taken to be the captive of Empire, rather than its offspring.) *Life & Times*, then, may be said to emerge from a struggle to release the potential of writing from the double burden of imperialism and history, and celebrates in its way a limited freedom of textuality and narration (Attwell, 1993: 88).

The issue of textuality leads to the third level, where Attwell follows Dovey's statement on the freedom of writing, and detects, in Michael K, a Derridean theme. The medical officer's frustrated attempt to interpret K – which generates his reflection on how 'outrageously a meaning can take up residence within a system without becoming a term in it' (1983: 228) – is hence the most critical moment in the novel:

> what is presented here is the capacity of the novel to 'get behind' itself and displace the power of interpretation in such a way that K is left uncontained at the point of closure. This is how one might speak of K as the narratological figure of the Derridean trace. Coetzee's metafictional frame produces the deconstructive gesture of erasure. K's 'essence' is allowed to slip back into the open-endedness of textuality from which it comes and to which it returns (Attwell, 1993: 99).

I sympathise with this textualised reading, even though Attwell may be accused of asserting it all too conclusively. This forcefulness is a paradoxical weakness here as well as in Dovey's and Mennecke's readings: they all seem to be *cornering* Coetzee's novel. I prefer instead to regard these analyses as starting-points that confirm the productivity of the narrative and enable an ironic and eternal return even to the representational aspects of the novel. The 'open-endedness' of K is precisely what invites us to produce new readings. That is to say, to reread *Life & Times* is to go with the grain of the novel, not against it, as has been the case with *Fools* and *A Sport of Nature*. I might go even further and claim that the *only* way to be 'true' to *Life & Times* is to continually produce an array of heterogeneous readings and thus obstruct the construction of a singular truth about the novel. This does not mean that anything goes, but it does mean that within the enclosure of the novel, no end needs to be in sight.

The ethics of reading

Such an ambition still begs the question, however: just *how* do I exit the hermeneutic impasse of either assuming the (ultimately failed) imperial authority of the medical officer or abdicating all ambitions to say anything but what the novel already says? This is where the Levinasian approach of recent Coetzee criticism comes in. Broached by Derek Attridge (1994: 59–82) and elegantly sustained by Mike Marais (1998a), this perspective rearticulates the reading/writing of alterity in terms of relation rather than appropriation.[8]

Marais introduces a full-scale Levinasian perspective and rereads Michael K as a consciousness that constitutes, in a phenomeno-logical sense, its own world. By closely comparing *Life & Times* with *Robinson Crusoe*, Marais argues that Michael K first assumes an imperial subject-position, but that he is ultimately 'held hostage' by the ethical imperative of caring, at which point he departs from the imperialist narrative. Subsequently, in the shift of point of view in Part II, Marais locates a self-reflexive manoeuvre that enables the novel to place its own representations in brackets and thus allow the idea of an infinite alterity that is absolutely beyond the reach of the text to be implanted in the reader (1998a: 132–192).

In pursuit of this argument, it must be stressed that Coetzee's novel posits structural correspondences between narration, representation, interpretation and knowledge. Each of these terms involves an act of conceptualisation on behalf of the knowing subject. Conceptualisation, in turn, involves the exercise of power over others. As an alternative to merely accepting the conceptual violence of interpretation, reading as relation would entail an ongoing response to and reflection on the alterity of the text – its irreducible *interruption* of my apparently sovereign being – without laying claim to its 'meaning'. This might sound like mere word-play: after all, what form of interpretation is not also a relation? And doesn't violence as such also count as a relation? The crucial point in Lévinas's argument is, however, that a relation with alterity *qua* alterity precludes violence *by definition* (1982: 90–95). Violence, appropriation and comprehension (the thematisation of the other in the terms of the Same) deny alterity. The additional objection – that no reading can ever *refrain* from the violence of comprehension or appropriation – therefore necessitates the constant reminder that the alterity of the text always lies elsewhere than in the reading.

If Coetzee, in Marais's understanding, writes with his eyes shut, then I shall try to read through the corner of my eye (Marais,

1998b: 43–60). My focus is always somewhat beside the mark, and *must* be so. It is by insisting on this predicament, and not by chasing the Holy Grail of a wholly non-appropriative form of reading, that a relation with alterity is made possible. Therefore, this relation does not really belong to knowledge, or interpretation, or philosophy, but to ethics.[9]

Blankness

Mindful of this dire qualification of the reading act, the Levinasian perspective *also* opens a number of interpretive possibilities, particularly with reference to the ambivalent status of Michael K's subjectivity. These interpretive openings lead in the same direction, however, as the foregoing discussion: they aim at simultaneously enabling and disabling a focus on alterity which, in turn, discloses the ethically sublime aspect of Coetzee's novel. In the chapters which follow I shall therefore conduct a combined close reading and philosophical argument with a view to establish, firstly, the narratory nuances of two divergent aspects of K's subjectivity – the intentional and non-intentional aspects – through a Levinasian critique of the knowing, sovereign subject; and then secondly, proceed to discuss how, at the level of 'war' and history, the novel performs a gesture of evasion and excess similar to the evasiveness of the figure of K. On both counts I argue that there are catachrestic elements, generally coded as 'blankness', that mark the formal conditions of (im)possibility for the narrative to fulfil its ethical project and clear a space for alterity. Although it gestures to an alterity that lies elsewhere than in the text, blankness itself should be understood as a formal quality that is read off from the linguistic construction of the narrative.

I distinguish between three types of blankness. The first is connected to K's subjectivity and can be construed either as a mental black-out, an absence – 'he felt stupidity creep over him like a fog again. He no longer knew what to do with his face' (1983: 88) – or as an intensity of being, of stillness and listening, of presence. A good example of the latter is K's experience in the mountains:

Everything else was behind him. When he awoke in the morning he faced the single huge block of the day, one day at a time. He thought of himself as a termite boring its way through a rock. There seemed nothing to do but live. He sat so still it would not have startled him if birds had flown down and perched on his shoulders (1983: 91).

The second type of blankness is not tied to the representation of the character's 'experience', his story, but rather to the way the story is told. Blankness is first of all inscribed in the primary signifiers of the story. It is there in the name 'Michael K', a combination of letters which is replaced by the even blanker 'K' – suffused intertextually with the anonymity of Kafka's K (Dovey, 1988: 265, 275; Merivale, 1996: 160) – or equally blank misnomers such as 'Michaels' or 'Mister Treefeller'. It is there, not least, in the ironic title with its reminiscences of English eighteenth- and nineteenth-century writing. In so far as the letter K is blank, so are 'his' life and times blank. (After all, whose life and times would this be?) Indeed, K could be seen as the negation of the novelistic convention of character, as Teresa Dovey claims, contrasting him to Alain Robbe-Grillet's ironic description of what goes into the construction of a character (name, property, parents, profession) (1988: 274).

It would, however, be fairer to say that the character convention is not negated, but stripped. K does, after all, have a name, but it is not used. He does have a mother, who dies. He does have a profession (as a gardener) but has been made redundant. 'K' is what remains when everything else has been removed – and what remains is not nothing.

Blankness, finally, in relation to every political, historical, even biological determination is what the curious slant of the narration incessantly produces. Nothing is ever explained in other terms than those that represent it in the first place – and when the medical officer enters with a wholly different narrative ambition, he too is forced to abandon the desire to explain and command. This point is borne out by Attwell:

> In a frenzied culture such as South Africa's [. . .] every sign, no matter how innocent, becomes a signifier at another level, pointing to the larger conflict. Within such a context there is no such thing as an irreducible element.

This is the context that makes the phenomenon of K – to use the Medical Officer's terminology – 'scandalous' and 'outrageous'. K is not a representative figure who models certain forms of behavior or capacities for change; rather, he is an idea floated into a discursive environment that is unprepared to receive it (1993: 100).

An idea that will not be received by its environment: isn't this the basic predicament of each of the three texts that I attend to in this book? Are they not all striving to articulate subjective and aesthetic options not provided for in the current historical context? And is this perhaps the point where the issue of blankness, of un-representability, becomes possible to historicise at a sufficiently general level that cuts across all three texts? I shall return to these questions in my Conclusion.

What needs to be added is that in *Life & Times* history itself undergoes the same significatory implosion as K's subject-position. History is in this respect not privileged, and the novel's blankness should therefore be read, at least initially, as an existential blankness in the Levinasian sense, undetermined by social circumstances. Specifically, the representation of Michael K corresponds to crucial moments in Lévinas's philosophy of the subject and the other.

To recapitulate: the disruption of representational expectations in blankness is what enables the novel to symbolically displace the discursive framework of colonialism/apartheid without envisioning the moment 'beyond' this framework. This reading supplements Marais's to some extent, but interrogates it also – my focus on the autonomous (and supposedly 'imperial') aspects of Michael K's subjectivity differs from his, and I view the tension between 'totality' and 'infinity' in different terms – as a tension not only between self and other, but also as a tension within the subject. Michael K is 'other' also to himself. As I proceed to the historical dimension of the novel, the analysis focuses less on the representation of subjectivity and more on textual manoeuvres that enable alterity to resist being appropriated by history. At this point, however, the novel's 'escape' from history will itself require historicisation. History, the 'rival' of Coetzee's writing, returns then to determine the conditions and limits of writing – not despite but because of the novel's ethical subversions. In the choice between history and its ethical erasure, in the choice between 'times' and 'life', I shall refrain from privileging any particular term and choose instead to uphold a sense of mutual crisis and aporia between the two.

CHAPTER 14

Lévinas and Passivity

THE REPRESENTATION OF Michael K corresponds specifically to crucial moments in Lévinas's philosophy of the subject and the other. Throughout his work, Lévinas returns repeatedly to the question of pre-reflective subjectivity. In opposition to Husserl's and Brentano's notion of consciousness as *intentional*, as always directed towards an object, and the privileging in Western philosophy of the *intellect* as the essence of subjectivity, Lévinas introduces the notion of *non-intentionality* in order to get behind this metaphysics of the self and grant precedence to alterity. In so far as the intentional subject is active and appropriative, non-intentional subjectivity should be taken as passive and vulnerable. Thus, he counters what Husserl called the *bonne conscience* of intentionality with the non-intentional:

> This implication of the non-intentional is a form of *mauvaise conscience*: it has no intentions, or aims, and cannot avail itself of the protective mask of a character contemplating in the mirror of the world a reassured and self-positing portrait. It has no name, no situation, no status. It has a presence afraid of presence, afraid of the insistence of the identical ego, stripped of all qualities. In its non-intentionality, not yet at the stage of willing, and prior to any fault, in its non-intentional identification, identity recoils before its affirmation (Lévinas, 1989: 81).[1]

Non-intentional, pre-reflective consciousness 'is from the start passivity' (Lévinas, 1989: 82),[2] a notion which is carried further in Lévinas's major work *Autrement qu'être ou au-delà de l'essence*. It now refers to an even more radical alterity – 'otherwise than being' – that forms the basis of the subject. Indeed, it is an alterity that precedes the subject and confers upon it a responsibility for the other that extends even beyond the death of the subject. Non-intentionality is the mark of alterity 'within' the subject. Alterity – and this has great consequences for the ensuing argument on *Life & Times* – is therefore operative in the subject as well as in the other person.

On such an understanding, the non-intentional inscribes the limits of the subject's powers. Early on, Lévinas makes a point of not only ascribing anguish to the solitary subject (as the existentialists did), but also pride, sovereignty, virility, 'the power to be able' (*pouvoir de pouvoir*) (Lévinas, 1979 [1948]: 35, 73). These capacities reach their limit in confrontation with the other. Or rather, the other is by definition *that which deprives the subject of its power*. The other signifies that the subject is 'no longer able to be able' (*nous ne pouvons plus pouvoir*) (Lévinas, 1979 [1948]: 62). This incapacity does not only emerge after the fact of the subject's emergence, but precedes it as well. Prior to the hypostasis of the empowered subject, there is always vulnerability, a moment of being *for* the other, rather than for oneself.

The radical thesis of Lévinas's thought is that the other cannot be *known*. Knowledge and understanding are both imperialistic categories, incommensurable with the ethical dimension of the face-to-face relation. The intentional operations of knowledge appropriate the other, totalise it and deprive it of its alterity. Instead, the other, *qua* other, surpasses understanding, surpasses philosophy with its traditional focus on the ego. The untotalisable other can only be compared to an irreducible infinity. Just as Descartes noted the paradoxical status of infinity as an idea – the event/thought that refers to it is infinitely smaller than its reality (the *ideatum*) and is incapable of containing it – so can the other not be captured or couched in philosophical terms but only be accounted for in terms of an irreducible ethical relationship: 'The idea of the infinite consists precisely and paradoxically in thinking more than what is thought while nevertheless conserving it in its excessive relation to thought. The idea of the infinite consists in grasping the ungraspable while nevertheless guaranteeing its status as ungraspable' (Lévinas, 1996: 19).[3] Thus, rather than giving us a philosophy of the subject as totality, Lévinas develops an ethics of the other as infinity, and the subject's subjection to the other.

At a metatheoretical level, Lévinas has come to be used *against* post-colonial reading. In a closely argued paper, Mike Marais criticises two post-colonial analyses of Coetzee and proposes Levinasian ethics as an appropriate alternative to the post-colonial approach (Marais, 1998b: 43–45). In the process, however, he reduces post-colonial studies to a straightforward case of resisting the 'centre' from the 'margin' (1998b: 44), an understanding which disregards the deconstruction of these terms precisely within the field of post-colonial studies (Hall, 1996: 246–250).

Rather than simplistically affirm the political cause of the other as defined by the metropolis, post-colonialism – as I have argued throughout this book – is an agonistic field of debate which, in its more sophisticated moments, unsettles the very logic of metropolis/periphery, centre/margin, same/other. This is why I argued in Part 1 for the appropriateness of Levinasian ethics in a post-colonial context. As Simon Critchley has put it, Lévinas's thinking is always double-edged, caught, as it is, in 'a double bind, belonging to the tradition and achieving a breakthrough that goes beyond the tradition' (1992: 69–70). In the present context, Lévinas's philosophy could therefore be regarded as a form of catachresis, akin to the catachrestic writing of Coetzee.[4]

CHAPTER 15

Michael K as Sovereign Subject

COETZEE'S NOVEL GENERATES certain generic expectations and then inverts them. Dovey has observed how Coetzee
fulfils certain demands inherent in the 'story about the oppressed',
but proves to be writing on the outer rather than the inner edge of
its arena (Dovey, 1988: 265–284). Thus, the other uncannily
precedes the Same, as in Levinasian ethics. My aim at present is to
pursue this argument as viewed from the narratory construction of
'Michael K'.

Other

There is a productive tension in the structure of *Life & Times*. There
is, first of all, an immediately observable difference between
viewpoints in the switch from Part I to Part II. The fictional
contract of Part I is that we are given access to K's own thoughts, as
well as his story, told in the third person. In Part II, it is the medical
officer who tells the story. In the very brief third part, finally, the
narrative returns to the first mode. Marais emphasises these shifts.
In fact, it is only in the tension between Parts I and II, he maintains, that the novel attains its metafictional level and places the
representation of Part I in question:

> By means of this structural contrast, then, the novel self-
> reflexively lays bare a 'dissonance' between its form and
> *ostensible* content and, in the process, establishes a
> homologous and supplementary relation between its form
> and those totalising forms which reduce an infinite 'reality'
> to a manageable, rational, coherent object. Accordingly, the
> novel points to a radical disjunction between the order of
> the other and a world of language and forms (Marais,
> 1998a: 175).

As for K's subjectivity, this reading posits a neat divide between ipseity ('sameness'; Part I) and alterity (Part II). Only in Part II, Marais contends, is K 'wholly other'; only there, through the refusal and failure to represent K, is there a relation of proximity to K (1998a: 174–175). Against this, I shall argue that such a reading is, in a sense, all too obvious in its acceptance of the novel's readerly bait. Instead, in my discussion of K as subject and other, I arrive at an additional complication: that the idea of infinity (or excess) does not emerge only in Part II, but is also present in Part I as a disturbance in the ipseity of K.

The obvious difference between narrative perspectives is bracketed by a less obvious play of difference within the horizon of each perspective. Therefore, the dual perspective on K as subject does not correspond to the Part I/Part II split. The alterity of K is also at play in Part I, as much as the ipseity of the medical officer is overrun by his own intimation of alterity in Part II.

In order to register this differentiality within Part I, it is first necessary to adjust the received view that the very 'essence' of Michael K's life is passivity. The notion of K's passivity does indeed grant us a point of encounter between *Life & Times* and Lévinas's ideas on passivity, but it is also questionable. K's passivity and alterity need to be qualified. For that reason I shall begin at the opposite end, by affirming his activity and power of initiative. Therefore I ask: what does K *do*, how does he *act*?

Mother

K is active in two general respects: he takes care of gardens and he takes care of his mother. Both actions denote respect, but describe different temporal vectors. To take care of your mother is to tend to your past, whereas gardening is directed towards the future, and is simultaneously at the mercy of the future. Gardening manifests a desire for what should and should not grow, but lacks the power to determine what will grow. In both actions, both manifestations of his capabilities, K is paradoxically held 'hostage' in the Levinasian sense.

K's care for his mother Anna sets the narrative in motion. In order to deliver her from the turbulence in the Peninsula, K builds a rickshaw of sorts. From that point onwards, K is almost constantly in motion. A few times, as a prisoner in internment camps, and for a brief season of farming, he stops moving. Otherwise, he is always wandering, drifting, cutting laterally across the face of society and landscape.[1]

K willingly exerts himself when caring for his mother. His painstaking work on the wheelbarrow/rickshaw provides a crucial example of his resourcefulness, of his ability to appropriate the world:

> now he returned to the project of using the wheels from his bicycle to make a cart in which to take his mother for walks. But though the wheel bearings slid smoothly over the new axlerod, he had no way of preventing the wheels from spinning off. For hours he struggled without success to make clips out of wire. Then he gave up. Something will come to me, he told himself (1983: 21).

> He worked all afternoon; by evening, using a hacksaw blade, he had painstakingly incised a thread down either end of the rod, along which he could wind clumps of one-inch washers. With the wheels mounted on the rod between the washers, it was only a matter of tightening loop after loop of wire around the rod to hold the washers flush against the wheels and the problem seemed to be solved. He barely ate or slept that night, so impatient was he to get on with his work. In the morning he broke down the old barrow platform-seat and rebuilt it as a narrow three-sided box with two long handles, which he wired in place over the axle (1983: 23–24).

The passage describes single-minded determination. Despite impoverishment, despite the lack of appropriate tools, K succeeds in bending the world to suit his needs. There is one brief moment of passivity ('something will come to me'), that places activity in question, but it is no more than a moment's pause in the flush of initiative.

As I have argued, however, K's intentional activity is not purely sovereign, but conditional on the mother–son relationship. In K's own understanding, his mother is his reason for being-in-the-world: 'he had been brought into the world to look after his mother' (1983: 9). Cleaning up the ransacked home of his mother's employers, he muses: 'I do what I do, [. . .] not for the old people's sake but for my mother's' (1983: 19). This continual directedness towards his mother effects an ironical inversion: he becomes his mother's keeper, his mother's parent, in fact. On their first outing with the barrow, the contraption is likened to a perambulator (1983: 27), and in his mother's hesitation – 'He had to coax her to get her in; it took a long time' (1983: 27) – we can sense how she intuits, and resists, the reversal of roles. Add to this the regressive rationale behind their trek: that his mother is returning to the place of her birth. This return is, however, ironically construed as his mother does not return after all (she dies along the way). K himself has no sense of an origin in Prince Albert, nor does he know where the farm his mother longed for lies or even what it is called. More than that, he understands that they probably won't make it, but lets his mother keep her illusions, as a parent might protect a child from uncomfortable facts (1983: 36). The only idea that K has of Prince Albert is a naïve, storybook image of rural bliss which smacks of the pastoral genre that Coetzee has repeatedly criticised and parodied (1988b: 62–81): 'He saw [. . .] in his mind's eye a whitewashed cottage in the broad veld with smoke curling from its chimney, and standing at the front door his mother, smiling and well, ready to welcome him home at the end of a long day' (1983: 11).

This dream-image must be accounted for, so stark is its *faux-naïf* colouring. The image extends an imaginary relationship with the mother into the future. It allows for the trip to Prince Albert to be not merely a duty performed, but also an attempt to reach this place of K's longing. But what kind of a longing is this? The preceding sentence states that just 'as he had believed through all the years in Huis Norenius that his mother had left him there for a reason which, if at first dark, would in the end become clear, so now he accepted without question the wisdom of her plan for them' (1983: 11).

In other words, K has habitually displaced his desire. He accepts that if his mother asserts the desirability of an undertaking, then he too should desire it. His desire is mediated.[2] Not only does he have no immediate access to 'reality' (Marais, 1998a: 136–137);[3] he does not even have immediate access to his desire. Unless he directly identifies with his mother's desire ('I do what I do [. . .] for my mother's [sake]'), or with the desire of some other figure of authority ('He did not know what was going to happen [. . .] there had usually been someone to tell him what to do next' [1983: 92]), his desire can at this stage only be expressed in imagery that is already available to everyone but no one in particular, in this case in the standard stock of children's drawings. As we can see, this mediation is also productive – it produces rather than expresses K's sense of what is real and desirable. This reiterates the irony of return that pervades the 'maternal' cycle of events: K's image of the farm cannot, at a flat, rational level, constitute a return for Michael K who has never been there, but formally, by being represented as already known, a ready-made, his naïve image does effect a return to the familiar. Just as Huis Norenius is called his 'father' (1983: 143), so can the image of the whitewashed cottage be said to pertain – in its specific conjunction of form and content – to the mother–child relationship.

The early travails of Michael K, the activity and intentional perception that he directs towards or on behalf of his mother, describe a circle. In Levinasian terms, K's intentional consciousness returns to the Same. His acts are acts of appropriation, enclosed within a tautological relation between parent and child (both subjects occupy both positions). Or, if not appropriations, then attempts at shielding the relationship from outright disruption by unforeseen occurrences, as when K fends off a pair of robbers (1983: 34). A drastic conclusion though it may seem, K's initial situation is akin to that of philosophical knowledge, in Lévinas's understanding:[4] 'Philosophical knowledge is a priori: it searches for the adequate idea and ensures autonomy. In every new development it recognizes familiar structures and greets old acquaintances. It is an odyssey where all adventures are only the accidents of a return to the self' (Lévinas, 1996: 14).[5] In his minimal way, K struggles while his mother is alive to ensure this return to the self by adequate means. When this order is at risk, the narrative registers the danger as humiliation. But it is first when K's mother dies that the order of the Same begins to be called into question.

Land

Just as the departure from the Peninsula was heralded by K's image of the cottage, so is his departure from his living mother accompanied by a pair of naivistic visions. Having been forced to leave her in a sorry state at a hospital in Stellenbosch, he sleeps alone and has a premonition of what awaits: 'He had a dream: his mother came visiting him at Huis Norenius, bringing a parcel of food. "The cart is too slow," she said in the dream – "Prince Albert is coming to fetch me"' (1983: 39). Later, after her death, he is summarily given a parcel containing his mother's few belongings along with a box that contains her ashes. The ashes shock K:

> So there is a place for burning, K thought. He imagined the old women from the ward fed one after another, eyes pinched against the heat, lips pinched, hands at their sides, into the fiery furnace. First the hair, in a halo of flame, then after a while everything else, to the last things, burning and crumbling. And it was happening all the time (1983: 44).

This second image seems to echo and invert a biblical scene – which would be reasonable in the context of K's strictly regimented childhood at Huis Norenius at which education in scripture would have been a standard feature. The women in the furnace recall the Old Testament story about Shadrach, Meshach and Abednego who are cast into a furnace. The phrase 'fiery furnace' corresponds to the choice of words in the *Standard Version Bible*. The significant contrast to that story is that here the old women burn, whereas in the 'Book of Daniel' the youngsters do not (Daniel 3: 13–27).[6] K's version excludes Providence: sheer entropy, no divine intervention. The significance of biblical allusion will emerge later in the chapter. For the time being, these visions simply emphasise that K's thinking – including both desire and repulsion – tends to function through mediated forms and images. K's intentional consciousness and sovereign subjectivity are undercut by a sense of predetermination; intentionality and sovereignty are 'set in place' by pre-existing forms. The sovereign subject which creates its being through intentionality is not autonomous but functions courtesy of a sovereignty constituted elsewhere. This predicament can be opposed only by surrendering sovereignty, as begins to occur after Anna K's death. Abandoned, Michael K's consciousness lapses sporadically into directionless. He is without a *raison d'être* in a literal sense: the loss of his mother means that he can no longer constitute his own being by directing it towards his mother. Within the context of my argument on intentionality, this is the single most consequential disruption in the narrative, more significant than K's arrival at the farm, or his periods of internment. And yet, 'disruption' is too definite a word for the process involved. There is no dialectic here, no reversal, just entropy, blankness, a petering out of intentionality. 'There were long periods when he sat staring at his hands, his mind blank' (1983: 45); 'Sometimes, as he walked, he did not know whether he was awake or asleep' (1983: 64). Lacking direction, he moves across the country at walking speed, sometimes following roads, sometimes not. His erratic physical movements correspond to his drifting between various states of consciousness. He is numb, drowsy at times, focused at others. It is in his repeated confrontations with bureaucratic and military force that his consciousness is coaxed up front, so to speak. At such moments he apparently summons an intention, points to the ashes he is carrying, and constructs a reason for his wanderings: he is headed for Prince Albert. The directedness of his consciousness continues to be mediated – through the ashes of his mother. Intentionality is summoned, it would seem, to *protect* the passivity in which K lingers.

In this part of the novel, prior to K's arrival at the Visagie farm, the road, the fence and the railway-line become signs of the coercions of intentionality. (I state this in philosophical terms now, but as we shall see later, it also contains an implied critique of history.) The road and the railway line enable action, motion, but they are couched within an expressly binary logic. Transported as one of a labour gang, K asks an elderly man where they are being taken. The man replies: "'Why does it matter where they are taking us? [. . .] There are only two places, up the line and down the line. That is the nature of trains'" (1983: 56). The road produces a similarly rigid logic. It is crucial for his (externally determined) ambition to arrive in Prince Albert, but it is also the cause of much trouble as a road means roadblocks and convoys. K learns to read the signs and avoid risks: 'When he heard the rumble of an approaching convoy he would creep away into the bushes' (1983: 54). Sometimes he abandons roads altogether and walks across country. He ignores not only the vectors of road and railway, but also the obstacles of fences. Fences are utterly conventional signs of unfreedom, but they are conflated with those conventional modern signs of freedom, namely, roads and railway tracks.[7] *The road also becomes a fence*, and the only gesture of release that remains is to cross it and ignore its direction.[8]

But if fences, roads and railway tracks are no longer opposing principles, does there emerge a new opposing principle? Yes, land itself, land which is charged with meaning in Coetzee's writing. Before *Life & Times* he dealt with the issue in all of his first three novels, and later he tackled the question head-on in *White Writing*. In *Life & Times*, the significance of land revises above all the approach to land in *Dusklands* and in *In the Heart of the Country*. In 'The Narrative of Jacobus Coetzee' (in *Dusklands*) the protagonist is famously overcome by the immensity of the land that he traverses:

> In the wild I lose my sense of boundaries. This is a consequence of space and solitude. The operation of space is thus: the five senses stretch out from the body they inhabit, but four stretch into a vacuum. [. . .] Only the eyes have power. The eyes are free, they reach out to the horizon all around. Nothing is hidden from the eyes. As the other senses grow numb or dumb my eyes flex and extend themselves. I become a spherical reflecting eye moving through the wilderness and ingesting it. [. . .] There is nothing from which my eye turns, I am all that I see. Such loneliness! Not a stone, not a bush, not a wretched provident ant that is not comprehended in this travelling sphere. What is there that is not me? (1974: 78–79).

Jacobus's hubris is generally read as philosophical parody. In his rovings across the face of the 'wilderness' Dovey recognises the Romantic inflation of the self (1988: 92). Watson (1990: 41), Attwell (1993: 37) and Marais (1998a: 89) point to the solitude of the rationalist Cartesian subject – which is also the imperial subject.

Following Descartes's severance of subject and object, the reasoning goes, the ultimate and logical consequence is Jacobus Coetzee's imperialist solipsism. In similar fashion, but sticking to the more immediate South African context, Michael Vaughan has read *Dusklands* as a devastating critique of liberalism (1982: 126). Whatever their specific formulation, each of these perspectives resonates with Lévinas's critique of Western philosophy. Jacobus's incessant reduction of everything to the same is an exemplary exposition of the workings of 'knowledge', as understood by Lévinas. The land becomes a 'theme' which is comprehended and cognitively domesticated. The obverse side of such magnificent egoism is alienation. Jacobus's only way of making contact with an alterity that surrounds him on all sides is through killing. The gun is his 'mediator with the world', his 'saviour', his mode of connecting to that which is not himself (Coetzee, 1974: 79).

Clearly, Michael K revisits the literary landscape of Jacobus Coetzee. Off-road, the sense of space and extension is similar. The Karoo has lost nothing in sublime potential, it would seem, in the space of two centuries. But this makes the differences all the more significant. Jacobus is an agent of modernity (in the most brutal sense) in a world coded as pre-modern (wild, unfenced) whereas Michael K is a postmodern figure traversing a fenced, modern space. In *Dusklands* we are confronted with the vertigo of boundlessness and the incessant expansion of a colonialist subject, in *Life & Times* it is the fact of boundaries and the radical contraction of the subject that constitutes the main vector of the story. However, Michael K should not be read as a mere inversion of Jacobus Coetzee. By implication, it is the latter's solipsistic experience of boundlessness that creates the boundaries of modernity. Therefore, K's position in the land is generally different but not antithetical to Jacobus's – it works according to another logic.

K is *not* the savage who approaches Jacobus from 'the fringes of the horizon', the wild other who crosses the threshold of his world and is subsequently subsumed and annihilated (Coetzee, 1974: 80). K does not belong in that conceptual register. As we follow his wanderings, we as readers cross a threshold in Western philosophy and approach (without attaining) the pre-reflective, hither side of consciousness. This is the aspect of subjectivity that is not reducible to consciousness, nor is it, as Lévinas is at pains to stress, equivalent to the unconscious. Whereas the unconscious, although clandestine, is made recuperable and thematisable through psychoanalysis, the hither side of consciousness – radical passivity – is unnameable, does not belong to being (as being is appropriated by thought) but precedes it always, is one of its conditions (Lévinas, 1996: 83). Such is the Levinasian notion of the 'otherwise than being' which has always already placed the subject in an ethical relation of absolute responsibility for the other. It is an irrecuperable level of subjectivity which does not ensure the return of the self to the self (that is, self-consciousness), nor is it possible to categorise since it eludes the object-status of categories, but is best thought of in the accusative, as vulnerability *to*, or responsibility *for*. It follows that reading a novel from the confines of such an elusive notion pushes the reader to the margins of representation. We will find that there are moments when the machine of representation blocks out its own function and, having stalled, burns a hole in the surface of the narrative. This is the significance of blankness.

Something occurs in the text as K becomes other than himself. What is effected in Part I is an oscillation between object and subject: between the apparently neutral mode of representing the actions of K and free indirect speech which presents the reader with K's thoughts. The 'otherwise than being' does not and cannot emerge in either of these modes, but the stalling of representation that I call blankness constructs a relation to it and is most striking in the subjective mode, that is, when K himself registers that he is other than himself, that there is a part of him that eludes his intentional consciousness.

But this argument is premature. We are not done yet with the transformations of K's intentionality, nor with the representation of his historical context. Following the progression of his intentional consciousness, his arrival at the farm constitutes a logical conclusion (but not closure – this is still in the first third of the novel). The passage from the Peninsula to the farm is the latter part of an odyssey, a homecoming which is consummated at the moment that K begins to cultivate the soil.[9] But what sort of a homecoming is it, and how do we read K's subjectivity as he arrives at the farm? Does he land in the familiar, as was prefigured by his naïve image of the farm? Is this the subjective odyssey that Lévinas has referred to, an adventure that ends in a return to oneself, or does it unsettle the very notion of a return?

Motherland

The questions that I raise are not easily answered, since K's sojourn at the Visagie farm involves a complex interchange between irony and gestures of depth and sincerity.

The situation as such is laced with irony. K does not know where his mother lived as a child. He tries two possible names of owners upon arriving in Prince Albert but neither is recognised. Instead, a shop-attendant suggests a third name, Visagie. In all likelihood, K's mother never set foot on the Visagies' place, but nothing definitely says that she did not. It is an abandoned farm that has not been attended to in years. It is a negation of the naïve cottage-Arcadia that K envisioned at the beginning of the novel.

And yet, K makes as if to settle there. A founding moment of this intention is when he blends his mother's ashes with the soil. In a first attempt to bury the ashes in the conventional way, he half-expects an epiphany: 'He closed his eyes and concentrated, hoping that a voice would speak reassuring him that what he was doing was right – his mother's voice, if she still had a voice, or a voice belonging to no one in particular, or even his own voice as it sometimes spoke to him telling him what to do. But no voice came' (1983: 80). The longing for a voice corresponds to earlier moments of mediated desire. K has hitherto required a stand-in, a representative or a representation, which validates his own actions or ideas. Even his most fervent moments of activity in preparing for their departure from the Peninsula were overshadowed at every turn by his mother. Now, when no voice comes, there occurs a break. On an unexplained whim, he spreads the ashes and turns them down into the soil. This act has a dual implication: it recognises the solitude which is the basic situation of the subject, and it effects an appropriation of the land. It follows that this 'was the beginning of his life as a cultivator' (1983: 81), in so far as cultivation involves activity in the most concrete sense, the activity of a sovereign existent manipulating the world to suit his or her needs. But there is also a sense in which the words 'beginning' and 'life' confer a peculiar meaning to the burial scene and to the act of cultivation. The reader is made witness to the construction of an origin, of the emergence of a human subject. Burial and cultivation belong, from an anthropological-cum-historical viewpoint, to the foundations of human culture. This implied understanding is contrasted in the novel by the contingency of the situation. There K stands, on a farm he has never seen before, with no inner voice to guide him – abandoned in a pre-ontological silence – enacting a ritual of inception, continuity and commitment. He makes of an arbitrary place a motherland, and thus binds his own being to the soil. He will later ask: 'But what if this farm was not her true birthplace?' (1983: 160). He tells himself that if 'my mother ever lived here I will surely know' (1983: 160), but his reflections just lead to the infinite regress of personal origins when he tries to imagine his mother's mother's mother's mother's, etc. mother. In other words, when he attempts to retrieve his roots and foundations, he confronts an abyss: 'the silence of time before the beginning' (1983: 161).

We can conclude that K's flagging intentionality after his mother's death is revived at the farm. But does this justify Mike Marais's argument that K's initial relation to the farm is marked by violence? (1998a: 142). And that his first acts – notably when he takes the farmhouse in possession and kills the goat – are equivalent to the coloniser's mastery of the wild? These are intriguing observations that fit in with the abundant intertextual links between Coetzee's novel and *Robinson Crusoe* (that proto-imperial narrative of the Western coloniser who cultivates 'islands without an owner') (Marais, 1998a: 145–157; Mennecke, 1991: 166–169). There are indeed many ways in which life on the farm-island at first runs counter to K's unfenced wanderings. The observation that he 'followed the perimeter fence all the way around the farm' (1983: 79), already describes a different situation, and the end of the same sentence – 'without meeting any living sign of neighbours' (1983: 79) – establishes a correspondence between the isolation of the farm and the isolation of the sovereign Cartesian subject. The fence inscribes a totality which is incapable of relating to alterity without reducing it to a term within totality. But the initial shift towards violence, possession and totality at the farm is more ambiguous than Marais will allow.

As stated, the farm is an indeterminate place which *passes* for K's mother's childhood home. When he spends his first night there, we read: 'Now I am here, he thought. Or at least I am somewhere' (1983: 71). The sense of minimal relief inscribed in the phrase 'at least' indicates an externally determined desire for situatedness. K knows that he ought to be *somewhere*, the underlying rationale being that if you are nowhere you are no one. The condition of possibility of the subject is closely associated with the rhetoric of physical presence – being *there*. This resonates indeed with a Levinasian critique of intellectualist ontology (in the sense that the intentional subject appropriates every place on behalf of its self-presence) – but is it an adequate approximation of K's initial subjective response to the farm?

His major act of violence, the killing of the goat, has nothing of Jacobus Coetzee's sadistic narcissism to it. As K kills the goat, he is not quite present in himself. He reflects upon his acts in a way which splits his subjectivity. 'I must be hard, the thought came to him. I must press through to the end, I must not relent' (1983: 73). This is not the voice of a confident expansionist subject. Rather, it is an ambivalent moment, at which K exercises violence with definite consequences, but does so without any strong conviction. This calls for a precise distinction *vis-à-vis* previous interpretations: K is at this point neither a wholly 'different kind of creature' from the coloniser, as Attwell has claimed (1993: 96), nor is he quite so close to the Crusoe/Jacobus paradigm as Marais maintains (1998a: 136). Thus, in the equation between self-consciousness and imperialist subjectivity (in an empirico-historical sense), the latter emerges as a logical but not necessary consequence of the former. The imperial subject's possessive relationship with the land is a position that is briefly open to K, but which he *does not* assume. He tries half-heartedly to assume this position at first, but even then it tends to repel him.

The point is borne out in the way that he relates to the house. His is an anxious appropriation: 'Though he continued to sleep in the house he was not at ease there' (1983: 80). Later on it is observed that he 'felt at home at the dam as he had *never* felt in the house' (1983: 135, emphasis added). The positions of proprietor and perpetrator of violence are prepared for him but do not appeal to his subjectivity. His strong intentionality when caring for his mother lacks a corresponding goal at the farm. For mere survival the goat is more than adequate and the house is inappropriate. 'There was nothing in the house of use to him' (1983: 78). 'The goat in the pantry was stinking. The lesson [. . .] seemed to be not to kill such large animals' (1983: 79). In leaving the large animals alone, K quickly turns to smaller game. At this stage, therefore, he functions according to the principle of adequation. Rather than be attracted to superfluous affluence, he shuns it. The power constructed in acts of goat-slaughter and his taking charge of the farmhouse is grand but meaningless. The challenge is to find ways of manipulating the world that appear meaningful in relation to the needs that cause them.

We find, accordingly, not an abandonment of the intentional subject at this stage, but an adjustment. K is turned not toward objects but towards meaning. Unlike Jacobus Coetzee, he does not succumb to the imperialism of the eye, nor does he endlessly postpone the loss of meaning by accelerating the pace of violence. Rather than appropriate as much of the world as possible simply because he is able (and he has proven himself to be able), he demands meaning of the acts he performs. This leads us to perceive a further dimension in K's treatment of his mother's ashes, which enacts a commerce with all-but-nothingness. Ashes are as far removed from being a concrete object while still remaining one as is imaginable. The ambivalent status of the box of ashes is remarked upon: his mother 'was in some sense in the box and in some sense not'(1983: 78). The box is the guarantor of meaning during his lonely wanderings. He cannot explain the purpose for wanting to reach the farm, but he points to the box (1983: 69), which in some sense contains the reason and in some sense not. The reason is unutterable. He cannot possess it but he can create a relation to it. His moments of failure as regards the box of ashes – when he expects its meaning and proper destiny to be revealed to him (1983: 79, 80) – are precisely due to a desire to possess the reason. It is when he relinquishes this desire that he is able to complete the burial and affirm the meaning of cultivating the ground. It follows logically that this is 'the beginning of his life as cultivator' (1983: 81). K is primarily directed towards the meaning of cultivation – rather than the possession of land – and this meaning is and is not gratuitous. It must be recognised as gratuitous but be treated *as if* it is not. Only then does K find it fit to bury the ashes and begin cultivating. When Dovey sees this purely as a dispersal of meaning and authority (dissemination) (1988: 295), and Mennecke ignores how K achieves his bond only when he no longer expects a transcendent authority to step in (1991: 163), both critics overlook the ambivalence of this firm-yet-ironic grounding of meaning.

It might even be a misnomer to call it ironic: it simply recognises meaning as ultimately blank but none the less crucial. Meaning thus becomes an other, in the Levinasian sense – inappropriable yet undeniable. And the person who claims possession of it is the one who per definition does not possess it. The boldness of refusing to possess meaning and yet rely on it, can be read in terms of profound ethical trust.[10] As I shall still argue, this trusting relation to alterity is enacted in the novel as a whole and emerges as the paradoxical prerequisite of its deconstructive scepticism. Trust in the future, trust in the non-text, trust in the reader: this is ultimately what enables the text to let alterity be, to refrain from legislating and asserting the imperial power of the hermeneut. The result of such trust might be labelled an ethically sublime mode of writing.

CHAPTER 16

The Alterity of Michael K

K'S RELATION TO meaning is redoubled in the text's relation to the alterity of K. Having said this, I also claim that the narrative does not escape the logic of intentionality but that it adjusts it.

Alterity functions catalytically in *Life & Times*. It causes disturbances in the regime of the Same (to which the order of narrative belongs) but is not, indeed cannot be, spent – in the sense that the representational manoeuvres of the narrative would 'spend' alterity by laying it bare. The narrative necessarily turns away from alterity but affirms its significance precisely in the act of turning away. Alterity is thus *brought to the reader's attention* without being appropriated. Or, to use Marais's terms, alterity is drawn but not represented (1998b: 51).

Stupidity, drowsiness, difference

In the first and third parts of the novel the alterity of K is approached/turned away from via K himself. The most transparent moments of alterity coincide with K's radical and deliberate descents into solitude, which occur during his stay at the cave – having fled the Visagie grandson – and during his second period at the farm. These two 'episodes' are paradigmatic. They code K's alterity, metonymically, in three ways: firstly, as stupidity/muteness; secondly, as drowsiness; and, thirdly, as a different mode of being (as regards eating, living, passing time).

In the first case it is registered by K as a loss, or a fall; in the second it is associated with sensual rapture; and in the third K *performs* difference – enacts a performative alterity – rather than responds to it. In the third case we might begin to speak of 'otherwise than being', of a state of subjectivity other than consciousness yet not defined *in contrast* to consciousness.

'Stupidity' tends to cause anguish. It emerges at specific moments when K feels cornered by the authorities, by the military, by the Visagie grandson. Not necessarily, though. It does occur that K *uses* stupidity at such moments, or rather the appearance of stupidity, to protect himself (1983: 55) but this is diametrically opposed to the more common fall into stupidity and muteness, when K is no longer in control. The fall into stupidity cannot be used since it marks the limits of K's power to be able: '[The grandson's] words [. . .] seemed to K to smother him. It is nothing but a manner, he told himself: be calm. Nevertheless he felt stupidity creep over him like a fog again. He no longer knew what to do with his face' (1983: 88). When confronted with medical authorities, he always feels lost (a crucial point if we consider that Part II is narrated by a medical officer): 'He stood before [the nurse] like a dumb dog while she wrote' (1983: 37). '"Do you want to make a phone call?" said the doctor. This was evidently a code for something, he did not know what. [. . .] People hovering over him made him nervous. He clasped his hands and stared hard at his feet. Was he expected to say something?' (1983: 41–42). '"How are you feeling today?" asked the doctor. K hesitated, not knowing what to say' (1983: 99).

Stupidity is the other of knowledge, muteness the other of speech – as defined within the realm of knowledge and speech. Both words converge in the English word 'dumb' and point to an aspect of K's subjectivity – point to it by rejecting it, giving it a derogatory name – which cannot be attained through the clarity of the reigning discourse. Above all, this inability involves a loss of freedom, hence the anguish.

Drowsiness, by contrast, is associated with freedom. Alone at his cave, K lovingly recalls a form of punishment exercised at Huis Norenius:

One of the teachers used to make his class sit with their hands on their heads, their lips pressed tightly together and their eyes closed, while he patrolled the rows with his long ruler. In time, to K, the posture grew to lose its meaning as punishment and became an avenue of reverie; he re-membered sitting hands on head through hot afternoons with doves cooing in the gum trees and the chant of the tables coming from other classrooms, struggling with a delicious drowsiness. Now, in front of his cave, he sometimes locked his fingers behind his head, closed his eyes, and emptied his mind, wanting nothing, looking forward to nothing (1983: 94).[1]

Drowsiness offers intense pleasure by facilitating the extinction of desire and intentionality. It is a condition of 'stupor' that K compares to 'bliss' (1983: 93). It is an experience that also emerges on the outside of clarity and knowledge, but without the threats or strict demands that cause 'stupidity'. Drowsiness requires solitude, or at least the right to retreat from social intercourse. It is, moreover, more similar to the indeterminacy of insomnia and the 'there is' than the definite state of sleep.[2] But not entirely similar. Insomnia is as helpless a condition as stupidity, whereas in the quotation above, K seems to invoke the blank state of drowsiness, or non-consciousness, actively. This is an important distinction. Such activity-in-passivity reaches its full-blown form in what I call K's performative alterity. Here, non-intentionality becomes not an 'experience' but emerges as agency. K achieves, in the words of Lévinas,

[duration] as pure duration, non-intervention as being that dare not be; the agency of the instant without the insistence of the ego [. . .] It has no name, no situation, no status. It has a presence afraid of presence, afraid of the insistence of the identical ego, stripped of all qualities. In its non-intentionality, not yet at the stage of willing, and prior to any fault, in its non-intentional identification, identity recoils before its affirmation. It dreads the insistence in the return to self that is a necessary part of identification (1989: 81).[3]

I shall demonstrate how this philosophical pronouncement corresponds, virtually segment by segment, to the most ascetic, 'other' moments of K's existence.

Duration as pure duration is an obvious point: few critics have refrained from commenting on K's escape from the calendar and the clock. During his sojourn in the Karoo, time 'was poured out upon [K] in [. . .] an unending stream' (1983: 139); time is 'flowing slowly like oil from horizon to horizon' (1983: 158); and K lives 'in a pocket outside time' (1983: 82). This is duration as pure duration. It is opposed to rational, recorded time which is explicitly associated with imprisonment: 'He had kept no tally of the days nor recorded the changes of the moon. He was not a prisoner or a castaway, his life by the dam was not a sentence that he had to serve out'⁴ (1983: 157–158). It is striking that K evades even the 'natural' time of the moon, a claim which calls into question Attwell's contention that cultivation is a deliberately conventional (and therefore insubstantial) theme and that K's 'temporal universe becomes the seasonal cycle' (1993: 96). Rather, K's unseasonal, 'untimely' cultivation, eventually carried out only at night, is demonstrably *un*conventional (1983: 139, 141). It has more to do with non-rational care and less with the rationale of farming.⁵ We should insist, therefore, that K's 'duration as pure duration' differs also from the seasonal cycle, which is, in its naming, already inscribed in an intentional logic.

As for the dread of insistence and affirmation expressed in 'the agency of the instant', this corresponds directly to K's timidity. Upon returning to the farm he is *determined* not to force his being upon the land. Determination opposes force. He refutes the logic of farming and mobilises a mode of agency that does something else than merely reproduces the behaviour of the colonising ego: 'whatever I have returned for, it is not to live as the Visagies lived, sleep where they slept, sit on their stoep looking out over their land' (1983: 134); '[the] worst mistake, he told himself, would be to try to found a new house, a rival line' (1983: 142–143). In fact, to live like the Visagies, to live in a house as such, is not to live at all (1983: 135). Therefore, K lives in a hole in the ground and seeks out transient materials: 'I am not building a house out here to pass on to other generations. What I make ought to be careless, makeshift, a shelter to be abandoned without a tugging at the heartstrings' (1983: 138). Indeed, 'his tools should be of wood and leather and gut, materials the insects would eat when one day he no longer needed them' (1983: 143). Stability, affirmation, the ego's return to itself in the regimented succession of generations: this is what K deliberately avoids.

In these passages we are still observing a reflective consciousness at work. It is drifting away from intentionality, it delivers itself to the earth rather than appropriates it, but it is still acting on intentions, and does so in a determined way. The path of least resistance would, after all, be to settle in the farmhouse and use all the tools that are available, but instead he laboriously carves his own dwelling out of the ground (1983: 137–138). However, there is a pre-reflective stage of subjectivity – which is also the final stage for representational strategies – at which reflection is abandoned.[6] Instead of reflection, the non-intentional and pre-reflective level is acted out, performed. This occurs only momentarily, but the diegesis of the narrative contrasts it clearly enough with the reflective level by shifting from direct and free indirect speech to external description. Thus, when embittered by the arrival of the Visagie grandson, K remarks that '[the grandson] thinks I am an idiot who sleeps on the floor like an animal and lives on birds and lizards and does not know there is such a thing as money' (1983: 85–86). K's resistance to such an imagined classification seems reasonable, but is contradicted by his own actions, since he does indeed eat birds (1983: 81), lizards (1983: 90), and ceases to relate to money. At other moments, he eats flowers, ant-grubs and bulbs (1983: 93), or, more commonly, simply forgets to eat. This forgetfulness of what he himself is doing points to a definite gap within K's subjectivity. All his concerted attempts to evade the logic of possession, coercion, and domination are still on that side of the reflective subject, of intentional consciousness. His determination to build a dwelling in the ground is intended not to rival the Visagie farmhouse, but his determination as such is still located in the logic of rivalry. By contrast, he is *not* in control of his moments of performative alterity – just as he cannot control the lapses into 'stupidity' (since he is at those moments not able to meet the external demands of the dominant rationality), neither can *his own* demands, *his own* determination, control his 'hither side of consciousness'. This, then, is also how I read the passage that follows K's own rationalisation of why he did not join the group of guerillas who camped nearby his dwelling:

Between this reason [that someone must stay behind and keep the idea of gardening alive] and *the truth that he would never announce himself,* however, lay a gap wider than the distance separating him from the firelight. Always, when he tried to explain himself to himself, there remained a gap, a hole, a darkness before which his understanding baulked, into which it was useless to pour words. The words were eaten up, the gap remained (1983: 150–151, emphasis added).

This is to say that the narrative establishes K already in Part I as radically exterior in relation to *himself.* His performative alterity is not 'otherwise than being', neither is his intentional consciousness. Rather, it is the unutterable distance between the two that is 'otherwise', the gap between K's determination to 'be other' and the represented acts of otherness – and this distance is coded as blankness in the representational structure of the narrative. The shift of point of view in Part II, quite drastic in technical terms, is therefore less drastic from a philosophical perspective. Whereas Marais sees a definite switch in the novel's relation to alterity as it is narrated by the medical officer – in the sense that it places the representation of alterity in Part I in brackets and highlights it *qua* representation – I claim that this relativisation, or intimation rather, also occurs in Part I (Marais, 1998a: 174–176).

But why is this nuance so important? In my view, it opens up a possibility for a more redemptive, or at least less crippling, relation with alterity than the purported Manicheanism of Part II, which places the reader in a strong imperial position. If, after all, there is a trace of an irretrievable alterity within the subjectivity of Michael K, an alterity that K senses, but which can only be turned away from, intimated through blankness, then there is a structural relation between totality and infinity within the subject that corresponds to the larger relations between reader and text, between subject and other, between Empire and land, etc. There is a level at which the colonising subject's predicament corresponds with the colonised subject.

Consequently, there is *less* of a disjunction between Parts I and II than immediately seems to be the case. The medical officer is just as incapable of explicating his own interest in Michael K, as K is unable to explain 'himself to himself'. In both cases, there is a radical loss of sovereignty. Neither K nor the medical officer are 'able to be able' in the face of alterity: in this they are similar, not different. The difference between them, in this regard, is the greater faith that the medical officer places in words, and thus his greater failure to relate to an unutterable alterity. The way in which he overstates his case, most emphatically in the 'letter' to K (1983: 206–208), is therefore not an aesthetic *faux pas*, but consistent with his more entrenched location in the Same, and thus his conviction that through words and knowledge, he will be able to enclose the essence of K. Knowledge is linked in this way to power. The medical officer is infinitely more powerful than K, but it is the very logic of power and appropriative knowledge that disables his relation to K. K, by contrast, relinquishes the desire for essences and definite knowledge. His inception of a motherland is therefore paradigmatic: he may have returned his mother to her home 'only by a trick of words' (1983: 160), yet it is this incredulous recognition that words are only words, that binds him more to that particular place than any bona fide legal or hereditary right. 'So, what is it', he asks himself, 'that binds me to this spot of earth as if to a home I cannot leave?' (1983: 171). It is, the novel seems to answer, the 'as if' that binds him, and enables him to be bound. 'As if' is a primary estrangement that saves K from the interminable estrangement of attempting to erase the 'as if'.

CHAPTER 17

The Plurality of Times

A S WE TURN to the 'times' of Michael K, we should choose our starting point in those frequent indications that the times could be something quite different than they are taken to be. This notion finds its most fluent articulation when K is isolated in the burrow. The issue at hand is the status of 'parasites' such as K himself or the camp-dwellers at Jakkalsdrif:

> Yet to K lying idle in his bed, thinking without passion (What is it to me, after all? he thought), it was no longer obvious which was host and which parasite, camp or town. If the worm devoured the sheep, why did the sheep swallow the worm? What if there were millions, more millions than anyone knew, living in camps, living on alms, living off the land, living by guile, creeping away in corners to escape the times, too canny to put out flags and draw attention to themselves and be counted? What if the hosts were far outnumbered by the parasites, the parasites of idleness and the other secret parasites in the army and the police force and the schools and factories and offices, the parasites of the heart? Could the parasites then still be called parasites? Parasites too had flesh and substance; parasites too could be preyed upon. Perhaps in truth whether the camp was declared a parasite on the town or the town a parasite on the camp depended on no more than on who made his voice heard the loudest (1983: 159–160).

Here is a vision of a specific order coming apart at the seams. Not through violence or force, since the order is precisely one of violence and force, but through something as seemingly unobtrusive as a change of focus. The alternative order of idleness is always there, but it is unacknowledged, *defined* as parasitical, insignificant, undesirable. The 'times' thus becomes a highly unstable signifier which could, feasibly, switch referent at a moment's notice, depending on 'who made his voice heard the loudest'. But as we explore the times represented in the novel, instability is extended also to the dominant historical paradigm itself, namely war. The war in the narrative is steeped in crisis, *is* crisis, but it is also turned away from crisis, randomly changeable. In this chapter I shall discuss just what is represented as pertaining to this war. In the process I shall also oppose representation with the conventionality of place-names as specific 'signs' of history. As will become evident, these conventional signs, along with the connotations they evoke, stand in a peculiar relation to the novel's representation of the times. They call, by implication, the certitudes of South African history into question and open up an ethical perspective that resists the imperative of political prescription.

Consequently, I am primarily concerned with 'history' *in* the narrative. This means that although the novel refers in any number of ways to a historically dense South Africa outside of the narrative, such reference may be read at first as serving the purpose of establishing an intradiegetic horizon (a textual 'universe') rather than commenting on what we take to be, discursively, the 'history of South Africa'. In this I follow Attwell, who argues that Coetzee is not concerned with history 'as such', but rather 'discourses of history, or the discourses of subjects positioned in history' (Attwell, 1990: 110). His remark finds renewed confirmation in the way in which *Life & Times* facilitates and blocks out the reader's access to the apparently real. The novel's 'ostentatious realism' (Attwell, 1990: 115), its assertion of what is discursively taken to be South African reality (that is, brutal oppression), is coupled partly with alternative representations of the real, partly with the foregrounding of the linguistic nature of the real, which is achieved mainly through an excessive employment of place-names.

War as/through deconstruction

The social upheaval in *Life & Times* is never explained. Instead, it is evidenced through a number of specific instances and occurrences.

It is also explicitly referred to as 'war', but in such a way that the word assumes common knowledge rather than explains to an outsider what it is all about. The actual term 'war' remains therefore curiously abstract, whereas the sense of violence and unease does not. We thus find a tension between 'telling' and 'showing'. Although these terms are imperfect as they stand, the distinction will help us to identify two different ways in which *Life & Times* relates to the notion of history.

We restrict ourselves at first to the narrative mode of 'showing', the accumulation of detail which is not different in principle from Nadine Gordimer's technique discussed earlier in Part 3. Characteristic of this mode is its tendency to present itself as unmediated, contingent, random. It is metonymical, alluding to a whole through the part. We find, in this manner, that signs of social deterioration rapidly accumulate in the novel. In the hospital where the reader first encounters Anna K, there are 'scores of victims of stabbings and beatings and gunshot wounds' (1983: 6). There is a curfew (1983: 8, 10, 14); public transportation is unreliable (1983: 8); new currency has replaced an old, valueless currency (1983: 9). All of these could be taken as signs of war – but not necessarily.

When Anna K dreams of escaping 'the careless violence, the packed buses, the food queues, arrogant shopkeepers, thieves and beggars, sirens in the night, the curfew, the cold and wet' (and her dream is mediated as K's longing as well, through his obligation to serve his mother) war-like conditions combine with a more generalised sense of unease (1983: 10), Likewise, there is a spontaneous and random outbreak of violence in the vicinity of Anna K's dwelling that has little to do with 'war' in the naïve sense of organised forces opposing each other (1983: 14–15). And yet, these events make K and his mother feel that 'the *real* war' has arrived (emphasis added). There is something definite implied by the word 'war' that is gainsaid by the contingent situations which K and his mother confront or avoid. 'War' becomes an elusive signifier which tries to square the circle by inscribing a radically indeterminate amalgam of situations. The word itself is thus involved in a semantic struggle, a struggle over the power to define the 'historical process' and thereby be seen to control it. The main (impersonal, collective) agent of this struggle is the state/military bureaucracy whose entire structure is geared towards control, but whose efforts to this end are frequently revealed as inadequate or futile. Despite 'controls on personal movement' – measures aiming at stasis – it is flux that dominates K's experience in the first quarter of the novel. Despite road-blocks, camps, curfews and raids, the 'parasites' live on. Despite a totalitarian 'totality' of repressive and disciplinary structures, the very subjects on whose behalf this totality functions – such as the Visagie grandson and the medical officer – lack faith in it.

War is intensified history. It is privileged in the novel's epigraph as 'the father of all and king of all'. It is, or is supposed to be, an ultimate signifier. Such power is, however, rendered impotent by what can justifiably be called a form of deconstruction: the war in the novel brings about an inversion, an implosion of power. Compare the war in *Life & Times* with a passage where Lévinas describes what occurred when France was occupied in 1940:

> A retreating military unit arrives in an as yet unsuspecting locality, where the cafés are open, where the ladies visit the 'ladies' fashion store', where the hairdressers dress hair and bakers bake; where viscounts meet other viscounts and tell each other stories of viscounts, and where, an hour later, everything is deconstructed and devastated; houses closed up or left with their doors open, emptied of their occupants who are swept along in a current of cars and pedestrians, through roads restored to their 'former glory' as roads when, in an immemorial past, they were traced by great migrations (Critchley, 1992: 151).[1]

This approximates the situation in *Life & Times*. Abandoned houses, roads and refugees, the retreat from hitherto semantically stable roles (covering the full range of gender, class and occupation) are main points of comparison. More important, however, is the context of the utterance itself: we are overhearing Lévinas's attempt to describe his experience of reading Derrida. This provocative metaphor – deconstruction as/through war – could also be applied to the war in *Life & Times*. The narrative's staging of a national crisis can be seen as facilitating a reading across, against, yet within the closure of a historical 'text'. As though war, which is 'history' and 'politics' in their most exacerbated forms, also undermines these terms and marks out their limits, relativises them.

I shall expand on this point, beginning with the most critical confrontation between K and 'the war', that is, when he is captured at the end of Part I. This is where the difference between the 'antagonists' is most extreme, with the war demonstrating its extreme appropriative power, and K languishing in his most radical moment of passivity. At the time of his capture, K's intentionality has been reduced to a minimum and he lapses frequently into the blank state of 'otherwise than being'. He lives in a burrow, he barely eats, he falls ill, he sleeps for days on end. A moment before he is picked up he is wandering about aimlessly, shivering with cold:

> He had no strength in his limbs; when he set one foot in front of the other it was tentatively, like an old man. Needing to sit all of a sudden, he sat down on the wet earth. The tasks that awaited him seemed too many and too great. I have woken too early, he thought, I have not finished my sleeping. He suspected that he ought to eat to stop the swimming in front of his eyes, but his stomach was not ready (1983: 165).

In terms of activity and intentionality, this is as close to nothing as we can get, short of sleep or death. But this is also where the military find K. At first 'they were ready to believe he was simply a vagrant, a lost soul the police would have picked up in the course of time' (1983: 165–166). But before long, these agents of 'war' close in on K. His house, or burrow, is found. Each of his few possessions is scrutinised, his pumpkins – which K has gone to great lengths to camouflage – are uncovered. Every detail fits neatly into an interpretive scheme, a hermeneutics of suspicion, that the soldiers have been trained at. One of them exclaims:

> 'You think there is nothing and all the time the ground beneath your feet is rotten with tunnels. Look around a place like this and you would swear there wasn't a living soul in miles. Then turn your back and they come crawling out of the ground' (1983: 167).

The hermeneutics is as much a part of the war as the acts of physical violence. The soldier *sees* only empty space, but he *knows* that this is a place of war, of a subhuman enemy that comes 'crawling out of the ground'. Such a superimposition of the known onto the seen repeats the imperialistic movement of the return to oneself. But the very confidence of this epistemic, bellicose imperialism transforms into the mark of arbitrariness. In Part II, the medical officer repeatedly refers to the area where K was found as a 'war zone' – as opposed to the Cape Peninsula (1983: 195). This is assumed to be common knowledge, but it contradicts Part I – as well as a statement by the medical officer himself (1983: 205) – in which K and his mother flee from the 'real war' (1983: 16) in the Peninsula, and the Karoo farm exists in a 'pocket outside time' (1983: 82). In this way, the novel simultaneously highlights and undermines the discursive aspect of war. Even as K is inscribed in the war and its discursive power seems absolute, we soon learn that the soldiers' understanding represents just one of several possible versions of the war. (By the same token, the novel calls its own representations into question. The confusion as to what is a 'war zone' makes the realism more provisional.)

This lesson is brought to its tragic culmination in the medical officer's narrative. It is tragic in the classical sense that he is destined to act against better knowledge. His agency is produced by and bound up with the bureaucratic structures of control, yet his writing is shot through with intimations of alterity within the war; of meanings, purposes, or possibilities that do not fit the official truth that he serves. The medical officer's irony betrays the pointlessness of 'rehabilitation'. K must recover so that he 'can rejoin camp life and have a chance to march back and forth across the racetrack and shout slogans and salute the flag and practise digging holes and filling them again' (1983: 183). Doubt, not faith, pervades the actions of the camp officials:

> Do any of us believe in what we are doing here? I doubt it.
> [. . .] We are given an old racetrack and a quantity of barbed
> wire and told to effect a change in men's souls. Not being
> experts on the soul but assuming cautiously that it has
> something to do with the body, we set our captives to doing

> pushups and marching back and forth. We also ply them with items from the brass band repertoire and show them films of young men in neat uniforms demonstrating to grizzled village elders how to eradicate mosquitoes and plough along the contour (1983: 183).

Rather than affirm the power over the soul exercised within this discursive framework, or, for that matter, the irreversible progression of modernity, the officer's tone evinces a radical lack of conviction.[2] His lack of faith is so abysmal that he does not even remember the official reason for fighting the war (1983: 215). 'The war' is thus shown to be a fragile concept at a relatively high level within the very bureaucratic structures that keep it going. By contrast, for the low-ranking foot soldiers who capture K, the war is a strong concept. For them, 'knowing' has precedence over 'seeing'. For the medical officer 'seeing' – seeing the prisoners, seeing K's face, seeing the futility of camp discipline – undermines propagandistic 'knowing'. But even this ironic knowledge does not really help him, since both 'knowing' and 'seeing' operate within the regime of the Same. What is seen is rapidly appropriated by the knowing subject, and the medical officer remains unable to escape the discursive logic of war. The significance of the weak status of the war lies elsewhere, over and above the individual horizon: even as the officer and K and everybody else are picked up by the war as by a tidal wave, there is a sense in which this wave – in its contradictory guises – disables and exceeds itself.

This is to say that far from hypostasising the discursive aspect of history, as we might all too hastily conclude from Coetzee's view of 'history as discourse' (Attwell, 1990: 102–103), this aspect is relativised, displaced, unsettled and rendered potentially weak within *Life & Times*. It is discourse that is disabled precisely where it should be strongest – in the Kenilworth camp. Schematically, within the novel, the concept of war moves from strong, clear-cut oppositions to radical ambivalence. The oppositions belong to Coetzee's understanding of 'history', whereas ambivalence pertains to writing. Yet 'war', which is history *par excellence*, covers both aspects. This apparent paradox requires that we recognise the inherent instability in war as a discursive and bureaucratic phenomenon. Ideology, bureaucracy and state policy legitimate the devastation and techniques of punishment; the hermeneutic activity of the soldiers leads them to capture K's body. However, this discursive ferocity exceeds its own determinations. The attempts by the state, the main agent of war, to contain difference through incarceration, roadblocks, camps, surveillance and 'rehabilitation' simply propagate difference. The war produces the parasitical other that eludes it, and the larger and more intense the war becomes, the more parasites it will (presumably) produce.

K and his mother do not flee until they feel that the 'real war' has arrived. They are constructed as refugees by the war; they are of the war at precisely the moment that they escape the war. In that sense, war as a semantic struggle with dire material consequences will always exceed and disable itself, in a double movement reminiscent of deconstruction's *différance* – the simultaneous construction of difference and deferral of meaning (Derrida, 1967: 98).[3] At the peak of its power, therefore, the 'king of all and father of all' reaches its lowest point. The war moves towards/causes/becomes ambivalence, in much the same way as Lévinas describes the self-generating ambivalence of the hierarchical regime of the Same:

> war and administration, that is to say, hierarchy, through which the State is instituted and maintained, alienate the Same, which they were supposed to maintain in its purity; in order to suppress violence, it is necessary to have recourse to violence. The Same does not recognize its will in the consequence of its vote. The mediation, which should have assured the triumph of the Same, is the source of a new alienation of the Same (1996: 15–16).[4]

We must, however, determine with greater precision the site (or sites) at which this alienation and ambivalence within the Same manifests itself. Generally, it would appear that ambivalence denotes a failure of cognition or an inability of language to pronounce definitely on something. This type of ambivalence is to be found in the medical officer's sense of irony and defeat. With regard to the war, however, we must rephrase this notion of ambivalence as an incommensurability between the discursive regime and its limits, notably the limit of the suffering body. The entropic fate of war as a concept (the impossibility for the bureaucratic structures to contain its meaning) comes about by way of what is represented as its material consequences. Whereas the bureaucracy remains discursively rigid, it is challenged by the radical indeterminacy of those bodies which are simultaneously its captives, its parasites and its 'offspring'. We see this most clearly in how the novel marks out K's body – not his mind or soul – as the primary site of ambivalence. This would imply that the forces of history and subjectification are both inscribed and evaded on K's body, singular and baffling though it may be. We might even suggest that the drama of 'differantial' war, of history, is enacted in the entire structuring of K as novelistic figure. His alterity would in such a reading not be due to an absolute separation between him and history, between 'life' and 'times', but rather to such a strong *subjection* to history that the instability of the discourse of history is exposed.

This brings us back to the mediated nature of K's thinking. Far from being the absolutely free soul that the medical officer sees, K's thoughts are already inscribed in and through dominant conventions – not least biblical, Christian conventions. K's words and thoughts are punctuated with allusions to Christian discourse: the 'fiery furnace' (1983: 44); 'It is God's earth' (1983: 53); 'Perhaps I am the stony ground' (1983: 65); his prayer of thanks (1983: 155).

The same can be said about the officer who speaks of the sparrows that are not forgotten (1983: 186); mentions a church choir that sings '*Loof die Heer*' (Praise the Lord) (1983: 196); envisions K gathering manna that has fallen from the sky (1983: 206); and refers to the Garden of Paradise (1983: 213). The camp commander's name is Noël, that is, 'Christmas', which also indicates a naturalised Christian frame of reference.

In this respect there is not much difference between the 'souls' of K and the officer. K's soul is already a captive of the same structures that operate through the Kenilworth camp. It is hardly viable to single out Christian discourse as a major cause behind the war in *Life & Times* – although Calvinism was instrumental in the ideological construction of apartheid (Davenport, 1991: 213), but it is significant that Christianity defines and works upon the soul in a narrative which turns repeatedly to the body/spirit or body/soul divide (1983: 66, 183, 207). K and the medical officer belong in this sense to the same discursive structures; they have the same 'father'. There is, consequently, a structural homology between 'soul' and the bureaucratic structures of 'war'. K does not, indeed cannot, resist the command that issues from the disciplinary structures. The fact that he never tells his story, despite the officer's admonishments, is less a case of resistance than of sheer inability, as K himself reasons at a later stage (1983: 247). As far as possible, his soul is obedient: 'In fact you did not resist at all. When we told you to jump, you jumped' (1983: 224). It is his body that resists instead: 'When we told you to jump a third time, however, you did not respond but collapsed in a heap; and we could all see, even the most unwilling of us, that you had failed because you had exhausted your resources in obeying us. [. . .] your will acquiesced but your body baulked' (1983: 224). Consequently, it is K's body, not he 'himself' that refuses to eat or digest the food that is offered to him. This creates a space of ambivalence – the ambivalence of a body turning against itself – contrary to the officer's understanding 'that the body contains no ambivalence' (1983: 224). K becomes an allegory not only of how 'outrageously a meaning can take up residence in a system without becoming a term in it' (1983: 228), but also of the war itself. His body exceeds the discriminations of his intentional consciousness and mediated desire. The discursive determinations of war, and of K's 'parents', are thus undercut, not by force, not through argument, but through bodily, material withdrawal.

My reading, then, does not oppose K and history – at least not in any unqualified way – but emphasises the possibility for both to exceed their own determinations without (impossibly) exceeding their own limits. The body is an absolute limit, but its limitations possess the capacity to challenge the limitations of the soul. (This recalls the finale in Ndebele's 'Fools', where Zamani's body succeeds in redefining the limits of his 'soul'.) History, likewise, is an absolute horizon, but this horizon far exceeds what history is *taken to be*.[5] The medical officer demonstrates how 'history' can be understood in different ways. His own understanding of 'currents of time swirling and eddying all about us [. . .], murkily at first, yet tending ever towards a moment of transfiguration in which pattern is born from chaos and history manifests itself in all its triumphant meaning' (1983: 216) is sophisticated, particularly in comparison to what he calls the 'childhood catechism' of history which is merely a collection of dates (1983: 216). Yet both war and K defy such quasi-Hegelian teleology. Instead, to the officer, 'with one ear to the banal exchanges of camp life and with the other to the suprasensual spinning of the gyroscopes of the Grand Design, time has grown empty' (1983: 217). Instead of meaning, war produces entropy, passivity, blankness. In relation to the unrepresentable 'absolute horizon', this production of blankness is yet another *version* of history. K's victory is his body's victory: it becomes the mark of possibility for this other history.

Place-names
What does the foregoing argument make of the alterity of Michael K? Is there not a risk that such a fixation of K's transgressive potential *vis-à-vis* history simply appropriates Michael K in the service of a pre-determined political programme, and that his alterity is once again elided? Mike Marais solves this problem by postulating a Levinasian tension between totality and infinity in the medical officer's narrative. Whereas the medical officer represents totality and is literally situated inside an enclosure, the way in which he responds to Michael K but fails to appropriate him achieves two things at once: it plants the 'idea' of infinity in the narrative, and rejects the attempt at representing infinity. It is, according to Marais, in the officer's narrative of failed proximity to K, rather than in the other two parts where the narrative approaches K's 'consciousness', that the reader is closest to the unutterable alterity of K (1998a: 175).

But what if we were to approach the problem not via K but via history? If, indeed, the notion of infinity as interruption and an intimation of alterity can be extended to the historical level, then the structural homology between K and history does not constitute an appropriation of K in a clear-cut 'resistance' against history, but becomes rather a double reading of a single textual movement. The representational level of 'war' discussed so far can be compared to the representations of K. The excess of war is not unlike K's blankness: both are moments of transgression. However, just as the idea of infinity is properly expressed in conventional terms – being self-consciously 'as if' – and not through any mystical sign that supposedly 'contains' it, so is the transgressive potential of history inscribed to an even higher degree through the conventional device of place-names than through representation *per se*.

Place-names abound in *Life & Times*. From specific locations such as De Waal Park (1983: 5), Somerset Hospital (1983: 9) and Kenilworth racecourse (1983: 206), to cities and towns such as Cape Town (1983: 18), Stellenbosch (1983: 36) and Prince Albert, the narrative conveys a distinct geography that corresponds to any detailed map of contemporary South Africa. There is nothing 'necessary' about this use of place-names. Rather, they are flaunted, used even at the barest excuse, as when Noël mentions Gordon's Bay in passing (1983: 211). Early on, the connotations of the place-names seem utterly incongruous. Chaos unfolds in luxurious neighbourhoods called Côte d'Azur, Côte d'Or, Malibu Heights, Copacabana and Egremont (1983: 16). Sitting in a ransacked apartment, K pages through 'picture-books of the Ionian Islands, Moorish Spain, Finland Land of Lakes, Bali, and other places in the world' (1983: 23). This brings to mind the affluent classes' hedonistic assemblage of global space in *A Sport of Nature*: the world as a selection of interchangeable pleasure-options.

Each of the place-names belongs to a phantasmagoria that is detached from the specificities of place and history. By the same token, the almost absurd emphasis placed on Prince Albert – to the point that the town takes on the qualities of a person (1983: 39, 67) – makes the linguistic appropriation of land by imperial discourse (which hypostasises the title and name of 'Prince Albert') seem not a little ludicrous. The supposedly straightforward, realistic practice of naming places reveals instead a distinctly 'unreal' aspect of reality.

However, rather than merely asserting in a pseudo-Marxian sense the 'artificial' or 'false' relation of the ruling classes to history, I wish to emphasise another aspect of place-names, namely, their formal challenge to representation. As a formal device, place-names in *Life & Times* are like words written on the surface of a figurative painting. Rather than 'showing', they are content to 'tell' of places, and thus assume a conventional historical/geographical knowledge of what these places 'are'.[6]

Whether the reader possesses such knowledge is, strictly speaking, less important. What is important is the assumption as such.

Place-names therefore do the same work at the historical level as the mediated, naivistic images of K do at the subjective level: they short-circuit the putative immediacy of realism by presenting the reader with a ready-made sign whose readability relies overtly on a context not circumscribed by the narrative. But over and above confusion, their factuality introduces a *different* approach to the real from the conventional illusionism of realism. The space of named places is, after all, physically accessible. The contemporary reader can easily move about physically in Prince Albert or Stellenbosch or on Beach Road, but can never hope to step inside the narrative. Such use of names (and only the names, not the representation of places) inscribes, I argue, a bodily notion of the real as against the cognitive, imaginary notions of realism: that is, the reader has at this level the very real option of assuring the text's 'correspondence' with reality by way of his or her bodily presence. Of course, the same could be said about any novel (such as *A Sport of Nature*) which happens to include names of 'real' places, but there are three specific reasons why place-names are so significant in *Life & Times*.

Firstly, their distinctness and implacability as opposed to the uncertainty surrounding K's name. Secondly, the sharp contrast between *Life & Times* and Coetzee's immediately preceding novels, *In the Heart of the Country* and *Waiting for the Barbarians*, where settings are nameless, vague or imaginary (the latter novel takes place in an unnamed, fictive empire). Thirdly, the role of place-names as hypostasised history, markers of an imperialistic and capitalistic capture of the landscape.[7] This means that place-names function, by way of their conventionality, as allegorical signs of history. The possibility for the reader to bodily corroborate the place-names, the erection of a concrete relationship between reader-body and text-body, refers allegorically to the juxtaposition of K and history, specifically of K's *bodily* response to the narrativising pressures of history. Just as it is K's body that ultimately escapes the structures of war/history/soul, so are place-names the site within the narrative where the narrative exceeds itself. It resists in this way its own determinations.

This is hinted at in the final section of the novel, where the pimp and the prostitutes ('sisters') who impose themselves on K recount how they move about in Sea Point:

> The stranger spoke of life in Sea Point. 'Do you think it is strange,' he said, 'that we are sleeping on the mountain like tramps? We are not tramps. We have food, we have money, we make a living. Do you know where we used to live? Tell Mister Treefeller where we lived.'
>
> 'Normandie,' said the sister in jeans.
>
> 'Normandie. 1216 Normandie. Then we got tired of climbing steps and came here. This is our summer resort, where we come for picnics.' He laughed. 'And before that do you know where we lived? Tell him.'
>
> 'Clippers,' said the sister.
>
> 'Clippers Unisex Hairdressers. So you see, it is easy to live in Sea Point if you know how. [. . .]' (1983: 239).

This exchange brings to mind once again Lévinas's image of the town where 'hairdressers dress hair' and how every role, every activity is abruptly dissolved and deconstructed (Critchley, 1992: 151). At Sea Point, places no longer stick to their initial definitions. Names remain, but their sense and meaning is up for grabs. This is what the pimp refers to by saying that 'it is easy to live in Sea Point if you know how'. Knowing how means being prepared to create meaning anew.

In this way, place-names become a blank space not through but on behalf of utopian projection. While refusing to assume the authority of political prescription, Coetzee's geographical insistence opens up, in a profound way which addresses the reader straight through and beyond the closure of the novel, the possibility of historical change. On the one hand, by placing familiar (to the South African reader) place-names alongside unfamiliar times, the reader's quotidian environment is relativised, released from hypostasis. On the other hand, and looking from the horizon of the narrative, place-names escape the narrative as much as Michael K escapes the determinations of war. The narrative has no control over place-names that 'exist' independently of this specific narrative. The place-names, in conjunction with the narrative, therefore constitute an additional element of ambivalence, placed simultaneously in the regime of the Same and a radically unknowable alterity. Coetzee's novel does not tell how this blank space of ambivalence should be filled: this goes beyond the novel's responsibility. Indeed, this is a historical challenge, ultimately concerned with redefining history *as it is known*, and it is the historical challenge that makes the novel unable to be able.

Consequently, by displacing the option of historical change from the imaginable but unreal realm of fictional representation to the unimaginable but real bodies of readers, and by prefiguring resistance and transcendence through K's body rather than his mind, *Life & Times* effects a critique of symbolic and intellectualist solutions to the historical crisis in South Africa. This amounts, in its way, to a critique of my entire project, dealing as it does with symbolic solutions to highly concrete conflicts. Or, more redemptively, it weaves itself into a dominant theme of this book, in which it has been a concern of mine to tease out attempts at symbolic solutions evident in specific narratives, but simultaneously to criticise them, to point out their inherent weaknesses and preconditions. As in *Fools* and *A Sport of Nature*, the intellectualist option is rejected for the benefit of a more corporeal perspective on historical agency, but the difference is that *Life & Times* also refuses the option of imagining a symbolic solution grounded in the body, since this too would be subsumed by the regime of the Same.

Throughout, the novel's critique of intellectualism and symbolic utopianism concurs with the Levinasian critique of the knowing subject, but at the same time this austere critique is re-engaged in a historical context. If Lévinas's project began in the Second World War but shunned the language of history for the qualified absoluteness of philosophical diction, Coetzee can be said to move *from* the stratosphere of theoretical critique into the raw ambience of historical crisis. In both cases, there is a critical edge against idealistic notions of subjectivity. The beginning of the subject is in the body, not in the mind. K's beginning is his body, and his body comes from his mother's body, not from the law of the 'father', Huis Norenius. However, his body is not present in any simple way.

In attempting to affirm, by an act of imagination, his own origin in a succession of mothers, he falls back on an infinite regress (1983: 160–161). Rather, his body is present only in its withdrawal, in its refusal to eat, in its withdrawal from consciousness, in its resistance to representation. This is K's story. Not the fictive construct that he half-despairingly wishes he could master, nor the story that he does tell (1983: 247). That these either seem paltry or unsatisfactory is simply due to the fact that they are not his. They belong to discourse, to the father of law/war. Only his body, and his body's story, are truly his – in so far as it withdraws from common discourse. His true story can never be told; the story that we read is always the wrong story.

What is striking in *Life & Times*, and what has not been emphasised in previous readings, is how this subdued appraisal of corporeality is repeated at the historical level of the novel. The 'life' and the 'times' converge at this point. Through the insistence on 'real' place-names, the narrative paradoxically, and ostentatiously, relinquishes control over its spatial disposition. It calls upon the unimaginable corporeality of the reader, insists on his or her relation to places that are named *in* the text, but lead far beyond it. The text concedes in this way its inevitable grounding in the discursive conditions of colonialism/apartheid, but opens a gap in the closure that will allow alterity to come into play on its own, inarticulable, terms. This counter-historical strategy is, however, marked by its own historical position.

Three factors constitute the text: a political interregnum, intense historical pessimism, and the refusal to pronounce authoritatively on what lies 'beyond'. Some twenty years after Coetzee's novel was published, the latter two subjective factors might feasibly still be operative (but for very different reasons), whereas the interregnum has definitely been surpassed. In that sense, the deconstructive thrust of *Life & Times* is, in its specific subversion of history, unequivocally part of its own historical moment. But this is hardly disabling. Rather it is this very struggle with history that makes the ethically sublime moment of the novel – its desire for a release from history and a non-appropriative encounter with alterity – all the more credible.

Conclusion

Writing in Crisis

IN A DENSE meditation on the current possibilities for literature in South Africa, Graham Pechey has suggested that 'writing' should be construed in programmatically heterogeneous and excessive terms:

> What I have called 'writing' [. . .] is that which can only by an act of hermeneutic violence be read as being *for* any one proposition and *against* another construed as its opposite. We are in the presence of writing in this strong sense when the discourse before us has no designs of assimilation upon other discourses; is unimpressed by the monopolistic claims of any one narrative, even its own; and loves the incommensurability of 'phrasal universes' above all else. The polar contest of apartheid and its antagonists needed for its own purposes to compel an infinity of disparate temporalities and identities into a totality. Writing is under no such necessity (Pechey, 1998: 63).

This is an audacious statement that refers specifically to the period after 1994, yet in its audacity it sums up a dominant concern of mine in this book: the potential of literature to challenge the underlying logic rather than just the effects of a particular historical moment. Those aspects of the narratives that I have discussed are indeed incommensurable with the political system under which they were conceived. The racist and positivist ideology of the South African government in the 1980s could certainly not accommodate the cultural self-reliance, spatial ambition and reappropriation of science evident in Njabulo Ndebele's *Fools and Other Stories*. Neither could the postmodern Pan-Africanism of

Nadine Gordimer's *A Sport of Nature* be readily accepted by a 'white' establishment that waged war against neighbouring African countries and identified with the anti-communist cause of the Cold War. Nor could the grand narratives of 'white' civilisation or the *Blut und Boden* ideology of 'ons vir jou Suid-Afrika' (literally, 'us for you, South Africa')[1] find any affirmation whatsoever in the deconstructive manoeuvres of J.M. Coetzee's *Life & Times of Michael K*. In this sense, and in many others, each of the texts under discussion is obviously *against* apartheid. But since being against apartheid is a bit like being against the devil, this offers only the most facile perspective on such writing. Instead, it is its resistance to and evasion of apartheid's determinations, its ability to displace symbolically the iron cage of history, that is its greater achievement.

But what of this historical moment? And what of today? If the future was the main concern in the 1980s, South Africa was in the 1990s weighed down by the gravity of the past and present. This decisive shift in political and cultural priorities also, inevitably, affected my work on this book. Having begun this project (in the form of my thesis) in earnest in 1993, a year before the 'miraculous' democratic breakthrough, my initial relation to *Fools and Other Stories*, *A Sport of Nature* and *Life & Times of Michael K* was somewhat continuous with the context in which they first were received. They dealt, bluntly speaking, with the yet-to-be-realised demise of apartheid. These were still contemporary texts. Once the political system changed, my focus shifted accordingly (although I didn't under-stand this at first) and I began to perceive them as historical documents, as evidence of irretrievably bygone days, whose strangeness would always disturb and offend latter-day readers.

True, even as I submitted my thesis-proposal of which this book is the final product, I had the ambition to fuse the contemporary/ historical aspect with strongly theorised close readings of the narratives. The assumption was, however, that their political address could be taken more or less for granted, whereas the theoretical/ formal aspect needed to be motivated all the more insistently. What happened over time was that the political dimension detached itself more and more from the pressing concerns that apparently governed the texts at the time of their publication, and was subsumed by the theoretical discussions that I entertain throughout. Apart from the historical sea-change in South Africa, this was also due to the continued institutional rise and diversification of post-colonial studies internationally, meaning that my mode of reading became less of a specialty and all the more engaged with central debates in the academe today, even viewed from a Swedish perspective. Theory, rather than politics, opened itself towards contemporaneity.

Given these shifts, the question is whether they have been detrimental or beneficial to my study. I believe the latter to be true. The gradual switch from obvious assumptions of a contemporary political challenge to the more vexed discussion of historicity (traces of a context rather than the assumed totality of a context) and post-colonialism opens rather than closes the texts in question. By allowing them a wider historical address than at the time of their initial reception, they speak far beyond the year 1994. In fact, and this comes as a surprise only in view of the critical intensity of the 1980s in South Africa, each of the three books can be shown to deal with dilemmas that endure much longer than day-to-day politics. Each of them is in various ways a 'sport of culture' that exceeds the determinations of their historical and cultural horizons.

A 'sport' is a game, but the dictionary also tells us that a 'sport' is an animal or a plant that deviates strikingly from the normal type, as indeed we are asked to understand Gordimer's Hillela. Both meanings are in play here. A work of fiction, no matter how serious, is always a game which follows certain rules – but it may also succeed in bending the rules. It may reassemble them and make different, provisional rules. This is what I read from the three works under discussion, in both a historical and formal sense. Being 'sports', they are *from* but not entirely *of* their own historical moment. They confound the cultural and political assumptions of their synchronic context; they perform a mode of *bricolage* by using the materials 'at hand' in South Africa at the time – the sense of severe conflict, the use of the English language, realistic form – and reassembling them so as to constitute an alternative position from which to regard the emplacement of the subject, the narratives of apartheid and imperialism, the question of difference and ethical responsibility. This makes these works essential reading in the pragmatic, non-utopian 1990s and 2000s, as well as in literary and theoretical contexts that exceed 'South Africa'.

For example, the epistemological challenge of *Fools and Other Stories* strikes at the heart of any debate over universalism and cultural relativism by refusing to privilege any single term. It secularises the 'universalism' of modernity by demonstrating how it must be grounded in local conditions, and offers a highly sophisticated perspective on the controversy over 'africanisation' at South African universities today. Rather than 'Africanise' along the lines of a strict binarism and discard everything 'Western', *Fools* implies that the post-colonial African subject should displace what the West has claimed as its own particular gift to mankind (science, technology, literacy) and situate it in the rationality of local cultures and experiences. Likewise, the postmodern-yet-post-colonial aspect of *A Sport of Nature* speaks in subdued tones to the current stage of cultural and economic globalisation in South Africa, which has exploded the severely limited scope of conflict produced by apartheid. In fact, Hillela's quirky progress reads more effectively as an attempt to salvage the notion and awareness of 'Africa' in the age of transnational media, than purely as a challenge to apartheid. The increased stigmatisation of 'Africa' in 'global' media since the end of the Cold War in 1989 indicates the urgency of such a project. *Life & Times of Michael K*, finally, remains a singularly stubborn disturbance in any regime of history and reading. Michael K's resistance to appropriation corresponds with the novel's resistance to being enlisted by any specified category, be it political or generic. This resistance evinces, however, a sense of profound ethical trust in the future, or rather in what lies outside of the Same.

The theme of representational ethics is particularly strong in Coetzee's novel, but in so far as it concerns central aspects of form in a post-colonial context, all three texts can be seen to engage with the issue. It is here that the similarities as well as the differences between them are registered most clearly. In *Fools*, the task is to find release from 'white' representations of 'black' society. The stories offer an alternative to the negativity of apartheid's definitions, but entertain at the same time a tension between affirmation and disablement which reaches its critical point in 'Fools'. At the end of the story, the affirmation of the 'black' community is displaced onto

Zamani's 'new' body that he erects in defiance of pain and violence. The new body is concretely represented and emerges at the culmination of a lengthy narrative. It is Zamani's climactic moment of 'embodiment' and a resolution of the conflicts that have bedevilled him. This is an affirmative project that can be understood along the lines of a Hegelian sublation, the negation of a negation that produces a higher synthesis. Even so, it is effectively an *unwritten* body that points beyond the narrative and beyond the historical moment of the narrative. It is understood to be a beginning for Zamani, but it is a beginning at the 'end', the spatial limit of the text. Hence, a blank body that challenges the closure of representation.

In *A Sport of Nature*, the issue is more complex. Here, too, there is a dialectical moment in the manifest desire to resolve historical conflicts by asserting realistically the transgressive nature of Hillela. At this level, it is fair to speak of a *failure* of representation, in so far as the text undermines its overt signification. Hillela's baffling, singular and concrete body is endowed with abstract qualities and subsumed by patriarchal categories. However, if Hillela is released from the requirements of realistic verisimilitude and deliberately read as an allegorical figure, she can be seen not so much as a 'white' revolutionary's wish-fulfilment as an indicator of an ultimately unrepresentable global and post-colonial 'text' made up of diverse historical and cultural time-frames. On such a reading, *A Sport of Nature* does not foreclose the future but retains instead the post-colonial subject as a blank space shielded by the conventional mask of allegory.

This particular quality of blankness is most consistently generated in the non-dialectical *Life & Times of Michael K*. It is also in my discussion of that book that the ethical significance of blankness is properly foregrounded as a mode of resistance – historically marked as post-colonial – to the appropriations of the imperial subject. Representation of difference is in this regard not viable, as the structures of representation elide difference once it is represented. Each narrative tends therefore to be most loyal to the notion of heterogeneity and difference in their moments of blankness.

By extension, this discussion demonstrates how all three texts can be placed within what I initially called the post-colonial metanarrative. As aesthetic artefacts, they all participate in the successive dismantling of the authority of the Western subject by resituating, symbolically, the foundations of subjectivity as well as literary form.

If I have hitherto insisted on these narratives' capacity to reach outside of their historical moment, it must be stressed that this does not refer to some form of idealistic transcendence. On the contrary, they achieve their transgression by being imbricated with their historical conditions, not by flatly disengaging themselves from the same. This is true even – and not least – of *Life & Times*. Although the suspension of representation in blankness so clearly moves away from the more obvious requirements of political mobilisation at the time, the fact that it reads as an ethical *response* to crisis indicates an element of irreducible historicity that singles out these texts *vis-à-vis* later writing. Above all, there is a sense in which, during the 1980s, the end of the social order known under the rubric 'apartheid' was inevitable *and* unimaginable in equal measure. For this reason the text must retreat from the unknown, yet, catachrestically, do something about the known: hence Ndebele's re-positioning of 'science', Gordimer's reassemblage of 'Western' and 'African' cultural traits, and Coetzee's deconstruction of crisis.

By comparison, South African English language literature has since the 1990s been less representationally pressured. It is, at least, tempting to make a broad developmental sweep and compare *Fools* with Mark Behr's *The Smell of Apples* (1993) and Johnny Masilela's *Deliver us from Evil* (1997); *Life & Times* with Ivan Vladislavić's *The Folly* (1993); and *A Sport of Nature* with Antjie Krog's *Country of My Skull* (1998). In the first case, Behr and Masilela deal with childhood under apartheid, much like Ndebele, but the pastness of the past is much more evident there than in *Fools*, where the recent past merges with the synchronic 'now' of the writing and is burdened by the same historical and representational limits as the agent of writing. For Behr and Masilela, in much the same way as I have described my own experience of working on my thesis, the past is irretrievably other. In fact, the past has become virtually unimaginable, but instead of pushing the limits of convention, these writers tend to construct readerly narratives. This gives the reader an unsentimental reconstruction (rather than a decon-struction) of a moment which once seemed impossible to transcend but has now apparently evaporated. Something similar is at work, moreover, in Coetzee's *Boyhood* (1997), an utterly straight-faced and delicate memoir of (what the reader assumes to be) Coetzee's own childhood.

In the second case, Vladislavić is easily paired with Coetzee as an adamant defender of the freedom and autonomy of writing. His novels, *The Folly* and *The Restless Supermarket*, as well as his short story collections, are not particularly readerly. They are metafictional and innovative to the same degree as Coetzee's writing, and place high demands on the reader's imaginative and suspicious intervention. Interestingly, the main character in *The Folly* is just as elusive and odd as Michael K, and the narrative could be read as a national allegory, not unlike the way in which the 'times' of *Life & Times* are first represented. However, whereas Coetzee's writerly freedom in *Life & Times* is extremely ascetic and consists principally of the deconstructive gesture of escape, Vladislavić's writing celebrates language. Although both writers share a similar understanding of representation and fictionality, and although both develop a comparable tautness of style, *The Folly* – with its indulgence in words, its wealth of narrative and stylistic ironies, its flat self-referentiality – does what *Life & Times* tries to clear a space for but could not practice on its own behalf.

In the third case, *Country of My Skull*, which is not a novel but a journalistic and essayistic account of the work of the Truth and Reconciliation Commission, forms a compelling counterpart to *A Sport of Nature*. Whereas Gordimer's novel ultimately desires to take a leap into the real, to actualise its utopian vision – as is indicated, not least, by its deployment of factuality – the 'real' is a given in *Country of My Skull*, but it is also controverted, or qualified rather, by Krog's deliberate use of various fictional and poetic devices. Krog appears in this case as a 'sport of nature' turned narrator, a post-colonial subject who is actively engaging with rather than skirting the national traumas of South Africa and who doesn't shy away from any textual options in order to consummate this engagement. Indeed, both *A Sport of Nature* and Krog's text are apparently governed by the 'white' subject's desire to identify fully with the nation (in Gordimer's case: the nation to be), but they are separated by the vast difference in their respective historical predicaments. Whereas Gordimer undertook in 1987 a flight of fancy that at the moment could not be anything but, Krog's leap of faith in 1998 was far more tenable (although hardly easier). In both texts, the body is centrally implicated in the process of identification – as indeed the very title of Krog's book indicates – but in *Country of My Skull* it is less fantastical, more vulnerable, more attuned to the violence acted out not only against the 'black' body but in equal or even greater measure against the female body. Furthermore, both texts deal with the insertion of a 'new' South Africa in a global circulation of media images, but what was a visionary moment in *A Sport of Nature* is in *Country of My Skull* a frustrating and bewildering everyday phenomenon which threatens to transform South Africa into just another simulacral 'story', thereby diminishing its *gravitas*. In short, the ordinary, in the mundane guise of globalisation, has returned with a vengeance.

Notes

INTRODUCTION

1. For a hard-hitting journalistic account of ground-level politics in the 1980s, see Joseph Lelyveld (1986).

2. In his survey of South African literature, Michael Chapman (1996: 327–331) refers to the interregnum as the period between 1970 and 1990, whereas I would restrict the interregnum to the years 1976–1990, that is, from the Soweto uprising until the unbannings in 1990. What particularly constitutes this period is the combination of crisis and stasis.

3. The most brilliant and seminal 'historical' study is Stephen Clingman's (1986) *The Novels of Nadine Gordimer: History from the Inside*. Other exemplary investigations that privilege historical contextualisation – with-in a liberationist-nationalist narrative – are Michael Vaughan's (1990) 'Storytelling and Politics in Fiction' (on Ndebele), and Susan VanZanten Gallagher's (1991) *A Story of South Africa* (on Coetzee).

4. See the studies mentioned in the previous note.

5. One of the most concise arguments against the concept of race is found in Anthony Appiah's (1986) essay 'The Uncompleted Argument: Du Bois and the Illusion of Race' (21–37).

6. Lewis Nkosi has recently argued that 'there exists an unhealed [. . .] split between black and white writing' also in post-apartheid South Africa (1998: 75). While this certainly holds as a general observation, for the very reasons that I cite above, Nkosi's contention that 'black writing [. . .] is [. . .] largely impervious for the most part to cultural movements which have exercised great influence in the development of white writing' (1998: 75), is inaccurate with regard to Njabulo Ndebele, or more recent writers such as Zoë Wicomb, Zakes Mda, Mandla Langa, Chris van Wyk, Andries Oliphant and Johnny Masilela. Hence the division between 'black' and 'white' writing is less clear than Nkosi makes it out to be.

7. Beauvoir explicitly compares 'woman' with 'Jews' and 'Blacks' in her introduction (1949).

8. In Latin America, however, Lévinas has long been discussed in theoretical discourse (see Walter Mignolo, 2002).

CHAPTER 1

1. The 1960s and 1970s were the critical decades with regard to bannings of literary works. As the chairmanship of the Publications Appeal Board changed in 1980, so did the definition of what was 'offensive'. This eased some of the immediate pressure on writers, while in fact censorship as a whole (specifically media censorship) was severely intensified in the 1980s (Brink, 1983: 231–256; Davenport, 1991: 385–386, 439; J.M. Coetzee, 1992: 315–332, 361–368).

2. I must admit, however, that the case of Abrahams is complicated. It is mostly in his knee-jerk responses to the politicised debate – as in the piece 'Down with English' (1988: 327–331) – that his views on literature transpire as rigid and unhelpful. Seen in isolation, however, his aesthetics are subjectivist and corporeal, rather than idealist. It is the body, the senses, the self that governs his outlook on writing and reading, and which results in fine poetry. What occurs when this view is confronted with the politicised debated, is that the aestheticising subject and body is *unproblematically* lifted out from the historical turmoil. The subject thus becomes an ideal subject, and the ensuing critical stance a version of idealism.

3. Coetzee does not refer explicitly to this term, but I use it to indicate a tacit assumption in his paper. 'The novel' and 'history' are in place before the writer, indeed, it is they who give birth to the writer rather than the other way around, as Roland Barthes argued: 'le scripteur moderne naît en même temps que son texte; il n'est d'aucune façon pourvu d'un être qui précéderait ou excéderait son écriture' (1994: 493). The difference between Barthes and Coetzee is the capacity to *choose* that Coetzee grants the writer (or perhaps the pre-writer).

4. Essays that employ this distinction between the two include: Glenn (1994: 11–32); Hewson (1988); and Pechey (1994: 151–171).

5. This conviction emerges – *mutatis mutandis* – repeatedly in her essays. See for example, Gordimer (1988: 27, 104–110, 114, 247–248). See also Lomberg (1990: 31).

6. Coetzee is, of course, not unique in this respect. The single most important proponent, internationally, of the discursive view of history is probably Hayden White, whereas of late Leon de Kock and David Attwell (significantly enough, neither is an historian in conventional terms), have developed this view in South Africa.

7. 'L'histoire se situe à des paliers differents [. . .] C'est dix, cent paliers qu'il faudrait mettre en cause, dix, cent durées diverses. En surface, une histoire événementielle s'inscrit dans le temps court: c'est une micro-histoire. A mi-pente, une histoire conjoncturelle suit un rythme

plus large et plus lent. [. . .] Au-delà de ce "récitatif" de la conjoncture, l'histoire structurale, ou de longue durée, met en cause des siècles entiers' (Braudel, 1969: 112).

8. This notion is related to Michael Green's 'resistant form', in terms of which a work of fiction will 'make of its historical material a moment of resistance that leads to an intervention with its own moment of production or consumption' (1997: 34). The difference is that Green investigates fiction *as* history – in accordance with his specific conception of history – whereas I posit fiction, that is, writing, as the space of negotiation between the writing subject and the subject's given historical horizon. My argument resonates likewise with David Attwell's (1993: 3) approach to Coetzee, that is, in his investigation of 'the relationship between *reflexivity* and *historicity*'.

CHAPTER 2

1. It refers, above all, to Macaulay's argument on anglicised Indians as 'a class of interpreters' (see Bhabha, 1994: 87).
2. See, for example, Ngugi wa Thiongo (1987).

CHAPTER 3

1. See, for example, Gyan Prakash (1990: 383–408).
2. On Sartre as the 'last' humanist, see Foucault (1994: 541–542; see also Lévi-Strauss (1962: 324–357); and Robert Young (1990: 28–47).
3. 'l'ethnologie n'est elle-même possible qu'à partir d'une certain situation, d'un événement absolument singulier, où se trouvent engagées à la fois notre historicité et celle de tous les hommes qui peuvent constituer l'objet d'une ethnologie [. . .]: l'ethnologie s'enracine, en effet, dans une possibilité qui appartient en propre à l'histoire de notre culture, plus encore à son rapport fondamental à toute histoire, et qui lui permet de se lier aux autres cultures sur le mode de la pure théorie. Il y a une certaine position de la *ratio* occidentale qui s'est constituée dans son histoire et qui fond le rapport qu'elle peut avoir à toutes les autres sociétés, même à cette société où elle est historiquement apparue' (Foucault, 1966: 388).
4. A brief, comprehensive introduction to this argument can be found in Emmanuel Lévinas (1991: 97–119).
5. The relation of Lévinas's philosophy to literary criticism has since been elaborated in great detail by Robert Eaglestone. Despite Lévinas's deep distrust of art and aesthetics, Eaglestone demonstrates how it is precisely the structure of the Saying and the Said that opens Levinasian ethics to literary criticism (1997: 156–170). See also Chapter 13, note 9.
6. 'Alors que l'âme platonicienne, liberée des conditions concrètes de son

existence corporelle et historique, peut atteindre les hauteurs de
l'Empyrée pour contempler les Idées, alors que l'esclave, pourvu qu'il
"entende le grec" qui lui permet d'entrer en relation avec le maître, arrive
aux mêmes vérités que le maître – les contemporains demandent à Dieu,
lui-même, s'il veut être physicien, de passer par le laboratoire, par les
pesées et les mesures, par la perception sensible et même par l'infinie
série d'aspects dans laquelle l'objet perçu se révèle.

L'ethnographie la plus récente, la plus audacieuse et la plus influente,
maintient sur le même plan les cultures multiples. L'oeuvre politique de
la décolonisation se trouve ainsi rattachés à une ontologie – à une pensée
de l'être – cette essentielle désorientation – est, peut-être, l'expression
moderne de l'atheisme' (Lévinas, 1964: 135).

7. This post-colonial critique of post-colonial studies, as it might
   paradoxically be called, unfolded all through the 1990s, notably
   exercised by academics situated in North America: Aijaz Ahmad, Anne
   McClintock, Arif Dirlik, Ella Shohat, Deepika Bahri, Gayatri Spivak.
   Some of the more common arguments has been that 'post-colonial' has
   no explanatory force (it is too vague, it elides differences between the so-
   called Third World countries) and that it confines the thinking on
   formerly colonised countries precisely to a Eurocentric, colonial frame of
   reference. In somewhat stronger terms, the latter position has served to
   accuse post-colonial theorists of commodifying the Third World for
   consumption on a structurally if not ideologically neo-liberal academic
   market. Each avenue of critique must rely, however, on its specific
   construction of the enemy, and therefore does not really disable a
   stipulated definition of 'post-colonial'. See Aijaz Ahmad (1992); Deepika
   Bahri (1995: 51–81); Dirlik (1994: 328–356); McClintock
   (1995: 9–17); Ella Shohat (1992: 99–113); and Spivak (1993: 53–76).

8. Although it apparently originates from the Pentagon, I borrow the term
   from Fredric Jameson (1981: 53–54).

9. Said's distinction '"imperialism" means the practice, the theory, and the
   attitudes of a dominating metropolitan centre ruling a distant territory;
   "colonialism" which is almost always a consequence of imperialism, is
   the implanting of settlements on distant territory' (1993: 8) – becomes
   vague here. The metropolitan centre still dominates South Africa in
   cultural and economic terms – not directly, but as a consequence of
   erstwhile colonial settlement. It is therefore not entirely clear what is
   included in one term and left out of the other. Instead, as discussed
   earlier in this Part, I use the qualifier 'Second World' to distinguish
   specific 'white' contexts in South Africa from the metropolis.

CHAPTER 4

1. As a way of foregrounding the social constructedness of 'blackness', I shall substitute 'subaltern' for 'black' as far as possible. Ranajit Guha, Gayatri Spivak and the Subaltern Studies Group in India are the main influence, but it is Gramsci who coined the term. The advantage, as I see it, is that 'subaltern' whatever its various connotations merely designates a relative position in society, and is devoid of millenarian as well as racist overtones.

2. Among unpublished works, I should mention Jacqueline Ruth Savage's M.A. thesis (1989).

CHAPTER 5

1. 'L'indigène est déclaré imperméable à l'éthique, absence de valeurs, mais aussi negation des valeurs' (Fanon, 1968 [1961]: 10).

2. The moment of *négritude* was of course the most spectacular breakthrough for outright cultural resistance, initiated through the publication of poems and articles by Aimé Césaire and Leopold Senghor in the 1930s and 1940s, and leading at a later stage to the celebrated *Anthologie de la nouvelle poesie nègre et malgache de langue française*, prefaced by Sartre, the conferences held in the 1950s and Fanon's seminal essays. Its emancipatory thrust is undeniable, but with the hindsight offered by later literary developments in Africa as well as Western Europe, *négritude* today is generally seen to have resulted from the parisian exile of Africans and West Indians in the period between the First and Second World Wars, and having been shaped in dialogue with contemporary French literature and philosophy. This 'voyage in', to use Said's term, this violation of formerly prohibited cultural spaces by the subaltern, is, as I have already argued, a necessary aspect of post-colonial writing, but it needs to be handled with utmost care. In its reversal of Descartes – 'I feel, therefore I am' – *négritude* held the colonial stereotype firmly in place by excluding African 'essence' from the realm of European reason, turning it into a mirror-image of hegemonic culture, rather than its substitution. For summaries of this debate, see Gérard (1986: vol.1: 342–393), and Ashcroft, Griffiths and Tiffin (1989: 123–124).

3. The Cattle-Killing Movement was a thaumaturgical attempt by the Xhosas to oust the British colonisers through massive sacrifice of (mainly) livestock (Peires, 1989: 122–138).

4. Moreover, the emphasis on English was in keeping not only with missionary policy but also with the Enlightenment tradition of identifying 'humanness' with the ability to write and compose literature (see Henry Louis Gates, 1986: 9–11).

5. It has, of course, affected writing in African languages just as deeply, if not more. We could mention Masizi Kunene's prolonged exile and the isolated status of his writing in Zulu.
6. As a case in point, see Frank Chipasula (1993: 38–55).
7. De Kock in particular argues for the agonistic view of 'black' writing (1996: 36–37).

CHAPTER 6

1. All page references in parentheses in this chapter refer to Njabulo S. Ndebele, *Fools and Other Stories* (1983).
2. In Mozambique, for example, the aim was for education to be 'secular and scientific, materialist, and train cadres to build a developed socialist economy and society' (Johnston, 1989: 128).
3. It is also worth noting that Mphahlele made the highly controversial move of realising this daydream in 1978, when he returned to South Africa.
4. Insensitivity to the cultural implications of science and technology is still rampant, as is exemplified by Karl Borgin's and Kathleen Corbett's polemical *The Destruction of a Continent* (1982).
5. I might also refer to the description of how gold-mining led to an influx of mainly British capital and scientific/technological know-how in Charles van Onselen (1981: 1–43), as well as to this exercise in progressivist apologetics in Borgin and Corbett: 'James Morris, in *Pax Britannica*, underlines the fact that "the British Empire was a developing agency, distributing technical knowledge around the world, and erecting what economists were later to call the infra-structure of industrial progress – roads, railways, ports, post and telegraphs."

   As long as the colonial powers ruled Africa, they constantly upgraded and modernized the technology they had built up on the continent. Even today, many years later, the products of what was at that time advanced technology can be seen all over Africa, and in most cases they are still functioning' (1982: 111).

CHAPTER 7

1. For recent South African research on the representational status of the body, see Rosemary Jolly (1996).
2. 'Dans le monde blanc, l'homme de couleur rencontre des difficultés dans l'élaboration de son schéma corporel. La connaissance du corps est une activité uniquement négatrice, C'est une connaissance en troisième personne. Tout autours du corps règne une atmosphère d'incertitude certaine' (Fanon, 1952: 109).

3. 'J'étais tout à la fois responsable de mon corps, responsable de ma race, de mes ancêtres. Je promenai sur moi un regard objectif, découvris ma noirceur, mes caractères ethniques, – et me défoncèrent le tympan l'anthropophagie, l'arriération mentale, le fétichisme, les tares raciales [. . .] [Je] me portai loin de mon être-là, très loin, me constituant objet. Qu'était-ce pour moi, sinon un décollement, un arrachement, une hémorragie qui caillait du sang noir sur tout mon corps?' (Fanon, 1952: 110–111).

4. In recent South African criticism, this line of argument has been pursued by Sue Marais (1992: 41–42).

5. This argument is indebted to the analysis of the 'grotesque body' in Michail Bakhtin (1968: in particular, 315–318).

6. Reams have been written on family and kinship in Africa. I refer in all brevity to John Middleton (1970: 149–188).

7. The concepts derive from Fedinand Tönnies. See *The Encyclopedia of Philosophy* (1967, vol.8: 149).

8. Ndebele touches upon this himself (1991: 74–98).

CHAPTER 8

1. 'La connaissance du corps est une activité uniquement négatrice' (Fanon, 1952: 109).

2. The Afrikaners commemorate their victory at Blood River in 1838 on 16 December. This, the Day of the Covenant, or Dingane's Day as it used to be called, was once the most politically volatile South African holiday. Since 1994, it has been renamed the Day of Reconciliation. In 1964, two years prior to the fictive date in Ndebele's narrative, the ANC launched its armed struggle against the apartheid regime on 16 December (see Davenport, 1991: 290, 364).

3. For more on this legislation, see Davenport (1991: 518–557).

4. Lokangaka Losambe also privileges this passage which, he claims, combines the rhizomatic and arborescent aspects of being (1996: 77).

CHAPTER 9

1. Admittedly, other novels such as *Burger's Daughter* and *A Guest of Honour* have certain openings for their 'white' protagonists, as Rose Pettersson has shown, but there the possible new positions are heavily qualified, whereas *A Sport of Nature* attempts to transcend even the constrictions of qualification. Hillela generally 'does' without having to consider what she 'is'.

CHAPTER 10

1. In Reich's view, constraints on bodily urges are purely repressive. The

revolutionary individual is therefore someone who unabashedly may follow his/her sexual instinct. For a discussion on Gordimer and Reich, see Pettersson (1995: 115–116).

2. All page references in parentheses in the body of the chapter refer to Nadine Gordimer (1987).

3. As far as apartheid is concerned, we could claim that the rigid attempts to adhere to the 'God-given truth' of racist essentialism within the framework of a modern state and an industrial economy repeatedly enacted their own failures. Two examples: firstly, the annual flow of several hundred individuals between the racial categories of apartheid indicated, if anything, their arbitrary nature; and secondly, the successive renamings of 'apartheid' as 'separate development' and 'plural democracy' revealed a significant degree of semiotic anxiety among apartheid's ideologues. To insist exclusively on the stasis of apartheid elides the perpetual crisis that it produced and 'managed'. As Graham Pechey has remarked, 'apartheid as a politics of permanent and institutionalised crisis has from the beginning been shadowed by its own transgression or supersession' (1994: 153).

4. In her Lawrentian celebration of sexuality, Gordimer's coy use of a personal pronoun is conventional. 'Do I make you grow big for me', as Ruth writes to her Portuguese lover (1987: 50). The curious thing in the passage about Hillela is the first person singular in third-person narration, not the pronoun as such.

5. 'La jouissance est in-dicible, inter-dite [sic]. Je renvois à Lacan ("Ce à quoi il faut ce tenir, c'est que la jouissance est interdite à qui parle, comme tel, ou encore qu'elle ne puisse être dite qu'entre les lignes . . .") et à Leclaire (". . . celui qui dit, par son dit, s'interdit la jouissance, ou courrélativement, celui qui jouit fait toute l'être – et tout dit possible – s'évanouir dans l'absolu de l'annulation qu'il célèbre").' (Barthes, 1994: 1504–1505).

6. On these narratological terms, see Gérard Genette (1983: 55–64).

7. Paradoxically, the consistency of this narrative mode hampers the argument, since I could cite thirty passages as well as one. I have chosen to focus on just one and leave it to the reader to corroborate the argument. A sample of places to look: pages 15, 82, 156, 200, 252.

CHAPTER 11

1. Brenda Cooper even speaks of the 'Pauline syndrome' when characterising Gordimer's view of white liberals (1990: 68).

2. Gates's description of Esu as the 'epitome of paradox', 'the dialectical principle' and one whose function is 'uncertainty or indeterminacy' (1988: 3–44), seems quite apposite in the case of Hillela.

3. See, for example, Gordimer's words on Turgenev (1988: 104–110), and on *War and Peace* (1973: 7).

4. I give due thanks to my colleague Ann Öhrberg who reminded me that 'Sasha' is the diminutive of 'Alyosha'.

5. I am thinking of Yeats's poem 'Easter 1916', written on the advent of armed, anti-colonial resistance in Ireland: 'All changed, changed utterly:/A terrible beauty is born' (Yeats, 1978: 203).

6. To substantiate: *The Brothers Karamazov* was written and published just a few years before the Berlin conference of 1884–1885 and the Scramble for Africa. The utilitarian, progressivist version of modernity that was the main target of the later Dostoyevsky's writing was essentially the same progressivism that fuelled imperialism and that much later has been lambasted by post-colonial theorists.

7. Indeed, Foucault even argues that psychoanalysis is one of the sciences that 'dissolves' Western man (1966: 385–388).

8. Such literary obsessions with the 'pathologies' of the self have, moreover, been criticised by Gordimer as immaterial to an African understanding of subjectivity (1973: 9–11).

9. For a particularly enlightening analysis of primitivism, see V.Y. Mudimbe (1994), especially Chapters 2 and 5.

10. Kathrin Wagner even claims that the representation of Hillela privileges 'a version of archetypal female prostitution' (1994: 94).

CHAPTER 12

1. I should qualify this statement: *A Sport of Nature* and *None to Accompany Me* (1994) span three and almost five decades, respectively, but their time-frames fit neatly into Nadine Gordimer's own professional life-span as a writer. Therefore, even when she writes about the late 1940s, it is still contemporary with her own work, and the focus of the narratives always returns to the contemporary context of the writing act.

2. On the 'Second World', see Chapter Two.

3. The idiomatic phrase is, moreover, 'go-go girl'.

4. And neither are they the only instances of error. Michael Wade has pointed out how the treatment of Jewishness – an otherwise suppressed theme in Gordimer's *oeuvre* – is marred (if that is the appropriate word to use) by some startling misrepresentations (Wade, 1993: 166–167).

5. In a strangely candid way, the very name of the country's largest mining conglomerate, Anglo-American, indicates precisely the main cultural, historical and economic affiliations of corporate South Africa.

6. Lévi-Strauss introduced the term *bricolage* in *La pensée sauvage*. For the *bricoleur*, 'la règle de son jeu est de toujours s'arranger avec les "moyens

du bord", c'est-à-dire un ensemble à chaque instant fini d'outils et de matériaux, hétéroclites au surplus, parce que la composition de l'ensemble n'est pas en rapport avec le projet du moment, ni d'ailleurs avec aucun projet particulier, mais est le résultat contingent de toutes les occasions qui se sont présentées de renouveler ou d'enrichir le stock, ou de l'entretenir avec les résidus de constructions et destructions antérieures.' In short, *bricolage* is not a question of creating something new *ex nihil*, but of making do with what is at hand and reassembling elements of older stuctures in such a way that their functions are redefined (Lévi-Strauss, 1962: 27).

7. The international sanctions on South Africa exacerbated the isolation, but can also be understood as an attempt at reversing the situation, that is, restricting the privileged classes' access to the global, but opening such access to anti-apartheid activists through various forms of exchange, clandestine support through IDAF, etc.

CHAPTER 13

1. Page references in parentheses in this part refer to J.M. Coetzee (1983).
2. This conclusion is not unprecedented in the growing corpus of critical work on Coetzee. As the first critic to appreciate fully the critique of reading that is latent in Coetzee's writing, Teresa Dovey (1988: 9–11, 58–62) famously claimed that the novels anticipate their masterful readers in a pre-emptive act of self-deconstruction. Dovey's view emerges from within a Lacanian frame of reference that sees language as the space of the Other, a realm external to both writer and reader, but simultaneously the only feasible site for the articulation of subjectivity. Furthermore, her argument requires that Coetzee's writing is read as though it recognises this too. Under those conditions, her readings are convincing. If we start interrogating any one of these conditions, however, it gets troublesome. A full-scale Lacanian analysis can only be conducted, it seems to me, from within the self-enclosed haven of highly specific Lacanian terminology. A major point in Lacanian analysis is of course that there can be no 'outside' anyway, no external point of observation and analysis. The reader is inevitably caught up in the same game of deferred desire as the text – hence Dovey's anxiety not to make false critical claims by exercising mastery over Coetzee's fictions. But as a paradoxical result, a new form of mastery emerges: either we submit to the regime of Lacanian terms, or our voice is not heard.

Reviewing the issue of textual production and reading in his monograph on Coetzee, David Attwell (1993) approached it in terms of authority and agency, rather than the Symbolic order. These terms also serve to highlight the techniques of evasion and autocritique that pervade Coetzee's writing, but do so from a broader philosophical base. As I state further down, Attwell could also be accused of assuming an all-too-authoritative position in relation to Coetzee's writing, but as a strategy this is successful, in so far as he effects a dialogue between text-theory, historiography and metafiction. The explanatory purchase of 'authority' and 'agency', terms which refer to the surreptitious manoeuvres undertaken by Coetzee to disarm and reform the sadism of print, thus emerges as much out of a contest between various discursive modes as from within any particular discourse.

Mike Marais has refined the argument on authority by demonstrating how Coetzee conflates the positions of author, reader and imperialist. Marais's pronouncement on the generic activity of the critic is particularly damning: 'Both reading subject and imperialist subject appropriate the threatening other and, thus, protect, fortify and confirm their own culturally-conferred identity' (1996: 71). Most recently, Derek Attridge (2004), has read Coetzee's entire *oeuvre* as an ongoing interrogation of the practices of reading, of canonisation and allegorisation.

3. A corresponding, yet harsher criticism is voiced by Z.N. (1984: 101–103). We should not mistakenly believe, however, that Gordimer's article is purely negative. As a discriminating reader, she places *Life & Times* at the most elevated of artistic levels, and only *then* does she voice her objection. With some fifteen years of hindsight the core of her achievement becomes clear: she historicises the novel, and points out why Coetzee is atypical in the context of oppositional writing in the 1980s. His resistance to political explicitness is 'a challengingly questionable position for a writer to take up in South Africa' (Gordimer, 1984: 6). Gordimer's acute awareness of the politically and ethically appropriate lends credibility to this statement.

4. The exception to paraphrase and comparison is Penner's discussion of 'being' and 'becoming' (which refers to Watson) (1989: 97–100).

5. I refer here to Ndebele's notion of spectacular representation (1991: 37–39). Gallagher notes Coetzee's 'lack of focus' on the war (1991: 145), but sees this – inconsistently, given the effort she has made to describe the sense of 'impending doom' of the times – not as a critique of the apocalyptic or spectacular mode, but as evidence of his simply having 'other concerns to address' (1991: 146).

6. Today, of course, they are not the exclusive exponents of a metacritical/metafictional reading. With specific reference to *Life & Times*, Marais and Parry (1996: 37–65) move in the same discursive

field – Parry a strongly critical vein – but Attwell and Dovey are the most thorough. See also note 8 below.

7. Dovey finds the term in Roland Barthes (1977: 49).

8. I should mention that my discussion restricts itself to what I regard as the major and paradigmatic studies of J.M. Coetzee. Even if we look merely at *Life & Times*, there are several highly qualified chapters and essays devoted to the topic, notably: Michael Green (1997: 268–272); Dominic Head (1998: 93–111); Sue Kossew (1996: 139–151); Michael Valdez Moses (1994: 131–155); and Derek Wright (1992: 435–444).

9. If we transpose these remarks from the metacritical to the critical level, it will become clear just how appropriate Lévinas's ethical imperative can be to the context of Coetzee's fiction. More than appropriate: it offers an elegant solution to a vexing problem. Whereas a deconstructionist such as Dovey (1988: 43) tends to appraise Coetzee's handling of alterity but falls short of dealing with the ethical dimension, a literary activist such as Gallagher eagerly appropriates Coetzee on behalf of an ethico-political project but forecloses on the deliberate evasions of his writing (1991: 1–22). Attwell deftly tackled this very problem, but his genetic approach excluded the typological option of using Lévinas. That is to say, whereas Coetzee never refers to this philosopher, and we cannot speak of the latter's direct 'influence' on the former, what Coetzee's writing *does* becomes much clearer if we take recourse to Lévinas. The crucial point is that Lévinas does not offer ethics as morality, but as the *refusal* to impose morality. Anyone familiar with Coetzee's writing can see how this corresponds to his often hotly debated refusal to impose political solutions on the reader. Or, as Mike Marais puts it, 'Coetzee's fictional project should not be understood in purely political terms as an attempt to "give voice" to the other, but rather in *ethical* terms as a refusal to do so.' It does not follow that this excludes political agency, but only that 'politics *begins* as ethics in [Coetzee's] fiction' (Marais, 1998: 45).

The argument on Lévinas and the ethics of reading has since been elaborated by Robert Eaglestone (1997). In his impressive *Ethical Criticism*, he demonstrates, perhaps surprisingly, how Lévinas's thought is explicitly hostile to aesthetics, art and literature since these are 'false' representations of being or, as he says later, only grants access to the Said and never to Saying. Yet, at the same time, precisely by honouring the argument on language in *Autrement qu'être* – which claims that language is a constant oscillation between the stasis of the Said and the ethical 'moment' of Saying – Lévinas does facilitate an ethical approach to criticism somewhat along the lines that I have elaborated above: as a continually interrupted practice of interpretation (Eaglestone, 1997: 129– 174).

CHAPTER 14

1. 'Mauvaise conscience que cette implication du non-intentionnel: sans intentions, sans visées, sans le masque protecteur du personnage se contemplant dans le miroir du monde, rassuré et se posant. Sans nom, sans situation, sans titres. Présence qui redoute la présence, qui redoute l'insistance du moi identique, nue de tout attribut. Dans sa non intentionalité, en deça de tout vouloir, avant toute faute, dans son identification non-intentionelle, l'identité recule devant son affirmation, s'inquiète devant ce que le retour à soi de l'identification peut comporter d'insistance' (Lévinas, 1984: 46).

2. 'Le non-intentionnel est passivité d'emblée' (Lévinas, 1984: 47).

3. 'L'idée de l'infini consiste précisément et paradoxalement à penser plus que ce qui est pensé en le conservant cependant dans sa démesure par rapport à la pensée. L'idée de l'infini consiste à saisir l'insaisissable en lui garantissant cependant son statut d'insaisissable' (Lévinas, 1991: 103).

4. A specific point of convergence is the paradoxical humanism of Lévinas. His thinking does not 'give up on humanism', it simply contests the notion 'que l'humanité de l'homme réside dans sa position de Moi. L'homme par excellence – la source de l'humanité – est peut-être l'Autre' (1991: 99). This is elaborated in another passage which, in effect, subsumes antihumanism:

> L'antihumanisme moderne, niant le primat qui, pour la signi-fication de l'être, reviendrait à la personne humaine, libre but d'elle-même, est vrai par delà les raisons qu'il se donne. [. . .] Son intuition géniale consiste à avoir abandonné l'idée de personne, but et origine d'elle-même, où le moi est encore chose parce qu'il est encore un être. A la rigueur autrui est 'fin' moi, je suis otage, responsabilité et substitution supportant le monde dans la passivité de l'assignation allant juqu'à la persécution accusatrice, indéclinable. *L'humanisme ne doit être dénoncé que parce qu'il n'est pas suffisament humain* (Lévinas, 1974: 164).

Rather than splinter the subject into a sheer play of differences, Lévinas anchors the subject in its inevitable responsibility, its being for the other, and then foregrounds the other in a double manoeuvre which postulates him or her as radically unknowable, but also – because of this – immeasurably profuse and paradoxically unifying. Thus, even when Lévinas exercises his harshest critique against the monolith of Western subjectivity, he is at the same time devising strategies to salvage uniqueness and unity 'beyond' philosophy. There is an element of faith in this way of thinking which differs from the main current of theorists who I have otherwise engaged in this book – and that are normally employed in critical work on Coetzee. Perhaps this element of faith is what enables Coetzee's writing, even in its most self-effacing moments.

CHAPTER 15

1. Perhaps one of the generic expectations that *Life & Times* works against is the picaresque. Moving laterally through society, in an era of historical flux, K would be well suited to play the role of the scoundrel, the picaro – but he never does. See, for example, the definition of picaresque in Ian Ousby (1988: 777).

2. On mediated desire – a term coined by René Girard – see Coetzee (1992: 127–138). Girard's own argument revolves largely around jealousy, envy, vanity and snobbishness, but he speaks also of the child–mother relationship in Proust in terms that could be applied to Michael K: 'Lorsque la mère refuse un baiser à son fils elle joue déjà le double rôle, propre à la médiation interne, d'instigatrice du désir et de sentinelle implacable' (Girard, 1961: 41). Desire is subdued in Anna K's and Michael K's relationship, but Michael K's torment when Anna is displeased, and his determination to take her where she wants to go, testifies to a mode of desire transferred from Anna to Michael K.

3. Marais's basic argument is that K is shown to conceive of reality through intentional perception. Reality isn't just 'there', independent of the perceiving subject.

4. The conclusion is not so far-fetched in the context of Coetzee's *oeuvre*. In *Dusklands* and *In the Heart of the Country* the characters Jacobus Coetzee and Magda are 'impossibly' conversant with the philosophy of Descartes and Hegel. The difference in *Life & Times of Michael K* is that Coetzee has refrained in Parts I and III from using outright philosophical terminology. This is of course significant in itself, as a decision to adhere to the generic expectations of realism, but it hardly prohibits a philosophical reading of the novel.

5. 'Le savoir philosophique est *a priori*: il recherche l'idée adéquate et assure l'autonomie. Dans tout apport nouveau, il reconnaît des structures familières et salue de vieilles connaissances. Il est une Odyssée où toutes les aventures ne sont que les accidents d'un reotur chez soi' (Lévinas, 1991: 99).

6. The image of burning, and the ashes that K carries with him, also have a more disturbing reference to the Holocaust.

7. It can be argued that there is a symbolic difference between the road and the railway track – the road is less pre-determined than the railway

line – but in the modern romance of escape, Jack Kerouac's *On the Road*, the road movies of Wim Wenders and Jim Jarmusch, etc., they carry a roughly equivalent symbolic import as the paths to freedom.

8. My argument resonates here with Mike Marais's contention that Coetzee's novel attempts to depict 'open space' (1998: 152).

9. Susan VanZanten Gallagher reads K's passage from the Peninsula to the Karoo as a rewriting of the mythology of the so-called Great Trek (1991: 151–153). It is an intriguing idea – K's barrow as a refurbished ox-wagon – but imprecise. After all, the trekboers generally *left* the Cape Province. The Karoo farm is almost as much a part of the old Dutch colony as the Cape Peninsula. With regard to the geographical vectors of history, then, Coetzee restricts himself to the transformations of the Cape – which of course is implicated in 'South Africa' in its entirety at a later stage, as well as in the historical time of the novel.

10. This is not unlike Attridge's (1994 and 2004) reading of trust in *Age of Iron*.

CHAPTER 16

1. Interestingly, there is a corresponding passage in Coetzee's auto-biographical *Boyhood* (1997: 132).

2. This distinction is crucial for Lévinas, but it is not consistently upheld in *Life & Times*.

3. 'Durée comme pure durée, non-intervention comme être sans insistance, comme être sur la point des pieds, être sans oser être; insistance de l'instant sans l'insistance du moi qui est déjà laps [. . .] Sans nom, sans situation, sans titres. Présence qui redoute la présence, qui redoute l'insistance du moi identique, nue de tout attribut. Dans son non-intentionalité, en deçà de tout vouloir, avant toute faute, dans son identification non-intentionelle, l'identité recule devant son affirmation, s'inquiète devant ce que le retour à soi de l'identification peut comporter d'insistance' (Lévinas, 'Philosophie Première', 1984: 46).

4. The association of appropriated time and imprisonment resonates with the perception of roads and railways as 'fences'.

5. Care being the theme that Marais stresses (1998: 141, 179).

6. Mennecke also sees this as the final stage of representation. K's capture saves the story as such from extinction: 'Das Erreichen des ersehnten Zustands der Losgelösigkeit von der Zeit ist [. . .] zugleich das Ende der Erzählung, da Thema und Material jeglicher Erzählung in der historischen Zeit bestehen, ohne welche keine Ereignisse denkbar sind. Die Auffindung Michael Ks ist nicht nur seine physische Errettung vor dem Tod, sondern die Rettung der Erzählung' (Mennecke, 1991: 164).

CHAPTER 17

1. 'L'unité militaire en retraite arrive dans une localité qui ne se doute encore de rien, où les cafés sont ouverts, où les coiffeurs coiffent, les boulangers boulangent, les vicomtes rencontrent d'autres vicomtes et se racontent des histoires de vicomtes, et où tout est déconstruit et désolé une heure après, les maisons, fermées ou laissées portes ouvertes, se vident des habitants qu'entraîne un courant de voitures et de piétons à travers les rues restituées à leur 'profond jadis' de routes, tracées dans un passé immémorial par les grandes migrations' (Lévinas, 1976: 66).

2. As Attwell has pointed out, there is a strongly Foucauldian tendency in the novel's rendition of discipline and power (1993: 95).

3. The notion of *différance* has been employed previously in connection with Coetzee's novels. It is developed at length by Claudia Egerer as the (de)structuring principle in *Foe* (1997: 111–138).

4. 'la guerre et l'administration, c'est-à-dire la hiérarchie, par lesquelles s'instaure et se maintient l'État, aliènent le Même qu'elles avaient à maintenir dans sa pureté; pour supprimer la violence, il faut recourir à la violence. Le Même ne reconnaît pas sa volonté dans les conséquences de son vote. La médiation qui aurait dû assurer le triomphe du Même, est source d'une nouvelle aliénation du Même' (Lévinas, 1991: 100).

5. Fredric Jameson's notion of history as an 'absolute horizon' has been used in similar fashion by Attwell to distinguish between 'history as discourse', which is always only accessible through texts and ideology, and 'actual' history (Attwell, 1990: 114).

6. This is not to imply that 'showing' is ever possible to achieve in verbal narrative without 'telling'. It merely indicates a relative diegetic tension in *Life & Times*.

7. This notion of language capturing the landscape has been elaborated by Coetzee himself in *White Writing* (1988b).

CONCLUSION

1. 'Ons vir jou Suid-Afrika' is an Afrikaner motto of allegiance to the South African nation, centrally placed in the Voortrekker Monument outside of Pretoria. It translates literally as 'us for you, South Africa', that is, 'we are prepared to sacrifice ourselves for you, South Africa'.

Select Bibliography

Abrahams, Lionel. *A Reader*. Craighall: AD Donker, 1988.

———. 'Revolution, Style and Morality: Reflections Around Nadine Gordimer's *A Sport of Nature*'. *Sesame*, 12, 1989: 27–30.

Achebe, Chinua. *Morning Yet on Creation Day*. London/lbadan: Heinemann, 1975.

Ahmad, Aijaz. *In Theory*. London: Verso, 1992.

Alvarez-Péreyre, Jacques. *The Poetry of Commitment in South Africa*. London: Heinemann, 1984.

Appiah, Anthony. 'The Uncompleted Argument: Du Bois and the Illusion of Race'. In Henry Louis Gates, ed., *'Race,' Writing, and Difference*. Chicago: Chicago University Press, 1986: 21–37.

Ashcroft, Bill, Gareth Griffiths and Helen Tiffin. *The Empire Writes Back: Theory and Practice in Post-Colonial Literatures*. London: Routledge, 1989.

Attridge, Derek. 'Trusting the Other: Ethics and Politics in J.M. Coetzee's *Age of Iron*'. *South Atlantic Quarterly*, 93(1), 1994: 59–82.

———. *Literature in the Event: J.M. Coetzee and the Ethics of Reading*. Pietermaritzburg: University of KwaZulu-Natal Press, 2004.

Attridge, Derek and Rosemary Jolly, eds. *Writing South Africa*. Cambridge: Cambridge University Press, 1998

Attwell, David. *J.M. Coetzee: South Africa and the Politics of Writing*. Cape Town: David Philip, 1993.

———. 'The Problem of History in the Fiction of J.M. Coetzee'. In Martin Trump, ed., *Rendering Things Visible: Essays on South African Literary Culture*. Johannesburg: Ravan Press, 1990: 94–133.

———. 'The Transculturation of English: The Exemplary Case of the Rev. Tiyo Soga, African Nationalist'. *Occasional Papers in English Studies*, 1. Pietermaritzburg: English Department, University of Natal, 1994.

Bahri, Deepika. 'Once More With Feeling: What is Postcolonialism?'. *Ariel*, 26(1), January 1995: 51–81.

Bakhtin, Michail. *Rabelais and His World*. Trans. Helene Iwolsky. Cambridge: The MIT Press, 1968.

Barker, Francis, Thomas Hulme and Margaret Iversen, eds., *Colonial Discourse/Postcolonial Theory*. Manchester: Manchester University Press, 1994

Barthes, Roland. *Le degré zéro de l'écriture*. Paris: Editions du Seuil, 1953.

———. *Oeuvres complètes*, vol.2, edited by Éric Marty. Paris: Editions du Seuil, 1994.

———. *Roland Barthes*. New York: Hill & Wang, 1977.

Behr, Mark. *The Smell of Apples*. Cape Town: Queillerie, 1993.

Beauvoir, Simone de. *Le deuxième sexe*. Paris: Gallimard, 1949.

Bhabha, Homi. 'Foreword: Remembering Fanon'. In Frantz Fanon, *Black Skin, White Masks*. London: Pluto Press, 1986: vii–xxvi.

———. *The Location of Culture*. London: Routledge, 1994.

Borgin, Karl and Kathleen Corbett. *The Destruction of a Continent: Africa and International Aid*. New York: Harcourt Brace Jovanovich, 1982.

Brantlinger, Patrick. 'Victorians and Africans: The Genealogy of the Myth of the Dark Continent'. In Henry Louis Gates, ed., *'Race,' Writing, and Difference*. Chicago: Chicago University Press, 1986: 185–222.

Braudel, Ferdinand. *Ecrits sur l'histoire*. Paris: Flammarion, 1969.

———. *On History*. Trans. Sarah Matthews. Chicago: Chicago University Press, 1980.

Brennan, Timothy. *Salman Rushdie and the Third World*. London: Macmillan, 1989.

Brink, André. *Mapmakers: Writing in a State of Siege*. London: Faber and Faber, 1983.

Carusi, Annamaria. 'Post, Post and Post, Or, Where is South African Literature in All This?' *Ariel*, 20(4), October 1989: 79–95.

Chapman, Michael. *Southern African Literatures*. London: Longman, 1996.

Chipasula, Frank. 'A Terrible Trajectory: The Impact of Apartheid, Prison and Exile on Dennis Brutus's Poetry'. In Abdulrazak Gurnah, ed., *Essays on African Writing 1*: A Re-Evaluation. London: Heinemann, 1993: 38–55.

Clingman, Stephen. *The Novels of Nadine Gordimer: History from the Inside*. Johannesburg: Ravan Press, 1986.

———. 'Revolution and Reality: South African Fiction in the 1980s'. In Martin Trump, ed., *Rendering Things Visible: Essays on South African Literary Culture*. Johannesburg: Ravan Press, 1990: 41–60.

———. '*A Sport of Nature* and the Boundaries of Fiction'. In Bruce King, ed., *The Later Fiction of Nadine Gordimer*. London: Macmillan, 1993: 173–190.

Coetzee, J.M. *Boyhood: Scenes from Provincial Life*. London: Secker & Warburg, 1997.

———. *Doubling the Point*, edited by David Attwell. Cambridge: Harvard University Press, 1992.

———. *Dusklands*. Johannesburg: Ravan Press, 1974.

————. *Foe*. Johannesburg: Ravan Press, 1986.

————. *In the Heart of the Country*. Johannesburg: Ravan Press, 1978.

————. *Life & Times of Michael K*. Johannesburg: Ravan Press, 1983.

————. 'The Novel Today'. *Upstream*, 6(1), 1988a: 2–5.

————. *Waiting for the Barbarians*. Johannesburg: Ravan Press, 1981.

————. *White Writing: On the Culture of Letters in South Africa*. New Haven: Yale University Press, 1988b.

Cooke, John. '"Nobody's Children": Families in Gordimer's Later Novels'. In Bruce King, ed., *The Later Fiction of Nadine Gordimer*. London: Macmillan, 1993: 21–32.

Cooper, Brenda. 'New Criteria for an "Abnormal Mutation"? An Evaluation of Gordimer's *A Sport of Nature*'. In Martin Trump, ed., *Rendering Things Visible: Essays on South African Literary Culture*. Johannesburg: Ravan Press, 1990: 68–93.

Couzens, Tim. 'Introduction'. In Sol T. Plaatje, *Mhudi*. London: Heinemann, 1978: 1–20.

————. *The New African: A Study of the Life and Work of H.I.E. Dhlomo*. Johannesburg: Ravan Press, 1985.

Critchley, Simon. *The Ethics of Deconstruction: Derrida and Lévinas*. Oxford: Blackwell, 1992.

Davenport, T.R.H. *South Africa: A Modern History*. London: Macmillan, 1991.

De Kock, Leon. *Civilising Barbarians*. Johannesburg: Witwatersrand University Press, 1996.

Derrida, Jacques. '"Eating Well", or the Calculation of the Subject: An Interview with Jacques Derrida'. In Eduardo Cadava, Peter Connor and JeanLuc Nancy, eds., *Who Comes After the Subject?* London: Routledge, 1991: 96–119.

————. *De la grammatologie*. Paris: Les Editions de Minuit, 1967.

————. *La voix et le phénomène*. Paris: Presses Universitaires de France, 1967.

Dirlik, Arif. 'The Postcolonial Aura: Third World Criticism in the Age of Global Capitalism'. *Critical Inquiry*, 20, 1994: 328–356.

Dovey, Teresa. *The Novels of J.M. Coetzee: Lacanian Allegories*. Craighall: AD Donker, 1988.

During, Simon. *Foucault and Literature: Towards a Genealogy of Writing*. London: Routledge, 1992.

Eaglestone, Robert. *Ethical Criticism: Reading after Lévinas*. Edinburgh: Edinburgh University Press, 1997.

Egerer, Claudia. *Fictions of (In)Betweenness*. Göteborg: Acta Universitatis Gothoburgensis, 1997.

The Encyclopedia of Philosophy. New York: Macmillan, 1967.

Fanon, Frantz. *Black Skin, White Masks*. Trans. Charles Lam Markmann. London: Pluto Press, 1986.

———. *Les damnés de la terre*. Paris: François Maspéro, 1968 (1961).

———. *Peau noire, masques blancs*. Paris: Editions du Seuil, 1952.

Ferguson, Russell, Gever, Martha, Minh-ha, Trinh T. and West, Cornel, eds. *Out There: Marginalization and Contemporary Cultures*. Cambridge: The MIT Press, 1990.

Foucault, Michel. *Dits et écrits 1954–1988, I*. Paris: Ed. Gallimard, 1994.

———. *Les mots et les choses*. Paris: Ed. Gallimard, 1966.

———. *The Order of Things: An Archaeology of the Human Sciences*. London: Routledge, 1970.

Gadamer, HansGeorg. *Wahrheit und Methode*. Tübingen: J.C.B. Mohr, 1960.

Gallagher, Susan VanZanten. *A Story of South Africa: J.M. Coetzee's Fiction in Context*. Cambridge: Harvard University Press, 1991.

Gates, Henry Louis. 'Introduction: Writing "Race" and the Difference It Makes'. In Henry Louis Gates, ed., *'Race,' Writing and Difference*. Chicago: Chicago University Press, 1986: 1–20.

———. *The Signifying Monkey: A Theory of African-American Literary Criticism*. New York: Oxford University Press, 1988.

Genette, Gérard. *Nouveau Discours du Récit*. Paris: Edition du Seuil, 1983.

Gérard, Albert S., ed. *European-Language Writing in SubSaharan Africa*, vol.1. Budapest: Akadémiai Kiadó, 1986.

Gilman, Sander L. 'Black Bodies, White Bodies: Toward an Iconography of Female Sexuality in Late Nineteenth-Century Art, Medicine, and Literature' In Henry Louis Gates, ed., *'Race,' Writing and Difference*. Chicago: Chicago University Press, 1986: 223–261.

Girard, René. *Mensonge romantique et vérité romanesque*. Paris: Edition Bernard Grasset, 1961.

Glenn, Ian. 'Nadine Gordimer, J.M. Coetzee, and the Politics of Interpretation'. *South Atlantic Quarterly*, 93(1), 1994: 11–32.

Gordimer, Nadine. *The Black Interpreters*. Johannesburg: SPROCAS/Ravan, 1973.

———. *Burger's Daughter*. London: Jonathan Cape, 1979.

———. *The Conservationist*. London: Jonathan Cape, 1974.

———. *The Essential Gesture: Writing, Politics and Places*. London: Jonathan Cape,1988.

———. 'The Idea of Gardening'. *New York Review of Books*, 2 February 1984: 3, 6.

———. *July's People*. Johannesburg: Ravan Press, 1981.

———. *None to Accompany Me*. London: Bloomsbury, 1994.

———. *A Sport of Nature*. New York: Alfred Knopf, 1987.

Green, Michael. *Novel Histories: Past, Present, and Future in South African Fiction*. Johannesburg: Witwatersrand University Press, 1997.

Gurnah, Abdulrazak. 'Introduction'. In Abdulrazak Gurnah, ed., *Essays on African Writing 1: A Re-Evaluation*. London: Heinemann, 1993: v–xiv.

Guy, Jeff. 'Class, Imperialism and Literary Criticism: William Ngidi, John Colenso and Matthew Arnold'. *Journal of Southern African Studies*, 23(2), 1997: 219–242.

Hall, Stuart. 'When was "the Post-Colonial"? Thinking at the Limit'. In Iain Chambers and Lidia Curti, eds., *The Post-Colonial Question: Common Skies, Divided Horizons*. London: Routledge, 1996: 242–260.

Head, Dominic. *J.M. Coetzee*. Cambridge: Cambridge University Press, 1998.

———. *Nadine Gordimer*. Cambridge: Cambridge University Press, 1994.

Hewson, Kelly. 'Making the "Revolutionary Gesture": Nadine Gordimer, J.M. Coetzee and Some Variations on the Writer's Responsibility'. *Ariel*, 19(4), October 1988: 55–72.

Huggan, Graham and Stephen Watson, eds. *Critical Perspectives on J.M. Coetzee*. London: Macmillan, 1996

Ingram, Forrest L. *Representative Short Story Cycles of the Twentieth Century: Studies in a Literary Genre*. The Hague: Mouton & Co., 1971.

Jameson, Fredric. *The Political Unconscious: Narrative as a Socially Symbolic Act*. Ithaca: Cornell University Press, 1981.

———. *Postmodernism, or, the Cultural Logic of Late Capitalism*. Durham: Duke University Press, 1991.

———. *Signatures of the Visible*. London: Routledge, 1992.

JanMohamed, Abdul R. 'The Economy of Manichean Allegory: The Function of Racial Difference in Colonialist Literature'. In Henry Louis Gates, ed., *'Race,' Writing and Difference*. Chicago: Chicago University Press, 1986: 78–106.

Jolly, Rosemary. *Colonization, Violence, and Narration in White South African Writing*. Athens: Ohio University Press, 1996.

Johnson, Diane. 'Living Legends'. *New York Review of Books*, 16 July 1987: 8–9.

Johnson, Karen Ramsay. '"What the Name will Make Happen": Strategies of Naming in Nadine Gordimer's Novels'. *Ariel*, 26(3), July 1995: 117–137.

Johnston, Anton. *Study, Produce, and Combat! Education and the Mozambican State, 1962–1984*. Studies in Comparative and International Education, 14. Stockholm: University of Stockholm, 1989.

Kossew, Sue. *Pen and Power: A Post-Colonial Reading of J.M. Coetzee and André Brink*. Amsterdam: Rodopi, 1996.

Krauss, Jennifer. 'Activism 101'. *The New Republic*, 18 May 1987: 33–36.

Krog, Antjie. *Country of My Skull*. Johannesburg: Random House, 1998.

Kunene, Mazisi. 'Some Aspects of South African Literature'. *World Literature Today*, 70(1), 1996: 13–16.

Lehmann, Elmar. 'Liberation and Fiction's Problematical Endings: On Recent South African Novels'. In Geoffrey V. Davis, ed., *Crisis and Conflict: Essays on Southern African Literature*. Essen: Die Blaue Eule, 1990: 133–142.

Lelyveld, Joseph. *Move Your Shadow: South Africa, Black and White*. London: Michael Joseph, 1986.

Lema, Antoine. *Africa Divided: The Creation of 'Ethnic Groups'*. Lund Dissertations in Sociology 6. Lund: Lund University Press, 1993.

Lenta, Margaret. 'Fictions of the Future'. *English Academy Review*, 5, 1988: 133–145.

Lévinas, Emmanuel. *Autrement qu'être ou au-delà de l'essence*. La Haye: Martinus Nijhoff, 1974.

———. *Basic Philosophical Writings*. Edited by Adriaan T. Peperzak, Simon Critchley and Robert Bemasconi. Bloomington: Indiana University Press, 1996.

———. 'Éthique comme philosophie première'. *Justifications de l'éthique. XIXe congrès de l'association de sociétés de philosophie de langue française*. Bruxelles: Editions de l'Université de Bruxelles, 1984: 41–51.

———. *Ethique et infini: Dialogues avec Philippe Nemo*. Paris: Fayard, 1982.

———. *The Lévinas Reader*. Edited by Séan Hand. Oxford: Blackwell, 1989.

———. *Noms propres*. Paris: Fata Morgana, 1976.

———. 'La signification et le sens'. *Revue de métaphysique et de morale*, 2, 1964: 125–156.

———. *Le temps et l'autre*. Paris: Quadrige, 1979 (1948).

———. 'Transcendance et hauteur'. In Catherine Chalier and Miguel Abensour, eds., *Emmanuel Lévinas*. Paris: Editions de l'Herne, 1991: 97–119.

Lévi-Strauss, Claude. *La pensée sauvage*. Paris: Plon, 1962.

Lomberg, Alan. 'Withering into the Truth: The Romantic Realism of Nadine Gordimer'. In Rowland Smith, ed., *Critical Essays on Nadine Gordimer*. Boston: G.K. Hall & Co., 1990: 31–45.

Losambe, Lokangaka. 'History and Tradition in the Reconstitution of Black South African Subjectivity: Njabulo Ndebele's Fiction'. In Emmanuel Ngara, ed., *New Writing from Southern Africa*. London: James Currey, 1996: 76–90.

Macaskill, Brian. 'Placing Spaces: Style and Ideology in Gordimer's Later Fiction'. In Bruce King, ed., *The Later Fiction of Nadine Gordimer*. London: Macmillan, 1993: 59–73.

Manganyi, N.C. *Being-Black-in-the-World*. Johannesburg: SPRO CAS/Ravan, 1973.

Marais, Mike. 'The Hermeneutics of Empire'. In Graham Huggan and Stephen Watson, eds., *Critical Perspectives on J.M. Coetzee*. London: Macmillan, 1996: 70–83.

————. *Towards a Levinasian Aesthetic: The Tension Between Implication and Transcendence in Selected Novels by J M. Coetzee*. Unpublished dissertation. Johannesburg: Rand Afrikaans University, 1998a.

————. 'Writing with Eyes Shut: Ethics, Politics, and the Problem of the Other in the Fiction of J.M. Coetzee'. *English in Africa*, 25(1), May 1998b: 43–60.

Marais, Sue. 'Ivan Vladislavić's Re-vision of the South African Story Cycle'. *Current Writing*, 4, 1992: 41–56.

Masilela, Johnny. *Deliver Us from Evil: Scenes from a Rural Transvaal Upbringing*. Cape Town: Kwela Books, 1997.

McClintock, Anne. *Imperial Leather: Race, Gender and Sexuality in the Colonial Conquest*. London: Routledge, 1995.

Mennecke, Arnim. *Koloniales Bewusstsein in den Romanen J.M. Coetzees*. Heidelberg: Carl Winter Universitätsverlag, 1991.

Merivale, Patricia. 'Audible Palimpsests: Coetzee's Kafka'. In Graham Huggan and Stephen Watson, eds., *Critical Perspectives on J.M. Coetzee*. London: Macmillan, 1996: 152–167.

Merleau-Ponty, Maurice. *La phénomenologie de perception*. Paris: Gallimard, 1945.

Middleton, John, ed. *Black Africa*. London: The Macmillan Company, 1970.

Mignolo, Walter. 'Rethinking the Colonial Model.' In Linda Hutcheon and Mario J. Valdés, *Rethinking Literary History: A Dialogue on Theory*. New York: Oxford University Press, 2002: 155–193.

Miller, Christopher. 'Theories of Africans: The Question of Literary Anthropology'. In Henry Louis Gates, ed., *'Race,' Writing, and Difference*. Chicago: Chicago University Press, 1986: 281–300.

————. *Theories of Africans*. London: Routledge, 1990.

Moretti, Franco. *The Way of the World: The Bildungsroman in European Culture*. London: Verso, 1987.

Morphet, Tony. 'Ordinary – Modern – Post-Modern'. *Theoria*, Octobre 1992: 129–141.

Moses, Michael Valdez. 'Solitary Walkers: Rousseau and Coetzee's *Life & Times of Michael K*'. *South Atlantic Quarterly*, 93(1), 1994: 131–156.

Mphahlele, Ezekiel. *The African Image*. New York: Praeger, 1974.

Mudimbe, V.Y. *The Invention of Africa: Gnosis, Philosophy and the Order of Knowledge*. London: James Currey, 1988.

————. *The Idea of Africa*. London: James Currey: 1994.

Nationalencyklopedin. Stockholm: Bokförlaget Bra Böcker, 1992.

Ndebele, Njabulo S. *Fools and Other Stories*. Johannesburg: Ravan Press, 1983.

————. *Rediscovery of the Ordinary: Essays on South African Literature and Culture*. Fordsburg: Cosaw, 1991.

————. *South African Literature and Culture*. Manchester: Manchester University Press, 1995.

Neill, Michael. "'Groping Behind a Mirror": Some Images of the Other in South African Writing'. In Geoffrey V. Davis, ed., *Crisis and Conflict: Essays on Southern African Literature*. Essen: Die Blaue Eule, 1990: 157–182.

Newman, Judie. *Nadine Gordimer*. London: Routledge, 1988.

The New Princeton Encyclopedia of Poetry and Poetics. Princeton: Princeton University Press, 1993.

Nkosi, Lewis. 'Postmodernism and Black Writing in South Africa'. In Derek Attridge and Rosemary Jolly, eds., *Writing South Africa*. Cambridge: Cambridge University Press, 1998: 75–90.

————. 'South African Fiction Writers at the Barricades'. *Third World Book Review*, 2(1–2), 1986: 43–45.

Ngugi wa Thiongo. *Decolonising the Mind*. Harare: Zimbabwe Publishing House, 1987.

Nkrumah, Kwame. *Africa Must Unite*. London: Heinemann, 1963.

Nyerere, Julius K. *Ujamaa: Essays On Socialism*. Dar es Salaam: Oxford University Press, 1968.

O'Brien, Anthony. 'Literature in Another South Africa: Njabulo Ndebele's Theory of Emergent Culture'. *Diacritics*, 22(1), 1992: 67–85.

Ousby, Ian, ed. *The Cambridge Guide to Literature in English*. Cambridge: Cambridge University Press, 1988.

Oxford English Dictionary. Oxford: Oxford University Press: 1989.

Parry, Benita. 'Speech and Silence in the Fictions of J.M. Coetzee'. In Graham Huggan and Stephen Watson, eds., *Critical Perspectives on J.M. Coetzee*. London: Macmillan, 1996: 37–65.

Pechey, Graham. 'Introduction'. In Njabulo Ndebele, *Rediscovery of the Ordinary: Essays on South African Literature and Culture*. Manchester: Manchester University Press, 1995: 1–16.

————. 'PostApartheid Narratives'. In Francis Barker, Thomas Hulme and Margaret Iversen, eds., *Colonial Discourse/Postcolonial Theory*. Manchester: Manchester University Press, 1994: 151–171.

————. 'The PostApartheid Sublime: Rediscovery of the Extraordinary'. In Derek Attridge and Rosemary Jolly, eds., *Writing South Africa*. Cambridge: Cambridge University Press, 1998: 57–74.

Peck, Richard. 'What's a Poor White to Do? White South African Options in "A Sport of Nature"'. *Ariel*, 19(4), September 1988: 75–93.

Peires, J.B. *The Dead Will Arise: Nongqawuse and the Great Xhosa Cattle Killing Movement of 1856–57*. Johannesburg: Ravan Press, 1989.

Penner, Dick. *Countries of the Mind: The Fiction of J.M. Coetzee*. New York: Greenwood Press, 1989.

Pettersson, Rose. *Nadine Gordimer's One Story of a State Apart*. Uppsala: Acta Universitatis Upsaliensis, 1995.

Posel, Deborah. *The Making of Apartheid 1948–1961: Conflict and Compromise*. Oxford: Clarendon Press, 1997 (1991).

————. 'Modernity and Measurement: Further Thoughts on the Apartheid State'. Seminar paper presented at the Institute for Advanced Social Research, University of the Witwatersrand, July/August 1996.

Prakash, Gyan. 'Writing Post-Orientalist Histories of the Third World: Perspectives from Indian Historiography'. *Comparative Studies in Society and History*, 32, April 1990: 383–408.

Said, Edward. *Culture and Imperialism*. London: Chatto and Windus, 1993.

————. *Orientalism*. London: Routledge, 1978.

————. *The World, the Text and the Critic*. Cambridge: Harvard University Press, 1983.

Savage, Jacqueline Ruth. 'A Study of Njabulo Ndebele's *Fools and Other Stories* with Particular Reference to the Complex Character as Developing Social Being'. Unpublished M.A. thesis. Durban: University of Natal, 1989.

Shohat, Ella. 'Notes on the "Post-Colonial"'. *Social Text*, 31/32, 1992: 99–113.

Slemon, Stephen. 'The Scramble for Post-Colonialism'. In Alan Lawson and Helen Tiffin, eds., *DeScribing Empire*. London: Routledge, 1994: 15–32.

————. 'Unsettling the Empire: Resistance Theory for the Second World'. *World Literature Written in English*, 30(2), 1990: 30–41.

Smith, Paul. *Discerning the Subject*. Minneapolis: University of Minnesota Press, 1988.

Spivak, Gayatri Chakravorty. *In Other Worlds: Essays in Cultural Politics*. New York: Routledge, 1988.

————. *Outside in the Teaching Machine*. New York: Routledge, 1993.

Todorov, Tzvetan. *La conquete de l'Amérique: La question de l'autre*. Paris: Editions du Seuil, 1982.

Van Onselen, Charles. *The Seed is Mine: The Life of Kas Maine*. Cape Town: David Philip, 1996.

———. *Studies in the Social and Economic History of the Witwatersrand 1886–1914, Vols. 1 & 2*. Johannesburg: Ravan Press, 1982.

Vaughan, Michael. 'Literature and Politics: Currents in South African Writing in the Seventies'. *Journal of Southern African Studies*, 9(1), October 1982: 118–138.

———. 'Storytelling and Politics in Fiction'. In Martin Trump, ed., *Rendering Things Visible: Essays on South African Literary Culture*. Johannesburg: Ravan Press, 1990: 186–204.

Vladislavić, Ivan. *The Folly*. Cape Town: David Philip, 1993.

———. *The Restless Supermarket*. Cape Town: David Philip, 2001.

Wade, Michael. '*A Sport of Nature:* Identity and Repression of the Jewish Subject'. In Bruce King, ed., *The Later Fiction of Nadine Gordimer*. London: Macmillan, 1993: 155–172.

———. *White on Black in South Africa*. London: Macmillan, 1993.

Wagner, Kathrin. *Re-Reading Nadine Gordimer*. Johannesburg: Witwatersrand University Press, 1994.

Watson, Stephen. *Selected Essays: 1980–1990*. Cape Town: Carrefour Press, 1990.

Weinhouse, Linda. 'The Deconstruction of Victory'. *Research in African Literatures*, 21(2), 1990: 91–100.

Welz, Dieter. 'Who Owns the Scenery?' *English in Africa*, 18(1), May 1991: 97–101.

Wicomb, Zoë. 'Five Afrikaner Texts and the Rehabilitation of Whiteness'. *Social Identities*, 4(3), 1998: 363–383.

Willan, Brian. *Sol Plaatje: A Biography*. Johannesburg: Ravan Press, 1984.

Winnett, Susan. 'Making Metaphors/Moving On'. In Bruce King, ed., *The Later Fiction of Nadine Gordimer*. London: Macmillan, 1993: 140–154.

Worthington, Kim. *Self as Narrative*. Oxford: Oxford University Press, 1996.

Wright, Derek. 'Black Earth, White Myth: Coetzee's *Michael K*'. *Modern Fiction Studies*, 38(2), 1992: 435–444.

Yeats, W.B. *Collected Poems*. London: Macmillan, 1978.

Young, Robert. *White Mythologies: Writing History and the West*. London: Routledge, 1990.

Z.N. 'Much Ado About Nobody'. *African Communist*, 97, 1984: 101–103.

Index